$$$$$$$$$$$$$$$$$$$$$$$$$

MAKING IT

MAKING IT
A GUIDE TO STUDENT FINANCES
WRITTEN BY HARVARD STUDENT AGENCIES, INC.

$$$$$$$$$$$$$$$ E.P. DUTTON & CO., INC. $ NEW YORK $ 1973 $$$$$$$$$$$$$$$

Published simultaneously in Canada
by Clarke, Irwin & Company
Limited, Toronto and Vancouver

SBN: 0-525-15045-5 (cloth)
SBN: 0-525-03930-9 (paper)
Library of Congress Catalog Card Number: 70-179862

CONTENTS

MAKING IT

PREFACE

You are a student, or you plan to become one. You share, with all other college students and the overwhelming majority of the human race, money troubles.

You need tuition money; money for books; money for room and board; or money to finance a Triumph, a new album, or a trip to Nepal. Perhaps you must depend upon your own efforts to secure all of the funds you will need in the course of your undergraduate career; perhaps you only worry about financing that occasional movie or concert. Whether your financial needs are vital or only troublesome, they are a matter of concern to *you,* and you may be looking for help as you struggle to solve your money problems. There are thousands of ways of making money, and if you want to, this book exists to help you learn how.

No one is unaware of the financial problems that face the college student. The average wage for students at Oberlin College in 1834 ranged from less than $.03 to $.10 an hour. At that rate, it required roughly 360 hours of work to earn the $18 yearly tuition! Happily, the student wage has now risen to over $2 an hour—so that earning tuition today would only require *800* hours of work. As college expenses continue to spiral upward, student employment and financial aid become increasingly important to growing numbers of students. At the same time, widespread unemployment, cutbacks in federal educational, and the withdrawal of major corporate scholarship support such as the Procter and Gamble program are coexisting factors that are bound to concern every student who is considering his strategy in the battle against the high cost of undergraduate life.

Despite these gloomy signs, the spectrum of term-time and summer jobs that are open to men and women in college is diverse, lucrative, and stimulating. During the late 1960's, the business boom and youth orientation combined to produce a flood of employment opportunities and financial assistance programs for American undergraduates, and there is no reason to believe that economic recovery will not bring about a revival and extension of these funds. More educational funding is available to needy students than ever before: billions of dollars—although the college population and its financial needs have outstripped even that gigantic sum.

This book was written *by* college students and recent graduates *for* college students who are currently in the predicament of financing an education. It was born from our conviction that undergraduates *can* find interesting, well-paid jobs on campus and off, during the summer and during the school year. Researching the facts behind this conviction has occupied many people for many months and has involved financial-aid officers, student employment-counselors, and, above all, individual students from all over the country. Small colleges and huge universities, rural academic havens and sprawling urban educational complexes, public and private institutions, schools from the North, South, East, and West—all have been examined in our search for a realistic picture of undergraduate employment.

From the first page this guide to student finance struggles toward a single goal: to present ideas and information that you, as an American undergraduate, can use in your own financial planning. It attempts to suggest the range and sources of scholarships, loans, and work-study aids that may be available to you as a buffer against the worst financial obstacles to your continued education. Students' skills, actual and potential, are reviewed for their marketability in today's economy, in the hope of drawing your attention to your own salable skills and the ways in which you might add to, combine, and profit from them.

Actual job possibilities have been divided into three spheres. Jobs that *you* originate, organize, and build are treated in the chapter on student business, which supplies the guidelines that many students have utilized in the past to start their own profitable enterprises. Term-time employment encompasses the jobs that you will hold during the many months of your college semesters; these jobs must conform to the limitations of your campus, community, academic schedule, and extracurricular activities. Summer vacations offer you your best opportunity for full-time employment and concentrated earnings, and challenge you to integrate your work plans with the possibility of travel and change of pace.

Finally, you will be confronted by many of the practical aspects of the student job search, as vividly recounted to us by our undergraduate informants: How do I prepare a résumé? When should I press for an interview, and how should I act? Where do I go, in my search for employment?

The investigation of students' experiences in each of these spheres has led to the discovery of many facts and trends, which are passed along to you in appropriate chapters. Hundreds of students, representing thousands of jobs and hundreds of thousands of hours of recent job experience, have contributed their reports from which we have culled details of wages, hours, duties, and working conditions for positions both on and off campus, all over the country. You will not recognize yourself in any specific reference or description, but it has been our continuing aim to present a variety of experience supplemented with ideas and suggestions for reapplying and extending these factual realities of past student employment to meet the present and future needs of individual readers.

Only you can synthesize this mélange of information to help meet your unique financial situation. In dealing with your needs, this guide will be of little help to you if you conceive of it as a mirror, which somewhere reflects your particular financial quandary and its resolution. On the contrary, we could never attempt such a task. What we *have* sought to provide is a window, through which you could look directly onto the reality of the current position of students in their pursuit of necessary funds. Stimulating opportunities, discouraging economic fluctuations, alluringly high salaries, underpaid drudgery—all of these factors are in plain view. This is the situation that you enter as a student looking for work, and in this book we attempt to provide you with a long look before you take the leap. In some instances, this look suggests caution. But you already knew that; with business in its current slump, high wages and intriguing work are not about to tumble into your lap. On the whole, however, we have been inspired by the example demonstrated by these thousands of fellow students and trust that this inspiration will be the major impact of our study on you.

There *are* jobs for students—good jobs, with satisfactory wages and satisfying aspects to the work itself. These jobs are available to freshmen and sophomores, juniors and seniors, students of every race, sex, and social class. You can find them throughout the country. What is more, you will find jobs that actually *interest* you or relax you or provide you with research material, career connections, or paths to a wider social life. If you work behind a typewriter or a broom for a while, that is par for the course—but eventually, you should be able to build something better.

Please don't read this book too carefully. *Making It* is a guide to student finance, a kind of field book, designed to provide you with the information you need in a convenient, straightforward way—so that you can act on it immediately and derive practical benefit from it. It is *not* a textbook on financial aid and student employment, and you won't gain much by studying it academically. Nor is it a "recipe" book, full of foolproof plans, carefully itemized in stepwise fashion, which are offered to you as blueprints for financial success. Our sole intent is to inform you and, hopefully, as a by-product, to excite you about finding a better job than you thought you could find, or land; a better job than the one you have right now. If you find an idea in this guide that really inspires you, put the book down, and go out to make the idea work for you.

Likewise, read what you need. If you are a high school senior, begin at the beginning, but if you are a college sophomore or junior who is already well versed in the possibilities of financial aid, start with the chapter on Student-Run Small Businesses—you still have two or three undergraduate years in which to make a bundle. Freshmen may want to consider the long-range planning implicit in the Skills chapter. If you know your skills and claim no entrepreneurial leanings, proceed to the two major topics: term-time employment (for your spring reading) or summer employment (if it's autumn). If you think we have our seasons inappropriately reversed, you have yet to learn the one essential rule in the successful organizing of student finances—*plan ahead*.

Imagination, initiative, and effort are the keys to financial comfort and employment satisfaction for college students. These are the ingredients that *you* add to the factual information in this book in order to produce concrete results in the form of cash and contentment. Our words are only catalysts. Listen as long as it means something or *until* it means something—then act. With every confidence, the makers of *Making It* turn their work over to you. It is our best effort; combined with *yours,* and with the best of luck (which we wish you), we have no doubt but that you've got it made!

Chapter One

FINANCIAL AID

Higher education is often presented to the high school student in the image of a financial investment. Fifty years ago, "college educated" was more of a class attribute than it is today. Decades of educational reform, pressed forward by thoughtful educators and by national legislation enforcing equal opportunity, have helped to alter the myth—and the reality—of college education as merely a "polishing" or "broadening" experience, or as "prep schooling" for professional training. Junior and community colleges as well as technical and paraprofessional schools have joined the traditional liberal arts and sciences colleges and universities to comprise a broader first level of postsecondary education. The range of associate and special degrees that have joined the B.A. are matched at the top of the educational ladder by an assortment of postgraduate programs leading to master's, doctorate, postdoctorate, and intermediate programs of specialized study. The extent and variety of opportunity is enormous.

This development, however, has only partial associations with the prestige of education, the satisfaction of study, and the pursuit of truth. It has economic roots. A sophisticated technological order of production and administration has generated a complex economy, and with it, a complicated society, demanding elaborate systems of goods and services. Educated, and indeed highly specialized, workers are required to keep our society and our economy functioning—even more are needed to advance it. The rewards to you, the high school student, for meeting this national need are most commonly brought home in terms of concrete financial facts.

In reporting on the incomes of men over twenty-five, as categorized by years of school completed, the 1970 Statistical Abstract of the Department of Commerce, Bureau of the Census, offers the following figures for the year 1968. Men who finished four years or more of postsecondary education earned an annual mean income of $12,938 and a lifetime income of $586,000, as compared with men who had completed only four years of high school who earned $8,148 as a mean annual income, with $350,000 estimated as their lifetime earnings.[1] Even those who had completed only one to three years of college demonstrated higher earnings: $9,397 in mean annual income and $441,000 in lifetime income. These figures suggest that the high school graduate who is willing to invest in four years of further education can expect an average, predicted lifetime return of $236,000 in extra income. This is indeed a handsome profit.

But is four years of patient study the only investment required? Every high school student and his family know that it is not. The accompanying table, prepared by *U.S. News and World Report* for an article in its issue of February 22, 1971, offers statistics to document the widespread publication of college costs.

An earlier edition of this guide, published in 1968, presented the following perception of the problem:

> College is expensive, and costs are rising. In 1958, the average tuition at four Big Ten schools was $301, and the average student budget ran approximately $1,450 for the academic year. In 1966, these figures had risen to $436 and $1,720 respectively. At the eight Ivy League colleges, the average tuition was $1,150 in 1958; the student budget came to $2,550; by 1966 these figures reached $1,900 and $3,400 respectively. Thus, in eight years, some costs have risen as high as 65%. The average annual cost of the least expensive private colleges is now about $1,850; even an inexpensive, urban public college, inhabited chiefly by commuters, now costs a student around $1,100 a year.

A comparison with the more recent figures makes a reading of this five-year-old discussion an exercise in nostalgia. Colleges across the country have announced tuition rises of 10 to 30 per cent for the year 1972, and increases in the cost of living have pushed room and board charges higher as well. *U.S. News and World Report* analyzes the rate of change in college charges with the following dire prediction: "At this pace, tuition and living costs alone will often mean $8,000 a year before the end of this decade."[2]

Although there is no reason to suppose that this upward trend will race on indefinitely and unchecked, it is clear that every undergraduate faces a real financial challenge. Few will have the personal or family resources to pay the bills for their college educations outright. Colleges make many efforts to keep costs down for their students, and in effect *every* student, even the wealthiest, receives indirect financial aid, since tuition charges typically represent only one-half to one-third of the actual amount of money spent by a college on educating any individual student. In terms of visible aid, although only about 20 per cent of all undergraduates receive flat scholarship grants, some schools aid as many as 50 or 60 per cent of their students *in some way*—through grants, loans, or guaranteed jobs.

This "package plan" has become the favored method of subsidizing the study of needy students in most American colleges. Whereas students and their families—and most educators—would prefer a "free" system of education, in which college costs were automatically met by sufficient funds granted with no strings attached, the adoption of such a distribution of current resources would mean that very few students could attend college. Since only a handful of low-income students could have their needs met completely and at no cost, the goal of equal opportunity in education would suffer even more than it does under present conditions. Colleges, cooperating with private scholarship sources and with federal and state assistance programs, now attempt to stretch their resources to aid the greatest possible number of needy students in a significant way. For some, this means a combination of loan and scholarship aid, plus part-time earnings from jobs that the institution has helped the student to find. Other students may benefit from only one of these three forms of aid or from a different proportion of the three. In every case, the college enlists the individual student in its effort to provide adequate and appropriate aid for the particular financial needs of that individual while keeping in mind the total requirements of the undergraduate population.

With the exception of a dwindling number of athletic scholarships and grants to students of exceptional academic achievement, there is little money that is likely to be pressed upon you, without your asking. If you are in need of money to finance your college education, you will have to ask for it—and there is an excellent and increasing chance that it shall be given to you. From the approximately $200 million in nationally available aid to undergraduates in 1958, current resources

Average Charges for Academic Year (1971) at Four-Year Colleges[3]

Public Colleges	1967	1971 (est.)	1972 (est.)
Total	$1,103	$1,417	$1,492
Tuition and fees	$ 326	$ 442	$ 472
Dormitory room	$ 304	$ 416	$ 441
Board	$ 473	$ 559	$ 579
Private Colleges			
Total	$2,314	$3,089	$3,281
Tuition and fees	$1,368	$1,924	$2,057
Dormitory room	$ 418	$ 539	$ 575
Board	$ 528	$ 626	$ 649

Averages do not include the cost of clothing, books, transportation, and incidentals and are far below the annual tab for a student in an elite institution. A typical Ivy Leaguer now spends $4,000 and up a year, and out-of-state students at top state universities lay out $3,000 and up. At present increases, college by 1980 would cost $8,000 a year in many places.

A Sampling of Anticipated Tuition Increases for 1972

Ivy League Colleges

	Tuition for college year starting September 1971	Increase over present year (1970)
Brown University	$2,850	$250
Columbia College	$2,700	$200
Cornell University	$2,800	$200
Dartmouth College	$2,820	$270
Harvard University	$2,800	$200
University of Pennsylvania	$2,750	$200
Princeton University	$2,800	$300
Yale University	$2,900	$350

Other Private Colleges

	Tuition for college year starting September 1971	Increase over present year (1970)
Agnes Scott College	$2,000	$100
Albion College	$2,020	$120
Austin College	$3,000	$150
California Institute of Technology	$2,560	$175
Case Western Reserve University	$2,385	$100
University of Chicago	$2,475	$120
Drake University	$1,970	$190

	Tuition for college year starting September 1971	Increase over present year (1970)
Emory University	$2,400	$225
Franklin and Marshall	$2,550	$150
George Fox College	$1,620	$219
George Washington University	$2,050	$150
Lehigh University	$2,450	$150
New York University	$2,700	$250
Northwestern University	$2,700	$300
Rice University	$2,100	$300
Stanford University	$2,610	$210
Williams College	$2,350	$100
Wittenberg University	$2,286	$165

Public Colleges

	Tuition for college year starting September 1971	Increase over present year (1970)
University of California		
(State residents)	$ 629	$141
(Out-of-state residents)	$1,829	$141
University of Maryland		
(State residents)	$ 589	$ 50
(Out-of-state residents)	$ 939	$150
State University of New York		
(State residents)	$ 550	$150
(Out-of-state residents)	$ 900	$300
University of Oregon		
(State residents)	$ 507	$ 99
(Out-of-state residents)	$1,575	$168

have mushroomed to at least $3 *billion*.[4] Funds in several forms are now available from many sources. The possibilities that are open to you will vary according to your background and interests—the eligibility requirements for scholarships and loans range from "resident of Dull County, majoring in Dull County history, with preference given to descendants of John Ebeneezer Dull" to "permanent resident of the United States." Between these two extremes are thousands of other categories, many of which you will probably fit. Whether you profit by a nationwide aid project that is millions of dollars in scope, or by the modest one-student-oriented efforts of a local PTA or club chapter, you should bear in mind that hundreds of programs and persons all over the country are seeking to keep you from giving up your plans for higher education because of insurmountable financial problems.

There is money, and this book was conceived in an earnest attempt to help you get as much as you need as an undergraduate. Although most of our concern has been with providing a picture of current student employment—showing what undergraduates can expect in the way of summer and term-time job opportunities, and what imagination, initiative, and the intelligent use of skills can achieve in this economic setting—we realize that many students will need some direct form of financial assistance to take the sharp edge off of their money worries before they can begin to deal with the problem of meeting the costs of a college education by means of personal employment. This chapter by no means lists or mentions in detail the multitude of sources of such financial assistance. We will, however, present a brief and general discussion of the three major forms of available aid: grants, loans, and earnings under the College Work-Study Program. It is our hope to indicate sources of funds and sources of information concerning funds so that the student will be able to form an idea of his needs and of the best strategy to adopt in meeting them. With some sense of what to expect, the undergraduate in need of money may be reassured that there *are* people to ask for what he requires—and this chapter may give the undergraduate a clearer idea of whom to ask, for his particular case.

Determining Need

As the children of more low-to-moderate income families continue their education past high school, and as college costs spiral upward, most undergraduates find themselves in a position of *financial need* as they confront their anticipated college bills. Although students will pinpoint their own degree of need in planning their individual undergraduate budgets, it is important to keep in mind the "official" definition of this term, as colleges, private programs, and government aid plans will apply it in their evaluation of your situation. The College Scholarship Service, which administrates the most widely used of the standardized need-analysis systems, offers the following definition.

Financial need can be defined most simply as the difference between the cost of an education at a particular institution and the amount of money an applicant, and his family, can make available from their income and assets to meet the expenses of that education.[5]

Note the flexibility of this definition. It takes into account the comparative interaction of income level and college charges. An expensive private university might make serious inroads on the finances of a family with above-average earnings, whereas a state-supported junior college, making far more modest demands, could put a low-income family in a comparable position of financial need.

According to the most recent government analyses, the median income for American families before taxes—that is, the figure below which half of all family incomes fall, and which half surpass—is approximately $10,600. At this level of income, about a quarter of the gross total income is taken in federal, state, and local taxes. Of the remaining net total of $8,100, current college expenses for even one undergraduate would require a giant share. It is clear from the preceding chart that without financial aid, a student from this average family would claim close to half of his parents' net income if he attended a private college and nearly one-fourth if he attended a public institution. Even if a family's net income rises to the affluent level of $20,000 a year, private college costs still claim a full fifth of this high total. And many families are faced with the dilemma of simultaneously supporting more than one child in college.

In the past, this financial bind has had a direct and predictable effect on college entrance rates, which show the following clear correlation with family income:

**Percentage of High School Seniors Entering College,
by Brackets of Annual Family Income[6]**

$15,000 and over	— 86.7%
$10,000–$15,000	— 61.3%
$7,500–$10,000	— 51.0%
$3,000–$7,500	— 37.7%
Less than $3,000	— 19.8%

The fact that families with highest earnings send more than four times as many of their college-age children to postsecondary programs as do families in the lowest income category points to a clear-cut situation of unequal educational opportunity. The roots of this problem are undoubtedly complex, but at least part of the discrepancy is a simple result of lack of educational funds on the part of the less wealthy families. Federal legislation, such as the Higher Education Act of 1965, has provided a legal impetus for the orienting of *all* financial aid toward economically disadvantaged students, and continued government commitment to this point has made not only direct gains but indirect changes in the distribution of state and private funds as well by influencing the criteria for financial need. It has also been the policy of the federal government to emphasize, as for example in the setting up of the massive Educational Opportunity Grants Program, the importance of identifying and encouraging college motivation in high school students of limited financial resources.

The effect of these financial realities, and the approaches that colleges, government, and other sources of aid have adopted toward them, have been presented as a prelude to considering how a student should assess his own financial need in preparing for a college education and how his parents can evaluate their fair share of the burden. It is apparent that student and family assessments will only be confusing unless they share the same approximate definitions of need as do the available financial assistance programs. Fortunately, this is generally the case.

The Student's Role—

You, as an undergraduate, are the direct recipient of the intellectual, social, and financial benefits of a college education. Yours is the burden of admission to college and of study once you get there. You also face the major challenge of responsibly dealing with the high finance of paying for your undergraduate years. If you are willing to work for part of that money, later chapters in this guide will offer you examples and suggestions of how to go about doing so. In arranging for grants and loans, however, you have less autonomy, and to deal with the distributors of funds successfully, your first step is to know where you stand.

Naturally, the high school senior—or junior—who is reading this section is in the best position to prepare for his future needs. College costs are so high that it is practically impossible to begin planning your strategy for meeting them too soon. But many college freshmen and even upperclassmen may benefit from taking another look at their financial position.

Begin with a budget. What do you anticipate as your *total costs* per undergraduate year?

Each student will come up with a different figure according to his own specific condition. Is your chosen college a private one or is it supported by government funds? If it is a state school, do you benefit by any decrease in fees for state residents? Are you considering only your basic expenses—tuition, room, and board—or have you realistically allotted sums to pay for books and school supplies, recreation, clothing, and the other personal expenses that do not disappear upon college enrollment? Have you figured on the cost of transportation to and from school in September and June and at the Christmas vacation? Even with student charter flights, a trip from Arizona to the University of Chicago or the University of Massachusetts involves a significant expense. If you are a commuting student, has your local transportation been taken into consideration? If you do not have to contribute to room and board at home, you must at least count on the expense of lunches and other meals eaten on campus. You may be discouraged to see the total bill mount as you add up these extra expenses, but it is far better to know *now* where you stand than to be surprised by your lack of money once you are at school.

The College Scholarship Service offers the following two approximations of typical college budgets for the year 1972–1973.[7]

	Private 4-Year College	*Public 4-Year College*
Tuition and required fees	$2,100	$ 500
Dormitory room	500	450
Board	600	550
Books	150	150
Miscellaneous personal expenses	400	400
Transportation (usually two round trips from home to college are included in a student's budget)	variable	variable
Total	$3,750	$2,050

Once you have prepared a realistic budget, you have a tool to use in your financial planning. If you have not yet decided which schools to apply to or how your financial requirements must interact with your personal order of preference in choosing between several institutions, a comparison of careful budgets prepared for each school may help you. Certainly your choice will depend to a great extent upon what concrete offers of financial aid are made to you—a private university (total budget: $3,800) that can provide you with a package of aid programs meeting your total need there may be better than a local public university (total budget: $1,900) that can only offer you 80 per cent of the assistance that you will need to attend it. Initial cost estimates are surely not the only important factor. On the other hand, it will undoubtedly be clear to you from your figures that some institutions will cost you more than others. Transportation charges, residence fees versus commuting costs, and benefits accorded by colleges operated by your home state are all sums to consider. Two more factors are important to your budget(s).

Can you estimate the length of your postsecondary education? Many high school seniors cannot, and your plans may, of course, change. The young woman who plans on a two-year associate degree in early childhood education, will have a different financial perspective from her sister who expects to complete a four-year Baccalaureate nursing degree, or her classmate who must count on at least eight expensive years of higher education before she achieves her ambition of beginning a career in medicine.

Can you estimate the degree of inflation that will affect the costs of the schools you are considering? This is a difficult question to answer, but sometimes colleges themselves, having analyzed these trends for the purposes of their own financial planning, will be able to pass on their estimates to you to help you with your own budget. California residents, for example, are justifiably proud of their excellent system of state-supported, "free" higher education. But a news magazine recently cautioned that at the University of California, as at many other public colleges, "the cost of tuition and fees is rising faster, percentagewise, than at private colleges."[8] In the autumn of 1972, it actually went up 28 per cent at that university. For state residents, charges for tuition, room, board, and fees rose to $1,774; for nonresidents, the average cost rose to $2,974. Such increases, if they can be anticipated, should certainly form part of your four-year projected budget.

Once your overall financial picture is clear to you, it will be easier to discuss college possibilities with your family, your guidance counselor at school, and the financial aid officers of the various public and private sources of funds. You should consider the extent to which you will borrow money to finance your education and should begin as soon as possible to accumulate savings from work during high school and in your prefreshman year summer to meet expected needs. Colleges generally expect a contribution of one-fifth of a student's accumulated assets during each academic year. If you manage to save $750 during high school, you will be asked to apply approximately $150 a year to your undergraduate expenses. In addition, ten to fifteen hours of term-time work (often fewer for freshmen) plus forty hours of summer work are usually counted upon as contributing wages to your financial deficit. Certainly your actual earnings will depend on you; this book was written in the hope that they will be high, and students who must help support their families will have to contend with understandably lower savings. But the College Scholarship Service offers the following estimates as guidelines to colleges for expected student earnings:

	Men	Women
Term-time (each year)	$600–$900	$600–$900
Prefreshman summer	$400	$300
Presophomore summer	$500	$400
Prejunior summer	$600	$500
Presenior summer	$600	$500

Note that women undergraduates cannot expect (or, at any rate, are not expected) to match the summer earnings of their male counterparts.

Many noncollege sources of scholarship aid are principally open to applicants not yet attending college, so it is worthwhile to begin investigating these possibilities early. The time you invest in financial planning will ultimately reward you with greater leeway in your decision between educational institutions and opportunities.

You should be aware that many students are denied college admission or financial aid *simply because they did not submit complete applications before the necessary deadlines.* All colleges and noncollege sources of funds have enormous volumes of applicants to evaluate, and fair judgment depends upon the processing and comparison of vast quantities of data. These institutions cannot make exceptions for individuals who are unprepared in their requests for aid. Competition is stiff enough—do yourself the favor of starting out even by applying accurately and on time.

The Parents' Role—

Few students attend college without the financial assistance of their parents. Whereas families with low incomes and heavy expenses may make only a token contribution, most undergraduates rely on their parents for at least half of their expenses while attending college.[9] In general, colleges expect each student's family to support his or her studies by making payments from its income and assets, at least to the extent of other families sharing a similar financial situation. Several systems are used by colleges and by noncollege financial aid programs to assess carefully and fairly the amount that a particular family can reasonably afford to spend for a child's higher education. These systems are helpful guidelines to parents, as well as colleges, if the family is not sure what is expected of it in terms of money.

By cooperating fully and freely in providing the *confidential* information concerning family finances by which such assessments are made, even parents with little or no concrete assistance to offer can look upon themselves as their child's principal financial ally in pursuing his undergraduate studies. Most parents will feel some reluctance to divulge the private financial facts of their lives to impersonal sources, but nearly all financial aid to students hinges upon the determinations of need made with the help of these facts. Families can be confident that their confidential data will be respected and will be turned over only to officials of the institutions and programs named to receive them by the individual family—never to high schools or other unauthorized recipients. It is essential, for the sake of the student, that the system of need-determination used by those schools and programs to which the student is applying be supplied with accurate family financial information—even if the parents do not wish to or expect to provide assistance that is commensurate with their actual monetary circumstances.

Three types of standardized systems are used by college and non-college financial aid offices to suggest to them what contributions a student's parents can reasonably make toward his higher education. One is a rule of thumb called the Income Tax method; the other two are need-analysis methods devised by large educational service corporations. One of these is the Student Need Analysis Service of the American College Testing Program (ACT), which computes comprehensive financial aid reports on individual students on the basis of information gathered from the students and their parents on the Family Financial Statement (FFS), a financial status form. The College Scholarship Service (CSS) of the College Entrance Examination Board (CEEB) gathers data by means of a form called the Parents' Confidential Statement (PCS), which it processes and reports on to the colleges and financial aid programs to which a student has applied. Although the ACT and CSS systems are similar, the latter, established in 1954, is used by the vast majority of institutions to which a student might apply. Hundreds of colleges, junior colleges, and universities require the completion and submission of the PCS from their financial aid applicants, and over 350 foundations, agencies, and other sources of scholarship aid—including the National Merit Scholarship Service and the Fund for Negro Students, and the George M. Pullman Educational Foundation—employ the PCS in determining the amount of assistance they will grant to each scholarship recipient. Fifteen state scholarship programs require or utilize the PCS in making their awards. In all, the PCS is used by over 4,000 programs and institutions, and 1,100,000 students made use of the service in 1970 alone. Because of its widespread use and the fact that its principles of financial need and family contribution are common to most sources of financial aid, we will discuss the PCS need-analysis system in some detail.

The object of the processing of the Parents' Confidential Statement is, in each case, to produce three estimates: the amount of money that the student's parents can reasonably be asked to contribute to the student's college expenses, the amount that the student himself may be expected to pay out from his own assets, and the student's financial need at each of the colleges from which he is seeking assistance. These estimates, along with photocopies of the raw data on the PCS itself, go to financial-aid officers at the colleges and agencies designated by the family. These officers in turn use the information and estimations *as they see fit* to *independently* determine which applicants they will assist and to what degree and in what form the aid will be provided. Agencies and scholarship programs make evaluations according to their own criteria; colleges weigh the needs of their current students against the competitive demands of all needy potential incoming freshmen and against the school's own resources. In each case, however, student need is defined—as discussed earlier—as the gap between college costs and the student's ability to pay. This part of the PCS estimate is easily understood, as is the contribution of student assets, by the one-fifth rule mentioned under "the student's role." An estimation of the parents' fair share of college costs is, however, more complex to arrive at.

This share is considered a function of "the total financial strength of the family. In this regard, the CSS recognizes that a certain level of income and assets is necessary to maintain the family."[10] In other words, an individual family's financial status is not merely evaluated in terms of two figures, income and assets. If this were true, no elaborate determination system would exist. On the contrary, a family's financial circumstances are analyzed on a highly individual basis.

The reported family income is considered. From this figure amounts representing totals of federal, state, and local taxes are subtracted and adjustments are made to account for unusual medical or dental expenses, for emergency expenses resulting from natural causes (such as hurricane damage to a home), for expenses incurred by supporting elderly relatives, and for such extraordinary circumstances as the illness of the family breadwinner. "In addition, while the income of working mothers is taken into account in the estimate of the family's total ability to pay, the CSS method makes certain allowances so that not all of a working mother's income is included in the computation of the parents' contribution."[11] In this way, families who are making special efforts to supplement their income to help their undergraduate children need not feel that their extra attempts are to be cancelled out by a lower estimate of their financial need. Similarly, families should not fear that different styles of living will affect the impartiality of the evaluation procedure. Two families of equal income will be treated equally, even if one is deeply in debt and must commit much of its earnings to paying off the debt—if the debt represents a choice of living styles on the part of the family (for example, expensive automobiles, vacations, or other elective expenses). An adjustment *would* be made if the debt reflected medical bills for an injured child, for example, or nursing home expenses for an aged grandparent; charges that are beyond the choice or control of the family.

Once these allowances and adjustments have been made, the remaining income is considered to be available to the family for the necessities of living. This remaining income is, however, considered in relation to family assets before it is evaluated for CSS purposes. Assets are considered to have three principal functions in family budgets. Some savings are allocated as retirement funds and are not expected to be tapped for educational expenses. Older parents who are closer to retirement age are allowed larger retirement deductions than couples who have longer to accumulate savings, and families with no male head receive special consideration. Secondly, certain assets may be earmarked for the discharging of debts such as those accumulated during past business enterprises or periods of unemployment. These payments are also thought of as inviolate assets, and are not considered in evaluating the parents' college contribution.

Once these sums have been subtracted from the net worth of a family (based on savings, investments, business assets, and real estate, including the family home minus outstanding mortgage payments), the remaining assets are considered to take on the third function; that of a *potential* income source for future spending. This amount is added to the adjusted *present* income to provide a base from which the family's capacity for making investments and purchases *of choice* can be evaluated. These "discretionary purchases" are the range of funds from which the parents' contribution to college costs is derived. According to official financial aid policy, "education is considered by the colleges, using the CSS to be the most important discretionary purchase that a family with college-age children can make."[12]

The accompanying chart is the scale by which the CSS computes parents' contributions in relation to their net, untaxed income. This chart takes into account the number of children in a family, but otherwise represents "typical" family arrangements in which there is one breadwinner, no dependent relatives (except for the children), and no medical or emergency expenses of any scope. Deviations from this pattern would result in an expected contribution that had been adjusted downward, as explained previously.

These charted contributions are based on the following rule of thumb derived from *Three Standards of Living for an Urban Family of Four,* a cost-of-living analysis prepared by the United States Bureau of Labor Statistics. This study asserts that $1,000 is approximately adequate to maintain a dependent child for a school year of nine months' duration. Families can afford this if their pretax income level is close to the national median cited at the beginning of this chapter: $10,600. A "typical' family of four with such an income is considered able to support an undergraduate child with a contribution of $1,000. If the family income is lower, the contribution drops; if the income is higher, some "discretionary income" must be added to the $1,000 figure. Should more than one child be in college at the same time, the extra contribution from discretionary income is to be divided equally among them, in addition to the basic $1,000 contribution for each child.

This involved discussion of a complex evaluation procedure indicates the lengths to which colleges and scholarship agencies go in order to insure the fair and equitable distribution of funds to deserving students *on the basis of need*. Need, as will be appreciated, is determined not by any intuitive or impersonal system but rather painstakingly and with a real commitment to equal educational opportunity.

This is one of the other two major systems used by colleges to determine parents' contributions when judging applications for financial aid, as well as of the CSS system. Similar in basic approach to the Parents' Confidential Statement evaluation is the Family Financial Statement (FFS), which was developed by the American College Testing program (ACT). It is important to note that the College Scholarship Service and the American College Testing Program are both private, nonprofit organizations that have become established in the testing and need-analysis fields. They are in competition with each other and each has a group of schools and programs that subscribe exclusively to it. If you apply to several colleges or scholarship agencies, you may have to use both services simultaneously. The processing fee for the PCS is $3.00 and for the FFS, $2.50. Additional charges may be added if reports must be made to several colleges. Applications for the ACT, which will consider individual fee waivers in particular cases of extreme poverty, should be made through your high school guidance counselor.

Finally, some colleges prefer to determine financial need on the basis

**CSS Expectation of Parents' Contribution from Net Income in a
"Typical" Family Financial Situation[13]**

Net Income before Federal Taxes	Number of Dependent Children				
	1	2	3	4	5
$ 5,000	$ 0				
6,000	280	$ 50			
7,000	550	280	$ 80		
8,000	820	510	280	$ 120	$ 50
9,000	1,080	730	470	300	220
10,000	1,290	960	660	480	390
11,000	1,530	1,180	860	650	560
12,000	1,800	1,400	1,050	830	730
13,000	2,100	1,650	1,260	1,010	890
14,000	2,440	1,920	1,490	1,210	1,060
15,000	2,810	2,240	1,750	1,420	1,270
16,000	3,240	2,590	2,030	1,660	1,490
17,000	3,660	2,980	2,350	1,930	1,740
18,000	4,070	3,390	2,710	2,240	2,010
19,000	4,480	3,800	3,110	2,580	2,320
20,000	4,890	4,210	3,520	2,960	2,670

of information provided by an applicant's parents directly from their federal income tax returns of the previous two years. An amount equal to the previous year's income tax payment, or an average of the two years' payments, is then expected as the parents' contribution to the undergraduate's expenses. If the family possesses net assets in excess of $10,000, the parents will be asked to add 1 per cent of that total to their college contribution. Helpful Addresses:

College Scholarship Service
College Entrance Examination Board
888 Seventh Avenue
New York, New York 10019

and at the following regional offices:

Midwest: Hollace G. Roberts, Director
990 Grove Street
Evanston, Illinois 60201

Northeast: Edwin T. Carine, Jr., Acting Director
Middle-Atlantic states
Robert J. Katds, Jr., Acting Director, New England States
888 Seventh Avenue
New York, New York 10019

South: Robert E. Stoltz, Director
Suite 200, 17 Executive Park Drive, N. E.
Atlanta, Georgia 30329

Southwest: John J. O'Hearne, Director
Suite 119, 3810 Medical Parkway
Austin, Texas 78756

West: Robert G. Cameron, Director
800 Welch Road
Palo Alto, California 94304
Suite 23, 2142 South High Street
Denver, Colorado

This service makes available the Parents' Confidential Statement (PCS) and two information booklets on its service and methods: *A Letter to Parents* (free) and *Financing a College Education: A Guide for Counselors* ($.25). These booklets, which are updated annually, are available through high school guidance counselors or directly from the

Publications Order Office
College Entrance Examination Board
Box 592
Princeton, New Jersey 08540

The American College Testing Program
P.O. Box 168
Iowa City, Iowa 52240

and at the following regional offices:

Western Regional Office
  J. Dan Recer, Regional Director
  Downtown Plaza Towers, Suite 515
  555 Capitol Mall
  Sacramento, California 95814

Mountain-Plains Regional Office
  O. W. Hascall, Regional Director

  Executive Office Building
  720 Pearl Street
  Boulder, Colorado 80302

Southwestern Regional Office
  Vernon L. Odom, Regional Director
  Coronado Building
  1626 50th Street
  Lubbock, Texas 79412

Midwest Regional Office
   Jack W. Goodner, Regional Director
   899 Skokie Boulevard
   Northbrook, Illinois 60062

Southeastern Regional Office
   Thomas C. Oliver, Regional Director
   20 Perimeter Park, Suite 101
   Atlanta, Georgia 30341

Eastern Regional Office
   Peter L. Fisher, Regional Director
   General Washington Building
   216 Goddard Boulevard
   King of Prussia, Pennsylvania 19406

This service publishes and processes the Family Financial Statement (FFS) and also administrates various guidance services and academic and vocational interest and ability tests that may be of interest to college-oriented high school students. The more general of these is the ACT Test Battery Program; the Career Planning Program is specifically designed for students headed toward vocational-technical education and two-year postsecondary institutions. For information about all ACT's services, contact the corporate headquarters in Iowa. The following free booklets relate to ACT's financial aid services: *Counselor's Handbook: A Guide for Using ACT Services in Pre-College Guidance, Financial Aid for College: A Guide for Students and Parents,* and *Financial Aid Services.*

Whatever the procedure is that provides guidelines to the particular college to which you have applied for financial aid, you can be confident that the institution will evaluate your case fairly and will do its best for you, insofar as its resources and the competitive demands of other needy applicants permit. Undergraduate financial need is a gap that billions of dollars are available in the United States to fill. Although the available funds do not yet satisfactorily meet the needs of every potential post-secondary student, you should make an investigation of all possible sources of aid that are open to you. The remainder of this chapter discusses the three forms that actual financial need can take once need has been determined: grants, loans, and jobs (most specifically, those subsidized by the College-Work Study Program; many other topics in the field of student employment occupy the rest of this guide). One or, more likely, a combination of two or more of these forms of assistance may make all the difference to your college plans.

Scholarships

Scholarships, or flat grants of money for which no repayment is required, are available to undergraduate students from five principal sources, including individual colleges and universities, the federal government, the armed forces, national scholarship organizations, and local sources including state scholarship programs. We will deal with each of these categories of grants, indicating briefly the nature of the scholarship and giving the appropriate addresses from which further, detailed information may be obtained.

Colleges and Universities—

Start your search for financial aid at the individual colleges and universities to which you are applying. The vast majority of financial aid—in all forms—that college students receive is administered through the colleges themselves, whether from their own resources or from federal funds that are channeled through the financial aid offices of individual institutions.

When you write to a college asking for admission materials, be sure to ask for a financial-aid application as well. Consult the information bulletin of the college carefully—financial-aid applications may have an earlier deadline than applications for admission alone. In addition, you and your family will probably need time to prepare and submit the PCS, FFS, or other information-gathering forms used by the schools that you select. Some colleges simply provide a special space on their admissions forms for financial-aid requests; others demand that an entirely separate set of papers be filed.

Asking for financial aid will *not* have any adverse effect on your chances for admission to a particular college. In almost every case, institutions keep their admissions and financial aid decisions separate.

Incoming freshmen have first priority in the distribution of college aid funds. Most schools, with the expectation that upperclassmen will be able to find higher-paying jobs, concentrate their aid on first-year students, since the freshman year is seen as a period of academic and social adjustment, and most first-year students are not expected to spend much time working at outside jobs. Flat grants, therefore, are often provided to freshmen in lieu of job offers or work-study funds.

Most college scholarships are unrestricted, and in those cases in which the original donor stipulated that the student's name, race, place of residence, high school, or subject of study be a factor in determining the recipients of the scholarship, schools have often petitioned the courts and escaped from the narrow terms of the original endowment. Consult the college catalogue, which will enumerate all special grants and scholarships, to see whether you fit the terms of eligibility for any restricted grants. In most cases, your single financial-aid application insures that the college will consider you for any and all of the scholarships for which you are eligible. Scholarships are sometimes donated for use by upperclassmen only; financial-aid officers can make you aware of any money for which you might apply.

The Federal Government

Federal money is available in the form of scholarships to aid many students who would not otherwise be able to continue their postsecondary education. Federal funds are distributed according to a policy of ensuring equal opportunity for higher education and are granted strictly on the basis of financial need.

The federal grant program that potentially applies to the largest range of students is the Equal Opportunity Grants program. Unlike many government-sponsored programs, the EOG program is not designed to promote any crucial field of study; any full-time undergraduate, pursuing any academic course, is eligible. The EOG program is exceptional, in comparison to most scholarship systems, in that scholastic achievement and potential are not even a contributing factor in the determination of the recipients. Sums from $200 to $1,000 a year, for up to four years, are made available to students solely for the purpose of enabling them to afford continued college study. Government requirements stipulate that recipients of EOG funds must receive at least a matching amount of other aid, either in the form of grants, loans, or jobs (other government sources may be tapped for this matching award).

Students do not apply to the federal government for these grants, but are selected by the financial-aid officer at the college to which they apply. If you are in doubt as to whether the institution of your choice is one of the hundreds that administer funds from this program, consult the pamphlet *A Guide to Student Assistance,* available from the U.S. House of Representatives Committee on Education and Labor. This book provides a chart indicating those colleges in each state that participate in the three main federal student-aid programs: EOG, the National Student Defense Loan Program, and the College Work-Study Program.

For further information, contact the Division of Student Financial Aid, Bureau of Higher Education, U.S. Office of Education, Washington D.C. 20202.

Several other federally funded scholarship programs provide money for undergraduate students who meet their particular eligibility requirements.

A student pursuing any full-time course of study, both high school and college, may receive Social Security cash benefit payments every month if a parent of which he is a dependent is deceased or receives Social Security payments for disability or retirement. The size of the student's benefits depends upon need, in each case, but typical payments amount to 50 to 75 per cent of the sum received by the parents in Social Security benefits. Only unmarried students, aged eighteen to twenty-two, may obtain such aid, and it is not granted automatically to eligible students; you or your family must notify the local office of the Social Security Administration if you think you qualify. The American Legion, in its pamphlet *Need A Lift?*, comments on these Social Security benefits as follows: "During the school year (1971–1972) more than one half million students . . . will receive 580 million dollars in benefit payments. . . . This source represents more funds to assist students to further their education than there are in scholarships at all colleges and universities in the United States."[14]

For further information, contact the appropriate district office of the Social Security Administration (look in the telephone directory under "United States Government") or the Office of Information, Social Security Administration, U.S. Department of Health, Education, and Welfare, Security Boulevard, Baltimore, Maryland 21235.

Under the Nurse Training Act of 1971, the federal government supplements its past programs of scholarship aid to nursing students of exceptional financial need. The annual stipend now available is $2,000 (previously $1,500), and half-time students now join full-time students in eligibility for benefits. Accredited diploma, associate degree, and collegiate nursing schools, which have agreed not to discriminate by sex in their admissions policies, are the administrators of these grants, and students should apply directly to the financial-aid office at their own institutions.

For further information, write to the Division of Nursing, Bureau of Health Manpower Education, National Institutes of Health, 9000 Rockville Pike, Bethesda, Maryland 20014.

Several other government grants support students training to enter various health professions.

The director of financial aid at individual schools can advise students on how to apply for Health Professions Scholarships. These pay up to $2,500 in any twelve-month period, depending upon financial need, and are administered by individual institutions. Although they are primarily oriented toward graduate students in the professions of medicine, optometry, dentistry, and the like, students studying for a bachelor of science in pharmacy are also eligible.

The Division of Health Manpower Educational Services, Bureau of Health Professions Education and Manpower Training, National Institutes of Health, Bethesda, Maryland 20014 has further information on this aid program.

College juniors or seniors who are engaged in full-time study with a major emphasis on work that will lead to some type of career related to the education of handicapped children—teaching, supervising, research, or other specialty—are eligible for traineeships from the Department of Health, Education, and Welfare. These range from $300 to $800 per year, plus tuition and fees for senior year trainees. A description of this program, including a list of participating institutions and state agencies (which administer these grants) is available from the Office of Education, Bureau of Education for the Handicapped, Division of Training Programs, U.S. Department of Health, Education and Welfare, Washington, D.C. 20202.

The traineeship stipends made possible by the Rehabilitation Services Administration are designed to increase the number of trained personnel available for rehabilitating the physically and mentally ill. Many of these grants are available only for graduate study, but undergraduates in the fields of physical therapy, occupational therapy, prosthetics and orthotics, and rehabilitation of the blind, deaf, and mentally retarded may also benefit. These stipends range from a few hundred dollars to over $1,000, plus tuition and fees, depending upon the subject of study. Recipients may not ordinarily be receiving any other *federal* financial aid. Individual institutions and agencies administer these grants. For a list of participating agencies in your specialty and for further information, write to the Social and Rehabilitation Service, Division of Training, Rehabilitation Services Administration, Department of Health, Education, and Welfare, Washington, D.C. 20201.

Nursing students who intend to study psychiatric-mental health nursing at the master's level or higher may receive aid while they are in their last two years of full-time undergraduate nursing study. These traineeships, in the form of stipends including tuition and fees, are available directly from participating schools. For a list of these institutions and further information, contact the U.S. Department of Health, Education, and Welfare, Public Health Service, Health Services and Mental Health Administration, National Institute of Mental Health, Rockville, Maryland, 20852.

If you are a full-time law enforcement officer, employed by a public police or corrections agency or by the courts, you may receive aid in the form of tuition and fees up to $300 per semester from the Law Enforcement Education Program. These grants are applicable only to courses that are related to the field of law enforcement, although recipients need not be enrolled for a degree. All awards are approved and granted by the individual colleges and universities participating in the program, listings of which may be obtained from the Law Enforcement Education Program, Law Enforcement Assistance Administration, U.S. Department of Justice, Washington, D.C. 20530.

Special categories of students may qualify for federal scholarship assistance regardless of their fields of study.

Students who are of one-quarter or more Indian blood, and who live on Indian reservations, are eligible for government scholarships if they demonstrate financial need and academic achievement. Application should be made to the area director of the local office of the Bureau of Indian Affairs or to the Branch of Education, Bureau of Indian Affairs, U.S. Department of the Interior, Washington, D.C. 20242.

Single children, aged eighteen to twenty-two, of deceased railroad workers may obtain benefits if they are full-time students in high schools or colleges. The Railroad Retirement Act, as amended in 1966, further stipulates that the payments to a retired railroad worker may be increased, if he has eighteen-to-twenty-two year old children who are full-time students. Contact the local office of the Railroad Retirement Board for further information.

Veterans and their dependents have several sources of federal aid available to them. Men and women who have served in any branch of the armed forces for at least 181 days during the period since January 31, 1955, may, whether or not they are still in service, receive certain benefits while continuing their education at the high school level or above. A veteran who served for less than 181 days may also receive benefits if a service connected disability terminated his active duty. Such benefits are payable for a maximum of thirty-six months, based on the rule of one and one-half months of benefits for every month of active duty. Payments are made at the rate of $175 a month to full-time students with no dependents; increases are made proportional to the number of dependents, and deductions are made if schooling is less than full-time. If a serviceman's discharge was on or after June 1, 1966, he has eight years from his discharge date during which to claim these educational benefits. Detailed information on this aid program is offered by the Veterans' Administration, Washington, D.C. 20420, or contact your local Veterans' Administration Office.

An unmarried student between the ages of eighteen and twenty-three who is the child of a deceased veteran of World Wars I or II, or of the Korean or Vietnam War, or of a veteran who was permanently and totally disabled while in active service in one of these conflicts qualifies for monthly benefits. In writing to the Veterans' Administration to check your eligibility, be sure to include the full name and claim number of the veteran in question.

Wives and widows of deceased and disabled veterans are also eligible for certain benefits. The particulars of eligibility are available from the Veterans' Administration.

Many other sources of aid to particular categories of soldiers and their relatives have been established. We will simply list several of the more important:

The U.S. Air Force provides financial aid to certain student dependents of Air Force personnel. Contact the personnel services officer at any Air Force base, and request details of Regulation 214–5.

The General Henry H. Arnold Foundation Fund, described in Air Force Form 105, provides some grants and a program of loans without interest for the postsecondary education of eligible students. Either the personnel officer at a local base or the Director of the Air Force Aid Society, National Headquarters, 1117 North 19th Street, Suite 700, Arlington, Virginia 22209, can provide you with forms and applications.

Children of active, retired, and deceased members of the U.S. Navy and Marine Corps may obtain information on available scholarship awards from:

The Chief of Naval Personnel
(Attention NAVPERS—15003–A)
Navy Department
Washington, D.C. 20370

The Navy Relief Society
801 North Randolph Street
North Arlington, Virginia 22203

Relatives of officers and enlisted men in the United States Army should consult the following:

The Army Relief Society
26 Federal Plaza
Room 1733
New York, New York 10007

Society, Daughters of the Army
c/o Mrs. Wesson Stone
2800 Woodly Road, N.W.
Washington, D.C. 20008 (for female children only)

Adjutant General
(Attn: AGMG–D), Department of the Army
Washington, D.C. 20314 (request Army Regulation 352–1)

Scholarships available without regard to the particular branch of the armed forces include the following, which are not necessarily federally funded:

La Verne Noyes Scholarships (available only at certain schools: consult the American Legion publication *Need A Lift?* for a comprehensive listing)

The Knights of Columbus
Director of Scholarship Aid
Drawer 1670
New Haven, Connecticut 06507

The Eagles' Memorial Foundation
4710–14th Street
West Bradenton, Florida 33505

Programs for the children of disabled veterans include:

AMVETS Scholarship Program
1710 Rhode Island Avenue, N.W.
Washington, D.C. 20036

Disabled American Veterans Scholarship Fund
3725 Alexandria Pike
Cold Spring, Kentucky 41076

Two specialized sources of funds are the following:

The United Daughters of the Confederacy Committee
c/o Mrs. Henry D. Ferris
2635 Woodside Road
Bethlehem, Pennsylvania 18017
(for lineal descendants of Confederate veterans or members of the Children of the Confederacy)

U.S. Submarine Veterans of World War II Scholarships
Pers P–511, Bureau of Naval Personnel
Navy Department
Washington, D.C. 20370

It is worth noting that many individual divisions of the armed forces offer scholarship benefits to children of men who served in them.

Two sources of information offer full listings of scholarships and other educational assistance that are available to veterans, armed forces members, and their dependents. These are the last section of *Need A Lift?* (American Legion Educational and Scholarship Program, Indianapolis, Indiana 46206; $.50) and the Department of the Army pamphlet Number 352–1, "Education Scholarships, Loans, and Financial Aids" (Superintendent of Public Documents, United States Government Printing Office, Washington, D.C. 20402; $1.00).

The Armed Forces—

Opportunities are offered by the armed forces for young men and women to work for their B.A. degrees while qualifying for commissions in the various branches of the Armed Forces. Each service has a slightly different program.

The Navy-Marine Scholarship Program selects its participants on the basis of nationwide competition, including an evaluation of scores on the required Scholastic Aptitude Test (SAT) or the American College Test (ACT). Applicants must be between seventeen and twenty-one years of age, physically qualified, and male citizens of the United States. They must have *"no moral obligations or personal convictions that will prevent their conscientiously bearing arms and supporting and defending the United States against all enemies, foreign and domestic"*—a stipulation that should be seriously considered by all potential applicants.[15]

Those men selected for the NROTC scholarship program are appointed midshipmen in the United States Naval Reserve and participate in naval science courses plus drills and summer training periods, in addition to their normal course of study. Upon receiving the B.A. degree, a participant in this program is commissioned as a Navy ensign or as a second lieutenant in the Marine Corps, where he serves on active duty for a minimum of four years. Such officers may apply for special training to prepare them for aviation, submarine, or nuclear propulsion specialization.

While a midshipman is an undergraduate the Navy pays the total cost of tuition, textbooks, fees, and uniforms, plus a $50 monthly subsistence. Although this probably will not cover the total cost of an undergraduate's education, it represents a major investment—up to $12,000 over four years. Study must be undertaken at one of the approximately fifty colleges and universities that participate in this nation-wide program.

Students may also participate in the NROTC Navy-Marine College Program, which carries no financial benefits but allows participants to share the same courses and draft deferment as NROTC Scholarship students. Those who finish the NROTC College Program may become Reserve Officers in the Navy or Marine Corps. Such students may, as undergraduates, shift into the subsidized NROTC Scholarship Program at any time, if they are selected through the annual competitions.

Two programs are offered by the United States Air Force, each resulting in commissions as officers in the Air Force. Acceptance of a commission involves a commitment of four years on active duty as a reserve officer or five years on active duty as a rated officer after the completion of flight training. The four-year ROTC program involves completion of a two-year General Military Course, followed by a medical examination, officer interview, and Air Force Officer's Qualifying Test. Those who complete these requirements successfully receive summer field training and then enter the two-year Professional Officer Course, which is taken during the junior and senior years. The two-year ROTC program simply involves competitive selection after the sophomore year, by means of the test and procedures listed previously. It essentially is the same program minus the General Military Course.

Four-year scholarships are offered to men only, as these scholarships involve a commitment to flight training, in which women are prohibited by law from participating. Although students may participate in the two- and four-year programs without scholarship benefits, both men and women are eligible for three- and two-year scholarships. All scholarships are awarded on a competitive basis, and 5,500 such grants are in effect nationwide at any given time (four-, three-, and two year-grants) with participation available at dozens of colleges and universities in forty-six states and Puerto Rico. Scholarship recipients are granted full tuition, fees, laboratory expenses, an annual book allowance, and a nontaxable monthly stipend of $100. Physical, academic, and personal qualifications for this aid are similar to those for the Navy-Marine ROTC program.

The Army ROTC program is similar to the Air Force arrangement. A two-year Advanced Course is supplemented for those in the four-year program by a two-year Basic Course taken in the freshman and sophomore years. Students in the Advanced Course receive $50 per month and may enter directly after a Basic Camp summer training period instead of the Basic Course. Students may receive Rescue or Regular Army Commission, with active duty service commitments of two and three years, respectively.

The Army ROTC awards 6,500 four-, three-, and two-year scholarships. Cadets who enroll via the two-year program are not eligible for these scholarships, which pay for tuition, books, laboratory expenses, and a $100 stipend for ten months of each school year. Scholarship recipients accept a four-year commitment to active duty when they are commissioned. More than 200 schools participate in the Army ROTC program.

Women interested in having their senior year of college subsidized by the Army may enroll in the Women's Army Corps College Junior and Student Officer Program. This involves a summer training period following the junior year; upon graduation, the women are appointed second lieutenants in the Army Reserve, agreeing to at least two years of active duty. Approximately $400 per month is available in benefits to such students during the senior year.

ROTC students who seek scholarships face only one obstacle beyond the standard academic competition. The Navy-Marine and Air Force requirements for physical condition are stringent; 20/20 vision (or vision correctable to 20/20, if your ability is deemed exceptional) is the most common stumbling block, but many physical defects and ailments, however minor, may disqualify a potential scholarship candidate.

If the armed forces appeals to you as a career or as a source of educational funding, you may consider the following advantages that ROTC programs offer beyond officer status and financial aid. Military service is deferred until your undergraduate education is completed, regardless of your draft number. Excellent training in special fields such as computers, nuclear engineering, and flight school are offered by the armed forces to ROTC candidates. Finally, you can expect subsidized graduate education in many fields—including medicine, business administration, and various technical specialties—if you remain on active or reserve duty beyond your initial commitment to the service.

Detailed information on requirements, benefits, service opportunities, schools, and applications are available from the following sources:

Army ROTC
Commanding General
U.S. Continental Army Command

Attn: ROTC/NDCC Directorate
Fort Monroe, Virginia 23351

The Navy-Marine ROTC College Scholarship Program
The Commander
Navy Recruiting Command (Code 314)
Department of the Navy
Washington, D.C. 20370

Air Force ROTC Office of Information
Maxwell Air Force Base
Montgomery, Alabama 36112

Women's Army Corps College Junior and Student Officer Program
Commanding General
U.S. Army Recruiting Command
Attn: USARCRO–W
Liberty Building
1520 Aberdeen Road
Hampton, Virginia 23366

It should be noted that the U.S. Coast Guard Academy (Director of Admissions; New London, Connecticut 06320) and the United States Merchant Marine Academy (Admissions Officer; Kings Point, Long Island, New York 11024) educate qualified young men at government expense to receive B.S. degrees plus officer status in the respective services. Admission is competitive, and further information can be obtained from the officers listed. Appointments to the U.S. Military Academy at West Point, New York, the U.S. Naval Academy at Annapolis, Maryland, and the U.S. Air Force Academy at Colorado Springs, Colorado, are obtained from nominations of qualifying men made by United States Congressmen. Graduation from each of these government-subsidized academies results in a B.S. degree and a commission as a Regular officer in the appropriate branch of the armed forces.

Civil Air Patrol members are eligible for undergraduate scholarships, ranging from $200 to $1,500, at colleges and technical and vocational schools. The National Board of the Civil Air Patrol offers both one-year scholarships and four-year renewable grants. Application forms are available from the National Headquarters, Civil Air Patrol, Attn: CPE, Maxwell Air Force Base, Montgomery, Alabama 36112.

Nursing students are eligible for three programs of aid sponsored by the armed forces. The Army offers nursing students up to two years of full pay and allowances as officers or enlisted personnel in the Army Reserve while they continue nursing school. This is the Army Student and Registered Nurse Program. The Walter Reed Army Institute of

Nursing Program selects high school graduates to pursue Baccalaureate studies in nursing, at government expense, with Army Reserve Nurse Corps commissions following graduation. Both programs can be further investigated by writing to Army Careers, U.S. Army Recruiting Command, Hampton, Virginia 23369.

The Navy subsidizes the education of third-year students in Diploma programs of nursing and of third- and fourth-year students in Baccalaureate programs. One year or less of benefits requires a two-year commitment to Navy service upon graduation; more than one year's training involves a commitment to three years of active duty service. Details of this program may be obtained from the Chief of the Bureau of Medicine and Surgery, Navy Department, Washington, D.C. 20390.

State Governments—

Every state in the Union and the District of Columbia and Puerto Rico have scholarship programs of some kind. Restrictions and qualifications for these scholarships vary enormously from state to state. Test scores or class rank may be significant factors or need may be the only determinant. States such as New York operate both competitive scholarship programs and systems of grants for particularly needy students. Many states have grant programs for the dependents of veterans or for veterans themselves. Future nurses or teachers qualify for grants in some states; blind students and Indian students may receive awards toward their higher education in others. States invariably limit their grants to state residents.

In most cases, grant money from the state is not expected to leave the state. Pennsylvania is a rare exception to this practice; recipients of Pennsylvania state grants may apply their awards to any school in the United States. By and large, however, state money is required to be used for study at a private or public college within the state. In many states, "grants" are in fact fee waivers, allowing a student to attend local state universities or public colleges without charge.

A great range of programs and combinations of programs are administered by the individual states. Often a State Department of Education offers one program while the State Department of Veterans' Affairs supervises another, and a local college oversees a third. State grant programs vary from year to year in requirements and in size, depending upon the appropriations by particular state legislatures. For all of these reasons, we have not prepared a comprehensive listing of state scholarship programs for this guide, since we expect to renew the guide only semiannually. Up-to-date information on your own state's offerings may be obtained by contacting the Board of Education directly or by consulting the financial-aid officers at the colleges that interest you. Detailed listings of state financial aid—scholarships and loans—to both graduates and undergraduates is undertaken in the following publications:

Federal and State Student Aid Programs
prepared by the
Subcommittee on Education
Committee on Labor and Public Welfare, U.S. Senate
available from the Superintendent of Documents
U.S. Government Printing Office
Washington, D.C. 20402 ($.40)

Need a Lift?
American Legion Educational and Scholarship Program
Indianapolis, Indiana 46206 ($.50)

National Scholarship Organizations—

Hundreds of nonpublic sources of financial aid administer scholarship programs. Many of these are directly concerned with assistance to students of particular minority groups, religious affiliations, or career choice. Those noted first are the most general in their objectives; more students may be eligible for them, but competition is stiffer than for those grants that are limited in intent.

Over $7.8 million in scholarship aid was distributed in 1971 by the National Merit Scholarship Corporation, a nonprofit organization designed to identify academically talented high school seniors and to channel money toward them to finance their higher education. One thousand of these awards were in the form of nonrenewable, one-time grants of $1,000, distributed according to a state-by-state selection pattern. Since each state's share of National Merit $1,000 Scholarships is determined to be proportional to that state's fraction of the total national number of graduating high school seniors, the winners of these scholarships represent the entire United States. More than 2,000 other awards, representing the remainder of the funds distributed, were four-year undergraduate scholarships, granted without regard to allocation by state. Two types of four-year scholarships are available: "standard" scholarships (sponsored by business, unions, industry, foundations, individuals, and professional groups, which usually involve criteria such as subject of study or relationship to an employee or member of the sponsoring organization) and "college-sponsored" scholarships, tenable only at the institutions granting them. Stipends for these scholarships range from $100 to $1,500 a year, for four years; although financial need is *not* a factor in selecting scholarship recipients, it *is* a decisive factor in determining the size of the stipends to four-year award winners. Candidates qualify for these one- and four-year scholarships by national competition on the Preliminary Scholastic Aptitude Test/National Merit Scholarship Qualifying Test (PSAT/NMSQT), taken in the junior year of high school. State semifinalists pass through a second qualifying stage; about 96 per cent of them emerge as finalists, and all are considered for the scholarships, which about one-fifth of the finalists actually receive. Detailed information on the scholarships—their sponsors, selection mechanism, and application procedures—can be obtained by writing to the

National Merit Scholarship Corporation
Attn: Educational Services Department
990 Grove Street
Evanston, Illinois 60201

Financial-aid officers at over 200 American colleges and universities award four-year General Motors Scholarships annually to entering freshmen. Over 300 of these scholarships are distributed, each carrying a yearly stipend of $200 to $2,000, depending upon the financial need of the winners. Only United States citizens are eligible, but there is no restriction as to major field of study. The General Motors Scholarship Program, 8–163 GM Building, Detroit, Michigan 48202 can provide detailed information.

The American Legion and its Auxiliary run two general nationwide programs of scholarship aid, only one of which is limited to the children of veterans. A National High School Oratorical Contest is held each year, with the winner and three runners-up receiving $8,000, $5,000, $3,000, and $2,000, respectively, in educational grants. Each state winner is awarded $500 in scholarship aid, and hundreds of local American Legion Posts have organized tie-in programs of scholarship grants, which compensate local finalists who miss the National Legion awards. All of these awards may be applied to higher education at any institution in the United States. The National American Legion Auxiliary annually offers ten National Presidents' Scholarships, five of $1,500 each and five of $1,000 each. These are awarded only to daughters of veterans, and need is a factor in determining the recipients. As in the previous case, local auxiliaries make many awards to girls who are not successful in the nationwide competition. Details of both scholarship programs may be obtained by contacting local American Legion Posts or Auxiliary Units, or from the Education and Scholarship Chairman or Department Secretary at each Legion State Headquarters.

During 1971–1972 736 undergraduates received over $529,000 in scholarship aid from the Elks Foundation Scholarship Awards program. This lodge distributes funds to students on the basis of academic achievement, personal qualities, and financial need. High school seniors and college freshmen, sophomores, and juniors at accredited institutions are eligible, as long as they are citizens of the United States. Individual awards range from $600 to $2,500. Local Elks lodges and State Elks associations have applications for these scholarships, which must be granted through the lodge foundation chairman of the applicant's home town.

Forty-five colleges and universities administer the Alfred P. Sloan National Scholarships. Each school has its own selection criteria and determines the size of the stipend—$200 to $2,500 annually—which each winner will receive, according to his financial need. Need, however, does not affect the actual selection of scholarship winners, and the sole restriction on recipients is that they must be male. About 150 of these scholarships are awarded every year. Application should be made to participation schools: for a list of these schools consult *A Guide to Student Assistance,* a pamphlet of the U.S. House of Representatives Committee on Education and Labor, available from the Superintendent of Documents, U.S. Government Printing Office, Washington, D.C. 20402 ($.60).

Several scholarship programs aim specifically at equalizing educational opportunity by providing funds solely for needy members of minority groups.

The Scholarship Officer at the Bureau of Indian Affairs, U.S. Department of the Interior, Washington, D.C. 20242 offers a list of the individual colleges, universities, and organizations that administer American Indian Youth Scholarships. Although the various institutions determine the size of awards according to their own particular standards, most pay the student's full tuition costs. Only students of Indian descent are eligible for this aid, and financial need is a definite factor. Information on these scholarships, which are granted directly by the participating schools, is also available from the Bureau of Indian Affairs Higher Education Program, Room 201, 5301 Central Avenue, N.E., Albuquerque, New Mexico 87108.

The most important distributor of grants to black students is the National Achievement Scholarship Program for Outstanding Negro

Students. This program, which was six years old in 1969–1970, has provided financial aid to over 1,700 black undergraduates in the amount of $6 million. Students participate in the Achievement Program simply by checking the appropriate space on the answer sheet for the Preliminary Scholastic Aptitude Test/National Merit Scholarship Qualifying Test (PSAT/NMSQT), which they take in the fall of their junior year of high school. Students entering the Achievement Program are simultaneously candidates for National Merit Scholarships; although a student's progress in one competition is independent of his standing in the other, no student may end up winning scholarships in both the Merit and Achievement programs.

Scholarships in the Achievement Program are awarded according to the general outline for the National Merit Scholarship Program discussed earlier. Over 200 one-time awards of $1,000 are distributed according to geographic representation. Rather than working on a state-by-state basis, distribution of these scholarships is based on six major subdivisions of the United States, which are assigned quotas of semifinalists and $1,000 scholarship winners according to their respective proportions of the black population, as ascertained by the most recent census. This ensures that Achievement scholarship winners are representative of the number of black students throughout the nation.

Semifinalists advance to finalist status as in the National Merit competition; approximately one-sixth of the finalists receive $1,000 awards. Over 100 four-year Achievement Scholarships are also awarded, regardless of geographical section, to individuals selected according to criteria supplied by the sponsoring industries, organizations, individuals, or foundations. Although home state or career choice is irrelevant to the selection for $1,000 awards, these factors may influence four-year grants. *All* grants are distributed without regard to financial need. Statements of need do, however, determine the stipend assigned to the winners of four-year scholarships, who may receive from $250 to $1,500 annually. The names of all Achievement Program semifinalists, whether or not they win scholarships, are sent to the news media and to colleges, universities, and certain scholarship agencies, where this record of merit may influence other possibilities for financial aid. A complete description of the National Achievement Scholarship Program may be obtained from the administrating organization: the National Merit Scholarship Corporation, Attn: Educational Services Department, 990 Grove Street, Evanston, Illinois 60201

A second, more limited, source of scholarship aid for black students is the National Scholarship Service and Fund for Negro Students

(NSSFNS). Although this organization is primarily designed to provide advisory and referral services to help black students gain admission and financial aid at interracial colleges across the United States, it also maintains its own program of supplementary scholarships. These awards, ranging from $200 to $600 per year and renewable for three years, are available to students whom NSSFNS has counseled and who have been awarded insufficient funds by their own colleges to meet their needs. Applicants are evaluated on the basis of school transcripts, extra-curricular activities, and test results on the PSAT/NMSQT or the Scholastic Aptitude Test (SAT) given in the junior and senior years, respectively. The National Scholarship Service and Fund for Negro Students is located at 1776 Broadway, New York, New York 10019.

Several sources of scholarship aid are church-affiliated.

The Aid Association for Lutherans provides financial aid for the 150 annual winners in its AAL All-College Scholarship Program. Recipients of this aid are chosen competitively on the basis of their high school records, extracurricular activities, recommendations, personal qualities, and scores on the Scholastic Aptitude Test (SAT), without regard to financial need. Need is a factor, however, in determining the amount of individual stipends, which range from $200 to $1,750 per year and are renewable for four years of undergraduate education at a Lutheran or any other accredited college or university. Every applicant must hold an Aid Association for Lutherans life or health insurance certificate in his or her own name before the application deadline, and must be a high school senior graduating in the academic year for which he applies. Winners must keep up their AAL membership in order to renew their grants. Applications are available from the Aid Association for Lutherans All-College Scholarship Service, 222 West College Avenue, Appleton, Wisconsin 54911.

The Lutheran Church in America offers two types of undergraduate grant assistance to Lutherans who demonstrate both academic achievement and financial need. Some of these scholarships are LCA opportunity grants that are offered to students of minority groups whom a Lutheran pastor or college has sponsored. Other grants go to undergraduates whose career plans are oriented toward active Lutheranism by means of the ministry, college teaching, or health and social services. The Lutheran Education Fund, which distributes these grants, is located at 231 Madison Avenue, New York, New York 10016.

The Office of Educational Loans and Scholarships Board of Christian Education, United Presbyterian Church in the U.S.A., 425 Witherspoon Building, Philadelphia, Pennsylvania 19107 offers information in the fall of each year concerning its scholarship program. These grants are available only to Presbyterian high school students who rank in the top quarter of their classes at the end of the junior year and who intend to study at one of the nation's forty-six Presbyterian colleges. Eighty awards are to be made for the 1972–1973 year with stipends up to $1,200.

Roman Catholic students may be interested in the Knights of Columbus "Pro Deo and Pro Patria Scholarship Trust." This trust provides awards of $1,000 per year, renewable annually, to entering Catholic college freshmen, on the basis of academic achievement without considering financial need. Five of these awards may be used only at Catholic University of America, Washington, D.C., and five may be applied to educational expenses at any Catholic college of the recipient's choice. Two similar $1,000 scholarships, one in each category, are also available to Columbian Squires. Applications for all grants should be requested from the Director of Scholarship Aid, Knights of Columbus, Supreme Council, Columbus Plaza, P.O. Drawer 1670, New Haven, Connecticut 06507.

Students who have been members of the United Methodist Church for at least one year and who have demonstrated leadership in Church activities while in school are eligible for up to two nonrenewable awards of $500 per year from the United Methodist Scholarship Fund. Every year 500 to 600 of these grants are distributed. They are applicable only to tuition and academic fees and are awarded through the United Methodist Scholarship Officer at each of the approximately 100 church-related colleges and universities to which these grants may apply. Scholastic record, financial need, and personal qualities are all evaluated in determining recipients. Details of the scholarship program and a list of participating institutions are available from the Student Loans and Scholarship Office, Board of Education, The United Methodist Church, P.O. Box 871, Nashville, Tennessee 37202.

The American Baptist Student Aid Fund, which is organized by the American Baptist Board of Education, Valley Forge, Pennsylvania 19481, exists to aid American Baptist students in meeting their college expenses in cases of financial need. Any college may be chosen, but awards are higher for students who attend institutions affiliated with the American Baptist Convention. High school seniors must be nominated by their hometown pastors; further information is available from the address given.

Many scholarship funds exist to assist students who plan to study a certain subject or pursue a certain career. Some of the most important funds of this type are indicated briefly.

Agriculture and/or Home Economics

The National Four-H Service Committee, Inc.
59 East Van Buren Street
Chicago, Illinois 60605

In 1971, 265 scholarships, valued at $179,000 were offered in the form of individual annual grants of $100 to $1,600. These awards are made only to present or former 4-H members who have either won a statewide competition in a particular 4-H project or who intend to study certain branches of agriculture, home economics, conservation, or animal science.

Education Department
The Ralston-Purina Company
St. Louis, Missouri 63199

Scholarships are awarded annually at land-grant colleges, with the specific goal of training specialists in animal agricultural technology.

The American Home Economics Association
2010 Massachusetts Avenue, N.W.
Washington, D.C. 20036

A list of state association presidents is available from this address; the association's scholarship aid is all channeled through its state affiliates.

The National Restaurant Foundation–Heinz Scholarship Awards Program

National Restaurant Foundation
1530 North Lake Shore Drive
Chicago, Illinois 60610

Five scholarships of $500 per year, supporting the last three years of a Baccalaureate program in food service management, are offered. Each recipient may gain up to $3,000 in total aid ($500 is allowed each summer as wages for employment in the food industry). Three awards of $500 per year are offered to students in two-year programs leading to an Associate degree in Food Service Management. Recipients of these scholarships may earn $500 in service employment during the summer, bringing the total grant to $1,500.

Club Managers Association of America
5530 Wisconsin Avenue, N.W., Suite 705
Washington, D.C. 20015

Scholarships are offered by this organization to students with academic potential and demonstrated financial need who are interested in careers as private club managers. Ten schools, offering courses in hotel, restaurant, and institutional management are the administrators of these funds; undergraduates should request further information from the financial-aid officer at the participating colleges. These awards are not ordinarily open to freshmen.

Institute of Food Technologists
221 North LaSalle Street
Chicago, Illinois 60601

Thirty $500 awards are available to freshmen and sophomores, and eleven $1,000 awards are offered to juniors and seniors. Students must be pursuing a course of study leading to a degree in food technology.

Sears-Roebuck Foundation Home Economics Scholarship Program
c/o Dean of Home Economics
local land-grant college in each state

More than 135 awards are distributed each year to further the education of home economics students.

Health

The National Easter Seal Society for Crippled Children and Adults
2023 West Ogden Avenue
Chicago, Illinois 60612

This organization administers two sorority-funded scholarship programs. The Alpha Gamma Delta program awards varying amounts, up to $500, to individuals, including undergraduates, who are studying in *summer* programs on minimal brain dysfunction (learning disabilities). Applicants are nominated by the schools where they intend to study. Senior students in the fields of occupational and physical therapy may be aided by one of the six $500 grants offered annually by the Kappa Delta Phi Scholarship Program. Again, students are nominated by their schools, and schools participate in regional groups on a rotating basis; not every school is eligible to nominate every year. Only United States citizens may qualify. Details of both programs are available at the address given.

The American Association for Health, Physical Education, and Recreation
National Education Association
1201 Sixteenth Street, N.W.
Washington, D.C. 20036

High school seniors seeking college preparation in one of the career areas that this association claims interest in may win grants of between $1,000 to $2,000.

American Fund for Dental Education
Suite 1630
211 East Chicago Avenue
Chicago, Illinois 60611

One-year Dental Laboratory Technology scholarships are available, with stipends ranging from $500 to $650. Five-year scholarships, which support *the senior college year* and four years of dental school, are available to undergraduates defined as "disadvantaged minority students." Depending upon the individual's financial need, such scholarships may pay up to $2,500 a year.

The American Pharmaceutical Association
2215 Constitution Avenue, N.W.
Washington, D.C. 20037

The association channels funds for scholarship grants to needy students through each of the nation's schools of pharmacy. It also provides information on other sources of funds that are open to pharmacy students, including John W. Dargavel Foundation aid.

American Society of Medical Technologists
Hermann Professional Building, Suite 1600
Houston, Texas 77025

The Education and Research Fund of this organization offers two scholarships to students pursuing a medical technology Baccalaureate degree program. High school seniors may apply for the $1,000 scholarship, paid in four installments over the first two undergraduate years. Sophomores may apply for the $2,000 Fisher Scientific Company award paid over the junior and senior years. Many American Medical Association-approved schools of medical technology, cytotechnology, and laboratory assistant schools are tuition-free.

National Committee for Careers in the Medical Laboratory
9650 Rockville Pike
Bethesda, Maryland 20014

A $500 scholarship is offered to community- and junior-college students in their second year who are planning to transfer to a two-year medical technology program.

Kappa Kappa Gamma Fraternity Headquarters
530 East Town Street
Columbus, Ohio 43215

Young women who are United States or Canadian citizens and who have completed their sophomore years at colleges that have a chapter of this fraternity are eligible for annual scholarship awards of $300–$350. These must be applied to the study of mental health, social work, speech, hearing, or physical or occupational therapy. Applications are available from the address given.

American Nurses Association–National League for Nursing
Committee on Nursing Careers
10 Columbus Circle
New York, New York 10019

Through its state units, a list of which is available, this organization each year distributes approximately 200 scholarships funded by the Allstate Foundation to nursing students.

Service and Technology

The Society of Exploration Geophysicists Foundation
P.O. Box 3098
Tulsa, Oklahoma 74101

The foundation awarded forty-seven scholarships to graduate and undergraduate students in 1971–1972, in individual stipends ranging from $500 to $1,500; the total amount of scholarship aid distributed is over $33,000. Application for this aid may be made by undergraduates or high school seniors and should be made directly to the foundation. Awards will be granted—and may be renewed—only if the student pursues a course leading toward a career in geophysics. Financial need is an important factor in determining recipients of this aid, but scholastic competence is paramount.

Science Service
1719 N Street, N.W.
Washington, D.C. 20036

The Westinghouse Educational Foundation contributes annual funding to the Science Service-administered National Science Talent Search.

Graduating seniors at United States secondary schools are eligible and must submit high school records, personal data, and any available national test scores, such as PSAT/NMSAT. The crucial factor in the competition is the submission of a short report on an independent, individual research project conducted by the student on some topic in mathematics, engineering, or the physical, biological, or behavioral sciences. Thirty nationwide winners receive awards of $250 each, and four-year Westinghouse Science Scholarships are awarded as follows: one $2,500 annually, two $2,000 annually, three $1,500 annually, and four $1,000 annually. Scholarships are awarded without reference to financial need and are tenable only as long as the recipient follows a college course in engineering or science. Forty-one states and the District of Columbia conduct coordinated State Science Talent Searches, leading to college recommendations and possibilities of financial aid.

Journalism and Graphic Arts

> National Scholarship Trust Fund
> National Printing and Publishing Scholarship Program
> 4615 Forbes Avenue
> Pittsburgh, Pennsylvania 15213

Graduating seniors, college undergraduates, and recent high school graduates who have not yet begun college are eligible for the more than twenty four-year scholarship awards of $100 to $1,500 annually made available by this fund. Awards are given on the basis of nationwide competition, which includes Scholastic Aptitude Test (SAT) scores, high school and college transcripts, recommendations, interviews, and personal data. Stipends may or may not depend upon financial need, according to the stipulation of the donating company or foundation. In some cases, preference is given to children of company employees, or in accordance with other particular standards. All award recipients must pursue courses of college study leading to graphic communication careers, such as education, science, design, engineering, or management. The Riegel Printing Trades Scholarship program (at the same address but requiring a separate application) administrates the award of grants from $100 to $2,000 to cover tuition, fees, and books for up to two years of trade and technical study of printing skills. Any recognized institution and course of appropriate study may be attended. Age and academic record are not an issue in this competition; financial need, potential, and interest in the field are the decisive factors.

William Randolph Hearst Foundation
Suite 218, Hearst Building
Third and Market Streets
San Francisco, California 94103

Undergraduate students at fifty-three of the fifty-six member schools of the American Association of Schools and Departments in Journalism are invited to take part in the foundation's six-month newswriting and photojournalism competition. Monthly awards for top articles and photographs run from $100 to $1,000, and over $60,000 is given away annually in this competitive scholarship program. In each case, the winning student's school receives a matching grant.

American Newspaper Publishers Association (ANPA) Foundation
Negro Journalism Scholarship Fund
750 Third Avenue
New York, New York 10017

More than sixty affiliated schools through their departments of journalism offer scholarship awards totaling over $20,000 to junior and senior black students studying newspaper journalism. Academic and professional promise and financial need are important selective factors.

The Newspaper Fund
Internship Scholarship Programs
P.O. Box 300
Princeton, New Jersey 08540

Juniors who work on their college newspapers and who are interested in a professional career in newspaper journalism may earn scholarships by participating in one of these two programs during the summer preceding their senior year. Applicants need not be journalism majors. Each program involves summer employment on a daily newspaper, at an approximate average gross salary of $126 per week. Forty internships in reporting are available, entailing twelve weeks of work and resulting in a $500 scholarship. Sixty internships are available in editing. Editing interns receive a free three-week intensive course, followed by nine weeks of work; they each receive a $700 scholarship. The Newspaper Fund also prepares the annual publication, *Journalism Scholarship Guide,* which presents comprehensive, updated, school-by-school information on all of the $2 million in grants and $4 million in loans available to journalism students from colleges and universities, newspapers, professional organizations, and journalism-related foundations. This booklet is free on request.

United Business Schools Association (UBSA)
Guidance Department
1730 M Street, N.W.
Washington, D.C. 20036

This organization offers a listing of over 500 member schools, together with information on the work-study and scholarship programs that they administrate, subject to UBSA controls.

Teaching

National Congress of Parents and Teachers
700 North Rush Street
Chicago, Illinois 60611

Preteaching education, librarianship, guidance and counseling training, and preparation for the teaching of exceptional children are some of the courses of study for which state and local PTA's offer scholarship and loan programs. The National Office serves as a clearinghouse for inquiries, forwarding requests for information to the appropriate local office.

Finally, the largest scholarship program in the world supported by individual contributors each year awards over 200 four-year scholarships to high school seniors who have demonstrated both academic potential and financial need. This is the Evans Scholars Foundation, funded by the Western Golf Association, Golf, Illinois. The terms of this foundation stipulate that awards shall only go to students who have been *golf caddies* for at least two years. Any field of study is open to Evans Scholars.

Other Sources

Many organizations are interested in seeing you get through college. As noted previously, local branches of the PTA, American Legion, Elks, and other national organizations offer grants to students from their states or immediate areas. You should explore other scholarship possibilities by inquiring in your home town about programs sponsored by business, industry, clubs, professional societies, lodges, religious groups, and farm organizations. The Kiwanis, Rotary, and Lions clubs frequently sponsor such programs. Individual churches, women's clubs, and school auxiliaries may offer scholarships. If one of your parents is affiliated with a national union local, contact that union or the AFL-CIO (Department of Education; 815 16th Street, N.W., Washington,

D.C. 20006) for scholarship information. Each union determines its own selection system and size of grant, but nearly every union of organized labor offers at least one award, in the range of $1,000–$2,500, to a child of one of its members. Members of the National Honor Society should talk to their high school guidance counselors to check on their eligibility for one of the $1,000 grants that the National Association of Secondary School Principals (1201 16th Street, N.W., Washington, D.C. 20036) awards to over 150 graduating seniors each year.

If you have decided to which colleges and universities you wish to apply, find out whether the alumni groups in your home town sponsor scholarships for local undergraduates. Many students finance their educations on the strength of local support. Fraternities and sororities also offer grants.

Numerous professional societies offer scholarships through their local or state chapters, and you may find it useful to consult articles in professional and trade journals for sources of scholarship aid. Libraries often have copies of pertinent magazines, and the *Reader's Guide to Periodical Literature,* which may be found in nearly every library, will help you to find the information you need. An extensive list of professional organizations providing career information is provided in the opening pages of *Need a Lift?* (American Legion Educational and Scholarship Program, Indianapolis, Indiana 46206; $.50); these societies will usually be glad to provide you with the details of financial aid possibilities for students in the field.

The nature of these grant possibilities varies enormously, but most will cover only tuition and academic fees. Some organizations grant aid only to students fitting narrow religious or ethnic criteria; others run broad-based programs of assistance. Grants are often made on a competitive basis and may involve essays on citizenship, Americanism, or the democratic ideal. Need may be a critical factor, or the award may be largely honorary. You will have to investigate your own state, county, and town potential for scholarship grants—but your efforts could pay off handsomely.

Loans

Scholarship funds have skyrocketed in the last decade, but not fast enough to keep up with college costs. If you cannot arrange sufficient funding in the form of grants to pay all of your undergraduate expenses, you are in a very common position. Since most scholarship funds are distributed on the basis of financial need, sons and daughters of middle-income families may find themselves too "wealthy" to qualify for substantial scholarship aid, yet priced out of the college market. The answer is often a student loan.

Some students and their parents are wary of going into debt over college expenses. This is understandable—but student loans are often necessary, and they may make sense for you. Loans are most likely to be taken out by students from middle-income families who are able to defer at least a part of the student's expenses. Extremely low-income families usually have their "income" bolstered by flat grants before they must apply for loans. In this way, students are rarely forced to borrow all the money needed for their undergraduate careers. Any student may also take on part-time work during the term as well as summer jobs to help lower the total amount he must borrow. Colleges are usually willing to guarantee jobs or work-study assistance to students whose financial needs compel them to take out loans. Student loans are usually not difficult to obtain, and are often granted at a low rate of interest. College itself is a financial investment for the student, as was described at the beginning of this chapter. Even if the amount of debt that an undergraduate has accumulated amounts, at commencement, to the price of a moderately expensive automobile, the purely monetary gains to be realized by the student by investing in a college degree far more than offset that debt.

Colleges themselves are the best sources of loans. Ask your financial-aid officer for information; loan applicants may be asked to fill out a set of forms that are separate from scholarship requests. Loan policies depend entirely upon the school's own financial situation; some schools have a small scholarship endowment and must substitute loans. The ratio of grant to loan funds that you receive will be influenced by several other factors. Most colleges and universities, for example, prefer to "insulate" freshmen from money worries with a cushion of flat grants, whereas upperclassmen are seen as better prepared to assume a burden of personal debt. Flat grants may be a reward for academic superiority at one institution, a compensation for extreme poverty at another. In any case, most colleges will offer you a "package" of loans, grants, and job possibilities that they calculate to answer your particular financial problem.

In the spring of 1971, Yale University instituted a "tuition-postponement" plan as an experiment in educational funding. Since this payment scheme has the potential to spread to other colleges and universities if it proves successful, its principal features are outlined here.

The Yale plan was conceived of as a way for students to defer part of their tuition and room and board expenses—that fraction that roughly corresponds to the increase in rates that the University expects to have to impose on its undergraduate students—until they are graduates, earning their own income. At present, Yale students may defer approximately $5,000 of their accumulated college expenses, and increased allowances are expected as tuition rates rise. After graduation, a former student will be required to pay the University back at the rate of $29 annually, as the minimum payment on every $1,000 owed to the college. This minimum is charged regardless of a graduate's income; usually, however, a student will pay four-tenths of 1 per cent of his annual gross income to Yale per $1,000 owed, this sum being larger than $29. The graduate may pay off his "postponed tuition" early, but if he does not, this income-related payment continues for twenty-six years, at which point liability for the debt ends. The total amount that an individual pays back on a debt will vary according to the fluctuations in his annual income; some graduates may end up with loans that are virtually interest-free, whereas others will find that they have paid the equivalent of 5, 6, or 7 per cent annual interest to Yale, over the long run. Presumably, a graduate with an income so high that four-tenths of 1 per cent of his income over twenty-six years amounted to an exorbitant rate of interest per $1,000, could afford to make the capital investment of total repayment. Even if a graduate pays only the $29 annual minimum, his debt to the university will be written off after thirty-five years. Yale has received foundation grants and private gifts to finance this funding venture; should it prove practicable, government financing might subsidize similar arrangements at other schools.

Most colleges have more traditional loan patterns. In general, college loans need not be paid back until after graduation, and the interest on them is kept to a minimum. Some schools allow for further deferment of repayment and the accrual of interest if a student goes on to graduate study or military service, or into the Peace Corps or Vista.

If your own institution cannot provide you with a large enough loan, there are several other sources to consider.

The Federal Government

Long-term loans are available from the federal government to post-secondary students who need financial aid to continue their educations through the National Student Loan Program. Students carrying at least one-half of a full-time program at colleges, universities, secretarial, vocational, and business schools are eligible to borrow up to $1,000 a year, although they must not borrow more than $5,000 under this plan during their undergraduate careers. No repayment of the loan is expected until nine months after the student ends at least his half-time study, although institutions have the option of deferring the repayment of NDEA loans made through them for up to three years if a student continues part-time (but less than half-time) study for degree credit. Interest is charged on loans at the rate of 3 per cent annually, and continues to accrue even if payment of the loan has been deferred for part-time study. The principal of a loan may ordinarily be repaid over a ten-year period, following the nine-month interval. No repayment is necessary, however, and no interest accrues for periods up to three years while the student is in the armed forces, Peace Corps, or Vista service.

Two other provisions are made in connection with the NDEA loan program, which allow for the cancellation or forgiveness of such loans under certain circumstances. The act encourages college students to become teachers, by the provision that 10 per cent of a loan may be canceled (plus interest) for every year that the borrower spends as a teacher in any nonprofit elementary, secondary, or postsecondary school. Up to half of the amount of a loan may be canceled in this way.

Increases in Numbers of Student Loans[16]

(These figures represent loans taken out by students in their own names; many undergraduates receive money from loans in their parents' names.)

School Year (beginning in September)	Number of New Government-Guaranteed Student Loans (Financed by Private Capital)	Total (in Millions)
1967	330,088	$ 248
1968	515,000	$ 436
1969	787,000	$ 687
1970	922,000	$ 840
1971 (estimated)	1,100,000	$1,000

School Year (beginning in September)	Number of New National Defense Student Loans (90% Federally Funded; 10% College Funds)	Total (in Millions)
1967	395,000	$ 222
1968	429,000	$ 234
1969	456,000	$ 246
1970	455,000	$ 287
1971 (estimated)	560,000	$ 364

If the teacher works in an elementary or secondary school that is located in a designated poverty area, or if he teaches handicapped children, the entire principal and interest of his loan may be canceled at the rate of 15 per cent per year of service. If an NDEA loan was made after April 13, 1970, up to 50 per cent of it may be canceled, at the rate of 12½ per cent per year, for each consecutive year of military service that a borrower has performed after July 1, 1970.

NDEA loans also require that the borrower willingly take an oath or affirmation to bear allegiance to the United States and to defend the country against domestic and foreign enemies.

Students who need these loans should contact the financial-aid officer of the institution where they are enrolled or plan to enroll.

The federal government, in cooperation with many states and non-profit agencies, has organized an extensive program to insure loans to postsecondary students, regardless of their family income. Students must be enlisted for at least a half-time course of study at a college, university, nursing, technical, or vocational school offering at least a one-year program. Some schools may require a full-time program for borrowers under this program. In any case, students are not eligible unless they are United States citizens or permanent residents.

Depending upon the state, a student may borrow up to $1,000 or $1,500 each academic year, although his total amount of guaranteed loans may not exceed $7,500. Repayment is not required until nine to twelve months after a student has ceased at least half-time study, and the repayment may last from five to ten years. Repayment of a loan is deferred while the borrower is a half-time or full-time student in the United States, a full-time student in an eligible foreign institution, or in full-time service with the armed forces, Peace Corps, or Vista, but unlike the NDEA loans, *interest accrues during this entire period.* Early repayment of the loan may be made at any time, of course, and the federal, state, or private insuring agency has the option of collecting one quarter of 1 per cent of the total outstanding loan in advance every year, as an insurance premium.

If a student's income is, however, less than $15,000 annually, the federal government may agree to assume the burden of the interest payments on the principal of a guaranteed loan, as long as the student is in a period of deferred payment—by virtue of school, military, or approved voluntary service, as noted previously.

These loans are among the most substantial forms of financial aid available to undergraduates. Once approval has been gained from the insuring agency—federal, state, or private—and certification of enroll-ment and academic standing are obtained, the student must approach a qualified lending institution. Banks, insurance companies, credit unions, savings and loan associations, and certain schools are qualified lenders, and accept or deny loan proposals at their own discretion; government supervision only affects approved loans.

Cuban refugee students who are in need of financial aid to pursue undergraduate studies, at least half-time, at an approved college or university may apply for a federally sponsored loan. Such loans, administered by the financial-aid officers of participating institutions, may not exceed $1,000 per year for undergraduate studies, up to a total of $5,000. Two years after the students cease at least half-time study, the repayment period begins, extending for ten years. Cancellation privileges for teachers, identical to those stipulated in the NDEA loan program, are available to holders of Cuban refugee loans.

To be eligible for such assistance, a Cuban refugee is defined as a Cuban national resident in that country for at least five consecutive years before his departure from Cuba (on or after January 1, 1959) and who is prevented by the government of Cuba from receiving financial support from within that country.

Further information on any of these federal loan programs may be obtained from participating colleges and universities, or from the Loans Branch, Division of Student Financial Aid, Bureau of Higher Education, U.S. Office of Education, Washington, D.C. 20202. Specialized loan programs are also available from the government.

Loans are available through the Health Professions Student Loan Program to graduate students in several health-related fields, as well as to undergraduates studying pharmacy. Citizens and permanent residents of the United States who are full-time students and in need of funds to finish their courses of study may apply for loans of up to $2,500 a year. The repayment period begins the year after full-time studies are completed, and at this point 3 per cent interest begins to accrue. The repayment period is ten years, and both the repayment and the accumulation of interest are deferred under the following conditions: three-year deferments for full-time service in the armed forces, public health service, or Peace Corps; and five-year deferments for advanced professional training. Pharmacists are not eligible for loan cancellation. Financial aid officers at individual schools administrate these loans.

The Nurse Training Act of 1971 authorizes loans of up to $2,500 per year to a total of $10,000 to full or half-time nursing students at accredited and participating institutions. Repayment of the loan begins nine months after the termination of studies and may extend over a ten-year period, with interest accumulating at the rate of 3 per cent per year. Deferment is possible on the same terms stipulated in the Health Professions Loan Program, but nurses may cancel all or part of their debt according to the following schedule: 85 per cent of a loan may be canceled at the rate of 15 per cent for the first three years and 20 per cent for the next two years of full-time employment as a nurse in a public or private nonprofit agency or institution. Full-time nursing practice in an area that is certified to be in need of nurses will result in cancellation of up to 85 per cent of all educational loans pertaining to the nurse's training (including other nursing student loan programs). In this case, the rate is 30 per cent annually for two years and 25 per cent for a third year.

Further information on these two loan programs may be obtained by writing to the Student Loan and Scholarship Board, Bureau of Health Professions, Manpower Education, Division of Physicians and Health Professional Education, National Institutes of Health, 9000 Rockville Pike, Bethesda, Maryland 20014.

The Bureau of Indian Affairs of the U.S. Department of the Interior, Washington, D.C. 20242 can give you information about the grant and loan programs that have been established by more than forty-five American Indian tribes to finance college education for their members.

Students who are engaged in full-time undergraduate studies leading to a degree in a field related to law enforcement may apply for loans from the Law Enforcement Education Program (LEEP) of the Law Enforcement Assistance Administration (U.S. Department of Justice, Washington, D.C. 20530). Up to $1,800 may be borrowed yearly to cover academic expenses, and loans may be paid back over a ten-year period, or at the rate of $50 a month, whichever is shorter. The interest rate on LEEP loans is 7 per cent. Periods up to four years of service in the armed forces may interrupt the repayment period, and no interest will accumulate during this time. Since this program is designed to encourage higher education for law-enforcement officials, preference in the distribution of these loans is given to professional policemen, correction officers, and court employees who are on leave of absence from their agencies. These loans aim to improve the American legal system by educating its members and are organized to serve students who intend to pursue or resume employment in this field once their studies are over. To this end, LEEP loans carry the provision that full-time employment in the criminal justice field will qualify a borrower to cancel his loan completely, at the rate of 25 per cent per year of service. Loans are made only through the individual schools that the borrowers attend, but a list of participating institutions and further information are available from the Law Enforcement Assistance Administration.

The States—

As noted in the scholarship section, various states have evolved their own programs of educational assistance for state residents, often with special emphasis on students who have particular financial need, who are enrolled at state universities, or who are veterans or dependents of veterans. State programs tend to vary with annual appropriations by the individual state legislatures, and thus they may change somewhat from year to year. Most states rely mainly on systems of flat grants and tuition waivers at public colleges and universities as a basis for their educational assistance programs, but states such as Mississippi, North Dakota, Wisconsin, Kentucky, and Alaska supplement this aid with student loans.

Your best source of information on the subject of state loans is the Office of Education in your own state government, but excellent summaries of state assistance programs (including loans) for students are available in the following two sources. Each includes relevant addresses, plus detailed information:

Federal and State Student Aid Programs
United States Senate Committee on Labor and Public Welfare
Subcommittee on Education
available at $.40 from
Superintendent of Documents
U.S. Government Printing Office
Washington, D.C. 20402

Need a Lift? ($.50)
American Legion Educational and Scholarship Program
Indianapolis, Indiana 46206

Private Sources—

Loans are available to students from many private sources. Most obviously, loans may be obtained from banks, savings and loan associations, and other general loan-administering institutions. Special rates are often available for educational loans, and students may enjoy special repayment terms. Commercial loans, however, often require collateral or some other form of security, and an undergraduate may have to rely on a parent's cosignature in order to make loan arrangements. In addition to the federal and state guaranteed loan programs discussed earlier, a private organization, the United Student Aid Funds, Inc. similarly insures student loans for private lending organizations.

The USA Funds is a ten-year-old private, nonprofit corporation that provides an alternative to federal funding for guaranteed loan programs to undergraduate students, both for the colleges and for individual students who might otherwise be unable to procure educational loans. The funds work on the principle that an established resource of reserve funds can act as a guarantor to private lenders who, confident that "collateral" funds are available, are then willing to make extensive loans to needy students. USA Funds, Inc. administrates such reserve funds and makes available an extensive list of those lending institutions—over 9,000, located all over the country—that are willing to participate in its program. Students are individually responsible for actually arranging their own loans and generally begin by contacting institutions in their home or college towns. Banks and other lenders may, however, make special stipulations within the scheme—such as only insuring local residents. Students must, therefore, be prepared to explore various avenues in securing USA Funds guaranteed loans.

United Student Aid Funds loans are subject to 7 percent annual interest, and in some cases the federal government absorbs these interest charges. Students may borrow up to $1,500 a year, by individual arrangement with participating lenders, up to a total of $7,500, and the repayment period begins ten months after studies are terminated.

Not all students are eligible to have their loans insured by USA Funds. Eligibility depends upon whether the student's *school* or *state* has established a reserve fund with USA Funds, since loans are guaranteed strictly on the basis of the existence of these reservoirs of "insuring" money. Close to 1,000 schools, located nationwide, have established such funds and their students may participate in the USA Funds guaranteed loan scheme, regardless of the state in which they legally reside. Eight states (Alaska, Hawaii, Delaware, Maine, Maryland, South Carolina, and Nevada; Louisiana, but only for residents attending out-of-state schools) and the Virgin Islands have contracted with USA Funds to administer their state programs of educational loans and have established reserve funds to that end. In addition, various organizations have provided money for Special Reserve Programs in order to insure that the children of their members or employees can always obtain necessary educational loans. Participants in the Special Reserve Programs include Texaco, Inc., the General Electric Company, the Mars Foundations, the

American Optometric Association, the Zeta Beta Tau Fraternity, and funds established for the Peace Corps Volunteers and the Job Corps.

Another organization that utilizes USA Funds administration is the Retired Officers Fund, although this fund may also provide interest-free loans to students who are unable to obtain commercial loans through USA Funds, Inc. Eligible students may be helped by the Association for years of undergraduate study. Applicants must be children of an active, retired, or deceased (while in service) member of the Public Health Service, National Oceanographic and Atmospheric Administration, or one of the branches of the armed forces. Further information may be obtained from the Secretary of the Scholarship Committee of the Association, 1625 Eye Street, N.W., Washington, D.C. 20006.

The United Student Aid Funds supports an additional program of financial aid: Guaranteed Opportunity Achievement Loans (GOAL). This program is aimed at disadvantaged young people seeking to build careers for themselves at community colleges and vocational schools, who cannot otherwise obtain educational funding. Reserve money comes from donors, and the program, which is currently operative in Washington and Kansas, is scheduled to be extended to California, Delaware, and other states in the near future.

In all, the USA Funds have made possible loans of more than $3 million to over a quarter of a million students in the course of its decade of existence. If you are unable to arrange federal or state guarantees for your loan, the USA Funds, Inc. is the first private organization to turn to. Extensive information, including an Educational Institutions Directory and a Lending Institutions Directory, is available upon inquiry from the USA Funds at 5259 North Tacoma Avenue, Indianapolis, Indiana 46220.

Several other private sources of funds are worthy of note.

Like state governments, the individual state and local posts of the American Legion administer an assortment of financial aid programs for the residents of particular states and communities. Legion assistance is almost invariably restricted to veterans and their wives, widows, and children, but this is the only requirement that is consistent from area to area. Listings of Legion offices and the funds that they administer will be found in updated form in the American Legion's annual booklet *Need a Lift?,* available for $.50 from the American Legion Educational and Scholarship Program, Indianapolis, Indiana 46206.

Eligible officers on active duty in one of the branches of the armed forces and their children may borrow educational funds from the Armed

Forces Relief and Benefit Association (Suite 700, 1156 15th Street, N.W., Washington, D.C. 20005). Five per cent annual interest is charged on such loans, which must be repaid within a year. The maximum single loan amount is $500, but additional loans may be made to the same individual.

Students who are or whose parents have been members of both the Disabled American Veterans and its Auxiliary for at least one year are entitled to borrow up to $250 a year from the organization's student loan fund. Such a loan is renewable for four years at any postsecondary school and is repaid upon the termination of studies in monthly installments. These loans are interest-free. For an application, contact the National Education Loan Fund, D.A.V. Auxiliary National Headquarters, 3725 Alexandria Pike, Cold Spring, Kentucky 41076.

Undergraduate students who are members of the United Methodist Church and citizens of the United States may be eligible for money from the United Methodist Student Loan Fund. Loan recipients must be full-time students working in accredited United States degree programs (although these may include foreign study), including schools of nursing, and must maintain a C average. Up to $500 a year may be borrowed by nursing students to a total of $1,500; undergraduates at four-year colleges may borrow up to $2,350 during their undergraduate careers, according to the following schedule: freshmen, $500; sophomores, $550; juniors, $600; seniors, $700. Junior college students whose school is affiliated with the United Methodist Church are likewise eligible for such loans; those in other junior colleges may borrow up to $250 a year. Loans are subject to 3 per cent annual interest, even when the borrower is still in school, and the six-year repayment period begins six months after full-time studies end. The United Methodist Student Loan Fund has assisted over 100,000 Methodist students with $25 million in loans during the hundred years since its founding; it is one of the world's largest educational loan organizations. If you are eligible and in financial need, contact the loan officer at your school; a list of appropriate persons at colleges and universities nationwide can be obtained by writing to the Office of Student Loans and Scholarships, Board of Education, the United Methodist Church, P.O. Box 871, Nashville, Tennessee 37202.

In the late 1930's, the Pickett and Hatcher Educational Fund was established. Since then it has recycled loans to needy undergraduates at over 400 American colleges, to the extent of substantially assisting almost 13,000 students, with over $13 million in educational financing. This nonprofit, noncommercial trust fund provides money, in the form of loans only, to United States citizens who are enrolled in liberal arts colleges. Students at vocational and business schools are not eligible, but students at liberal arts colleges may follow business or nearly any other course of study; prelaw, premedical, and pretheological school students are, however, not eligible for Pickett and Hatcher loans, because other sources of financial aid are particularly available to these preprofessional groups. The unusually large number of applications, in recent years, has prompted the fund to concentrate its efforts on helping students in its immediate area—the Southeastern United States. This is a temporary measure of expediency, not a permanent policy of the fund. Students only (not their parents) may borrow; applications are evaluated from the point of view of financial need, academic record, personal qualities, and, often, the results of an interview. The Pickett and Hatcher Fund will make loans of up to $1,000 per year, renewing the loan annually, under favorable circumstances, up to a four-year potential total of $4,000. Two per cent interest is charged on the balance of each loan while the borrower is in college, and this interest must be paid semiannually, although the principal of the loan need not begin to be repaid until six months after the student leaves school. At this point, the interest rate becomes 6 per cent annually, and the borrower must make monthly payments on the principal as well as his semiannual interest payments. Applications and a leaflet explaining the philosophy and mechanics of the Pickett and Hatcher Educational Fund are available by writing to P.O. Box 2128, Columbus, Georgia 31902.

Like our earlier enumeration of scholarship sources, this summary of loan sources for needy students is incomplete. Several of the organizations and agencies described in the subsection on scholarships also offer loans, and students seeking grants should inquire from each institution and organization they approach whether any other form of financial aid is available from that group; separate applications and evaluations are often required for different varieties of educational funding from the same source.

Programs of Study and Employment

The educational loan is undoubtedly the most common form of financial aid to undergraduates, whereas scholarship grants are the most desirable because they require no repayment. A third way of financing a college education, however, is universally acceptable, regardless of a student's school or course of study, and is a source of funds that need

never be repaid. This third form of "financial aid" is student employment, the subject to which most of this book is devoted. Hundreds of
thousands of American undergraduates—of every background, income,
and academic inclination—hold term-time and summer jobs every year,
supplementing their loans and grants, or simply providing for their own
spending money. As indicated at the beginning of this chapter, colleges
and universities have recently been meeting the soaring demand for
financial assistance on the part of undergraduates with a combination of
strategies. In many cases, outright transfers of funds in the form of
grants or loans is insufficient, and the school guarantees the student a
further portion of "aid" in the form of a job, the earnings from which
may be applied to the student's educational expenses. This type of job is
discussed briefly in this subsection: the job that is a part of an organized
system of cooperative education or a work-study financial aid program.
The most common student jobs—those that undergraduates arrange for
themselves with private employers—will be taken up in great detail in
the remainder of this guide.

Cooperative Education—

This type of program is based upon an alternating schedule of full-
time academic work and full-time employment. Several hundred colleges
and universities operate such programs, and each has different goals and
organizational principles. At some schools, the cooperative plan is
common to all students; at others, it is optional. Many schools consider
the work aspect of the program to be educationally vital, and the work
interval of the year is set aside for exploring potential careers or gaining
preprofessional experience. At other institutions, the employment interval is viewed primarily as a financial plan, to ease the monetary burden
on full-time undergraduates. Jobs, in this case, are evaluated more for
their remunerative than for their educational promise. Certain colleges
are committed to strict alternation of work and study at short (six- to
ten-week) intervals, whereas others allocate a designated or elective
semester as the yearly employment period.

Many liberal arts colleges function on the cooperative system, but
this plan is especially well-adapted to business, pharmacy, engineering,
nursing, and vocational programs. Two good examples of exclusively
cooperative institutions that provide coordinated work experiences for
their students are the General Motors Institute and the College of
Insurance.

The General Motors Institute, the only accredited undergraduate
college maintained by a private industrial corporation, prepares men and

women, by means of engineering and industrial management programs, for careers in the administration of General Motors. The curriculum leading to a B.A. degree at the Institute is five years long, involving four and one-half years in the cooperative phase. During this time, the student alternates six weeks of formal study with six weeks of coordinated work experience in one of the 150 General Motors plants across the continent. The final half-year of the degree program is spent preparing a thesis on a topic related to a concurrent full-time work assignment. Students may expect to earn a gross income of $4,450 during their first year, with appropriate raises as they progress toward their degrees. Because these substantial earnings are a direct result of the work aspect of the institute program, no scholarships are granted, but a loan fund is available to assist students who may have extraordinary expenses. Work wages ordinarily cover all undergraduate expenses. High school seniors who seriously seek the particular career preparation that this corporate institution offers should contact the Admissions Officer, General Motors Institute, 1700 West Third Avenue, Flint, Michigan 48502 for applications and further information.

Similar professional training programs, organized on cooperative lines, are the business/insurance and actuarial mathematics courses offered by the College of Insurance at 150 William Street, New York, New York 10038. Also a five-year program, the College of Insurance alternates four-month periods of work and study, and students in these Baccalaureate courses can expect to earn about $12,000 during their undergraduate careers. In addition, each student has two-thirds of his tuition paid by the sponsoring agency in which his work trimesters are scheduled, and if he remains with the firm upon graduation, the final third of his tuition will be restored to him by the company. More than forty large insurance firms, brokerage houses, and bureaus act as work-interval sponsors, enabling each student to gradually rotate through all the departments of a company and thereby master its practical organization. Inquiries about these courses should be directed to the Director of Cooperative Education at the College of Insurance.

Detailed listings of schools that operate cooperative education programs are available from two sources. The major one is the National Commission for Cooperative Education, 52 Vanderbilt Avenue, New York, New York 10017. A second reference is *A Guide to Student Assistance,* a pamphlet published by the House of Representatives Committee on Education and Labor, and available from the Superintendent of Documents, U.S. Government Printing Office, Washington, D.C. 20402 for a fee of $.60. This pamphlet contains a list of colleges and universities that offer cooperative education programs, grouped state by state, following which (since many of these institutions have coordinating work programs in only certain subjects) is a grouping according to the fields of study that are offered. Federal funding has helped to subsidize the development of the cooperative education movement, and the list of participating institutions has steadily grown.

In the specific program of federal government employment for cooperative education students, various federal agencies provide jobs for these students during their alternate work semesters. A wide variety of government employment may be sampled in this way, and the possibilities for linking term-time study to work-term duties are many. To be eligible for such jobs, however, students *must* meet Civil Service job requirements. The U.S. Civil Service Commission (listed under United States Government in the telephone book) can provide the details of eligibility procedures.

Another approach to cooperative education is exemplified by the W. Clement and Jessie V. Stone Foundation Scholarship Program, which is designed to pay tuition, supplies, costs, and academic fees for undergraduates who aspire to become professional workers with the Boys Clubs of America—and who are willing to work for at least ten hours a week as paid employees of the Chicago Boys Club while they are in school. Applicants may come from anywhere in the nation and should display both academic and career potential. The Director of Education, Chicago Boys Club, 304 West Randolph Street, Chicago, Illinois 60606 has application forms and information. Various other community and social service organizations invest in the training of their potential workers in this way; if any of such activities appeals to you as a career, contact the appropriate local agency and investigate the possibility of subsidized study.

Work-Study—

If your school does not run on the cooperative education plan, a different kind of organized study and employment scheme will often be operating on campus; namely, the federal work-study program. Hundreds of American colleges and universities, and vocational, secretarial, and business schools participate in this program; a state-by-state listing of these schools is included in the House of Representatives pamphlet *A Guide to Student Assistance,* mentioned earlier. The work-study program represents one aspect of the government's financial efforts to ensure equal educational opportunity; in this case, by making funds available to subsidize wages for the employment of students who demonstrate a need for money to enable these students to complete their educations.

The work-study program has the secondary goal of providing non-profit private or public agencies that are concerned with health, education, welfare, recreation, and research with additional personnel at low cost. The principle of this program is that the government pays part of a student's wage for working at such an organization if the student and his job are approved for the program by the financial-aid officer of the specific college. Students paid from work-study funds may be employed by any nonprofit organization or institution with the exception of political parties and groups and in the purely sectarian activities of churches and other religious bodies. In some cases students are helped by their school to locate appropriate jobs; in other instances, they are required, or have the option to, locate their own jobs.

If an employer employs a student employee through the work-study program, he will find that, although he must contribute the full employer's share of Social Security payments on behalf of the employee, he will be responsible for only a fraction of the student's wage—approximately 20 to 40 per cent, the remainder being paid by federal funds as channeled through the particular program. Of course, this is a boon to the employer, and the student benefits not only by the financial boost that his earnings bring him but often from the opportunity to work in an interesting situation, for a nonprofit agency whose strict budget would not have ordinarily permitted the hiring of an eager but untrained student employee. It is stipulated in the legislation that created this program, however, that such a student employee may *not* replace a regularly employed worker, nor may it interfere with existing contracts for services such as janitorial or food services. This provision protects regular personnel from the threat of displacement by students who, because of the program, can work for less than half of the ordinary salary. Often a student will have a position created especially for him in accordance with a particular project of his own—a sophomore sociology major, for example, did a statistical study on family patterns at a local day-care center, which provided a useful tool for the agency in assessing its role and objectives in the neighborhood and formed a part of its self-evaluation in a request for public support. In other instances, students may be hired as trainee-assistants who participate in the activities of the organization and develop skills while relieving permanent personnel from some of their work, in order that the permanent staff may take on extra projects appropriate to their training and experience. A premedical student who "ran errands" in the emergency room of an urban hospital,

with term-time work-study support, gained insight into his chosen profession and eventually picked up much practical medical knowledge
while his extra pair of hands eased a crucial shortage of attendants and
nurses.

Students interested in the work-study program must directly contact
the financial-aid officer of their own school, since it is only these officers
at the individual participating institutions who select the students who
are to benefit from the program. Legally, the only eligibility requirements are that the students must be engaged in full-time study and must
be permanent residents or citizens of the United States, or permanent
residents of the trust territory of the Pacific Islands. Students must also
need the work-study earnings to balance their budgets for college expenses, since this program was conceived as a form of financial aid
through self-help, but individuals are evaluated by their own schools to
determine this need. Family income and grants that have been awarded
to the student are considered, and the program seeks to help reduce the
amount that students must go into debt by taking educational loans. The
neediest students at each school are served first by the program, but a
financial-aid officer must also weigh a student's academic situation,
substituting other forms of assistance when he feels that a student's
standing may be damaged by devoting his time to a work-study job.

Schools determine many employment conditions as well as student
eligibility. They screen employing agencies and check job descriptions to
make sure that they correspond to legal requirements; the schools may
actually solicit work-study job inquiries for their students from likely
local organizations. They insist on supervisory feedback on the student's
performance. Although, under the law, students may work no more than
fifteen hours a week during the term and forty hours a week during the
summer, schools may limit these maximums for their own students.
Student wage rates must match the current legal minimum wage, but the
schools actually handle the work-study payrolls and it is they, and not
the actual employing agency, who determine student wage rates. At one
Midwestern university, the work-study pay scale for freshmen and
sophomores was $2.50 an hour, whereas upperclassmen received an
hourly wage of $2.75. A small college in the same city paid $2.25 an
hour to *all* its work-study students. In this way, the assistance aspect of
the earnings are emphasized, and the work itself may be selected for its
relevance to the student's interest, and not for competitive wages.

A college may also set a limit on individual earnings in conjunction
with its overall financial-aid policy. A private women's college with an

endowment large enough to provide adequate grants and loans for all of its needy students set a $200 limit on work-study term-time earnings and $400 on summer earnings, whereas an urban university with a smaller endowment allows its students to make $1,000 yearly through the work-study program. It should be noted that these guides do not prevent students from earning additional money at ordinary jobs nor do they prevent an agency that has hired a certain student under the work-study plan from rehiring him or keeping him on after the work-study earnings limit has been surpassed *if* the agency is willing to take on the full responsibility for the student's salary when it can no longer be subsidized by the school.

Colleges administer federal work-study funds with a considerable degree of flexibility. The government makes arrangements with individual schools, granting them blocks of money to disperse, and colleges exercise the many controls cited in channeling this money to students. Since government appropriations for this purpose are limited, most schools cannot secure sums as large as they would like to serve the needs of their students. Some colleges and universities may vary the proportion of salary paid to students by government and employer in order to extend aid to a larger total number of undergraduates. If the employer is asked to contribute 40 per cent of the wage, funds from the government will go 20 per cent further than if the government's share were set at 80 per cent and the employing agency's at 20 per cent. Such proportions will vary from school to school, and from year to year at the same institution.

At some colleges and universities (but *not,* by law, at the postsecondary business and secretarial schools participating in the program), the academic institution may itself be the student's employer. Because work-study jobs are ideally more than a funding device, additional qualities such as the public interest and the appropriateness of the employment to a student's career and academic goals should be considered in developing job possibilities, according to the legislation defining this program. As a result, such on-campus jobs as dining hall help, kitchen help, and dormitory porters and janitors are not usually subsidized by work-study funds. Library and research assistant positions may, however, be so subsidized if the student meets the federal criteria for need. In these instances, work-study and ordinary on-campus jobs are identical, differing only in the source of the money for the student's wages. Although some schools assign jobs arbitrarily, most colleges and universities allow students to choose their own jobs, and, often, students find that their potential work-study status, with its low cost to the employer, helps them to find especially stimulating or convenient positions.

Work-study has funded an enormous number of student jobs. Initiated by Congress in 1965, the program had approximately 290,000 student participants two years later. In 1968 it served about 314,000 students and added over 50,000 in the school year beginning in September 1969. Growth has continued steadily at this rate.[17] Likewise, the variety of different jobs funded is great, as indicated by the following examples.

Summer jobs offer the greatest flexibility, allowing students to work in different parts of the country and to make a substantial investment of time. An American Indian girl, attending a Massachusetts college, was able to land a work-study position for three months with the Southwestern Indian Development Program. She went to Arizona where she ran a children's library and did special tutoring. A fine arts major from Michigan spent a summer as an assistant to the curator at the San Francisco Museum of Art. An undergraduate interested in psychology worked for the Institute for the Study of Family and Youth transcribing and analyzing tape recordings of the home life of deviant families as part of a research project. Many work-study summer jobs involve research— whether with a student's biophysics professor, or in South American anthropological field work, or at a Cretan archeological excavation. Prelaw students have worked on legal referrals to a Mayor's Office of Human Rights; future physicians have tabulated data in a clinical drug-use study or worked on a laboratory project investigating cancer in children or served as administrative assistants to the American Heart Association.

Work-study jobs often help involve students in community action programs in their home or college towns. A junior who had volunteered during the term to do rehabilitative tutoring through his college's Prisons Committee was able to use his work with inmates as a reference and spent a work-study-funded summer creating a day-recreation program for delinquent boys. Upward Bound, a precollegiate tutoring program, and Urban CORE are nationwide programs that have employed many work-study undergraduates, but local programs probably provide excellent chances both for securing positions and for doing personally satisfying work.

Term-time jobs are somewhat limited by the short number of hours that students are free to spend at work. An English major who participated in her college's Teacher's Aide Program, working with third-graders in a local public school, found that her ten-hour weekly employment was a strong enough force to prompt a change of her major—to education. A biology major from Boston left his sophisticated laboratory experiments every Tuesday and Thursday afternoon in order to give walking tours to wide-eyed schoolchildren who were fascinated by the seals and sea turtles at the New England Aquarium. A junior from Minneapolis worked with individual teen-agers in a tutoring program sponsored by a ghetto church—only *sectarian* church activities are excluded by the work-study program. One student whose work-study job did not exactly reflect her educational goals was a classics major who spent her days deciphering Cicero and her nights sizzling hamburgers for her dormitory grill. Because the grill was financed by the college as a nonprofit student service, it qualified as a work-study employer. Because the hours were from 9:00 P.M. to 1:00 A.M. every night, and because the grill was located in the basement of her own dormitory, the convenience of this job dovetailed nicely with the student's schedule—and she earned the money she needed for her term bill.

The Package Deal

Financial aid has been a high priority for government and private organizations concerned with American undergraduate education, but it is still inadequate to meet the needs of all the postsecondary students who are seeking educational financing. If you are interested in continuing in school after your high school graduation, and money is a problem, you should expect to tap several sources of funds. Most colleges and universities offer students some combination of flat grants, long-term loans, and part-time job opportunities in order to meet their requests for financial aid. If you can think of other sources of aid that may help you, investigate them.

Can your religious organization or church sponsor you for grants or loans? Are your parents union members? Are they veterans? If they are, they may have access to special funds. Are you an athlete? Many schools offer athletic scholarships. What are the policies of your state legislature on educational assistance? Do you have a settled career goal? Many professional associations and private endowments exist to aid future members of various professions and trades in obtaining the necessary training. Is there a branch of the Rotary Club in your town, the Elks, the Lions, the PTA, or any one of the hundreds of local associations, lodges, clubs, and other organizations that support hometown students in their studies? What about competitive scholarships? Can you succeed on nationwide examinations such as the National

Merit Scholarship Qualifying Test or present a winning project in a science fair or a 4-H program? Are you a member of a minority group? Is your family income below $10,000, or does your situation reflect economic or educational disadvantage? The federal government has aimed most of its financial assistance efforts at an attempt to assure equal educational opportunity for you—look into its programs. Are you a veteran, or would you be interested in combining your college education with preparation for military service? Any branch of the service will welcome your inquiries concerning benefits and opportunities for its past, present, and future members. If you have considered all of the possibilities that you might explore in seeking flat grants, look over your list again, and think about loan possibilities in all of those categories.

Remember that your best ally in seeking educational funding is (for high school students) your high school guidance counselor who will have information on careers, colleges, and finances, and (for college students) the financial-aid officer at your school, whose business it is to allow you whatever the college can afford to offer in the way of endowed and federal monies, and to direct your attention to all of the other routes to educational financing that are open to you as an individual.

The major rule in a search for financial aid is identical with the principle that guides all successful financial organizing: *plan ahead.* This foresight will help you to maximize your chances of receiving the assistance you need, in the best form for you, and it is certainly your best guide to the employment preparation and job-finding that is discussed in the remainder of this book. Whatever stage of the search you are at, think about what you need to do and start early. If you are considering college and career possibilities, investigate the concrete opportunities and examine your own talents and inclinations. If you know your general educational plan, begin immediately to assess its financial challenges and to consult with your family, guidance counselor, and others as to how to best meet them. Gather all of the information you can—from people, books, pamphlets, library resources, and direct inquiry to institutions and organizations. When you know to whom you must apply for funds, obtain the necessary forms as soon as possible and return them promptly. Arrange to take required examinations—PSAT/ NMSQT, Scholastic Aptitude Test, ACT exams, and College Entrance Examination Board exams. These examinations may be important to your chances of college admission or financial-aid approval, and they must all be registered for weeks in advance of the few dates each year on which they are given. You must also arrange to have your examination scores, high school transcripts, and personal recommendations forwarded to any source of aid that may request them. You and your parents will probably have to provide *some* family financial information to your aid sources; obtain the proper form and complete it. File all applications on time and fulfill all application requirements. Above all, start early. Filing early cannot be overemphasized, because it is the key to successful competition for the limited sources of aid. In no other way will you be able to sort out the programs that are most likely to help you from the diverse mass of assistance possibilities in time to concentrate your energies on prompt and effective requests for financial aid.

The American Legion quotes significant statistics, based upon a survey that was conducted by Richard McKee for the United States Office of Education, in its booklet *Need a Lift?*[18] From the 2,115 colleges and universities surveyed, it was discovered that over $130,850,000 was dispersed annually in the form of flat grants to more than 300,000 undergraduates. Loans, excluding those funded by federal and state programs, went to over 60,000 students in the amount of nearly $24 million. Private, state, and corporate funds for financial aid run into the hundreds of millions of dollars each year, and the federal government's commitment to this field is massive, if fluctuating. Billions of dollars are available annually to needy undergraduate students in the United States. This chapter has tried simply to give you a sense of the breadth of aid opportunities and a start in your exploration of the specific sources of assistance with your personal educational expenses.

Organization and perseverance on your part are bound to bring you at least a portion of the educational funding that you seek, even if it is in one form of long-term student loans. Whatever your success, however, in applying for financial aid—and we hope it is complete—you will probably need more money. This may sound like a contradiction in terms, but complete success in educational funding cannot be expected to pay for more than tuition, room and board, fees, books, and some miscellaneous expenses. No university, federal program, or private foundation is about to finance your stereo system, 1968 Volkswagen, or Saturday night movie. Personal expenses are almost invariably left to the individual student, and you will almost always need to find a way of financing such purchases. You will need a job.

Many students, especially those whose families cannot afford to contribute much toward their educations, will find themselves forced to earn much more than even their school's work-study limit in order to keep up with their educational bills. Others will be granted scholarships on the condition that they contribute a certain sum or percentage of their summer earnings to the cost of their schooling. A third group will see term-time and summer employment as a way to avoid incurring further educational debts by way of loans.

Even the landed aristocrat and the doughnut-shop chain heiress, whose Porsches and polo ponies are amply subsidized, may not be able to withstand the lure of the chance to work with a favorite professor or to start their own lucrative student business. Many students will view their undergraduate jobs as a potential basis for later employment as well as a source of present earnings. Some students will welcome an opportunity for financial independence, career exploration, change of pace, academic interest, humanitarian service, social contacts, or simple work experience—an undergraduate job may provide any or all of these. A substantial number of students will find that their employment experiences mean as much to them and have as much educational value as any other experiences of their undergraduate careers.

Whatever your reason, you will probably want to join the majority of your fellow American college students and take on *some* job *some* time during your postsecondary school years. The following chapters are intended to help you prepare for that job, to find it, to secure it—and to get the most out of it, whatever of your needs your job is meant to fulfill.

Notes

[1] These figures are cited in the American Legion Educational and Scholarship Program booklet, *Need a Lift?*, 21st edition, Indianapolis, Indiana, p. 4.

[2] *U.S. News and World Report*, February 22, 1971, p. 25.

[3] *Ibid.*, p. 26.

[4] *Financing a College Education: A Guide for Counselors*, College Scholarship Service of the College Entrance Examination Board, New York, 1971, p. 2.

[5] *Ibid.*, p. 8.

[6] Figures from the U.S. Census Bureau, presented in *U.S. News and World Report*, March 8, 1971, p. 44.

[7] College Scholarship Service, *op. cit.*, p. 2.

[8] *U.S. News and World Report*, February 22, 1971, p. 28.

[9] This and all other concrete figures, charts, and information concerning the use of the Parents' Confidential Statement, as described in this subsection "The parents' role," are derived from College Scholarship Service, *op. cit.*, pp. 7–12.

[10] College Scholarship Service, *op. cit.*, p. 10.

[11] Sidney Margolius, "A Letter to Parents," College Scholarship Service of the College Entrance Examination Board, p. 4.

[12] College Scholarship Service, *op. cit.*, p. 10.

[13] College Scholarship Service, *op. cit.*, p. 11.

[14] American Legion Educational and Scholarship Program, *op. cit.,* p. 15.

[15] "1972 NROTC Bulletin," Princeton, N.J., p. 10.

[16] Chart based on figures cited by *U.S. News and World Report,* February 22, 1971, p. 25. The magazine's source was the U.S. Office of Education.

[17] *U.S. News and World Report,* February 22, 1971, p. 27.

[18] Twenty-first edition (revised, Fall, 1971), American Legion Educational and Scholarship Program, Indianapolis, Indiana; p. 2.

Chapter Two

SKILLS

"Sorry, Charlie, but if you don't have a *high school diploma*—buzz off!" Surely this punch line has moved you many times as you closed the cover of your matchbook, before striking. It always comes at the end of a touching vignette concerning the fortunes of an unemployed cartoon character, who always discovers that "statistics show that a high-school diploma will be worth $100,000 to you in your lifetime because you will be able to qualify for better jobs at higher pay," not to mention "prestige." Even as a college freshman, you have that high-school diploma and should start getting your hands on some of that $100,000.

Even if your only "skill" is the fact that you finished high school and are now attending college, it is an important one. You probably speak, read, write, compute, and catch on to new responsibilities faster than the greater part of the labor pool, and, most significantly, you have your achievement as a college entrant to demonstrate this fact to a potential employer. Don't underestimate this college "image"—it not only bespeaks your real ability but adds an immeasurable psychological advantage to your sales pitch. The United States has associated higher education indivisibly with intelligence and upward mobility. The possession of that college diploma may actually render you *over*qualified in the eyes of one range of employers, but as long as you're pursuing your degree, you have a head start in convincing the personnel manager that you are bright and eager. Your lack of concrete skills may seem glaring to you, but you are probably comparing yourself with college classmates of similar ability. An employer, on the other hand, weighs your background and potential against that of *all* his other applicants, and your positive attributes will be apparent to him.

However, the student who brings a natural talent or a special skill to college is very fortunate. He will simply earn more money than his unskilled roommate as can be seen from the following examples. The camp sailing instructor ($800 per summer) and waterfront director ($1,000) may make more than twice as much as a regular counselor ($300)—even though all three may be chemistry majors at the state university. The free-lance student artist who spends her vacation from nursing school drawing summer layouts for a town merchant will earn more than her classmates who clerk in the store—and she will enjoy her work more, as well. One freshman spent his extra time learning how to arc-weld in his high school shop class and applied his skill in a local ironworks at $3.70 an hour during the summer. He will carry a lot more cash back to college with him than his metal-shop buddy, who never really bothered to master the skills—he was forced to work nights as a busboy at a restaurant.

After four years of high school and some time at college, it may surprise you to realize how little your liberal arts education alone has qualified you to do. Cheer up: most of your competition is in the same situation. More important, few college students have the fact that they are college material as their only skill. Most students—and you are included—do at least one thing well, and usually that one thing can be turned into money. This chapter suggests ways to make your skills and interests pay.

Even if your main skill lies in an area that is not ordinarily marketable, you may figure out a way to profit by it financially. For example, a Rutgers junior who enjoyed chess invented a game called "Round Table Chess," with a round board of concentric circles. He borrowed $250 from the student business organization (which received a promise of repayment, plus 5 per cent of any profits) and began marketing the game through college bookstores at $2.75 a set. He got back his initial investment from the sales at a single store—the rest was "gravy." A Portland, Oregon, student parlayed his numismatic acumen into a $500,000 retail business specializing in old coins. In these cases of available skills that were not in great demand by the economy, the students used their imaginations to start their own businesses, thereby creating their own demand.

Most skills, however, can be used profitably by existing organizations. The following sections describe the types of jobs you can obtain with different kinds of skills and give you ideas on where to go if you want to learn new skills or polish up old ones.

Identifying Marketable Skills—

Although you probably already possess marketable skills, it is sometimes difficult to find out just what you can do well and how you can use these skills to get a job. Don't be afraid to credit yourself with all of your talents and to push them; a skill with which you may be dissatisfied often seems impressive to an employer, who is not as sensitive as you are to its imperfection. You may not have attended design school, but your flair for color and pattern may be worth cash to the shop owner who is looking for imagination to apply to his window displays. Give yourself a chance—so that he can give you a chance.

Many resources are available to help you discover your own skills. It is often a good idea to talk to a counselor at school about what kinds of jobs you might do. Many schools have student placement offices with qualified counselors and others run student employment programs through the dean of students or the financial-aid office.

You might try checking into your school's testing program if you are uncertain about what you can, or want to do. Several measures of interests and aptitudes, such as the Kuder Interest Index, can tell you which professional group you are closest to in interests and attitudes on the basis of your answers to test questions. Aptitude tests may show you in what direction your skills lie and which ones might be worth developing.

Another source for aptitude tests is your local state employment service. These services often administer such tests and will also give you typing, filing, and stenography exams to measure your speed and accuracy in business skills. Such scores can be an asset in applying for office employment, but you are the only one who need see these test results; they will not be reported to anyone else unless you request it. State employment services usually have counselors who will be able to give you advice on job hunting as well. Remember, though, that a test is only as useful as its interpretation. If you score 75 in math aptitude, is that 75 out of 100, out of 800, or out of 75? And what does that result mean to you in terms of your native ability, learned knowledge, and possibilities of future employment? If you take any of these tests, be sure that the scores are explained to you by a qualified interpreter who will help you plan your future on the basis of the test results.

Another way of discovering your own skills is by composing your résumé. (See "Nailing a Job.") When you write your résumé, begin by putting *everything* in it. Try to step back and see if there is any general trend or orientation in your background. Have your activities been slanted toward public contact, toward individual research, or toward creative activity? You will not want to leave *all* of your activities in your final résumé but perhaps this overview will help you decide what general area you would be most interested and effective in.

What if your high-school employment record is a patchwork of short-term efforts to earn spending money that bored you utterly at the time. The summer you washed greasy pots at the White Star Diner, that winter you typed invoices in your dad's warehouse, those stints of baby-sitting for the Jones twins—do these jobs really reflect your talents and ambitions? Probably not—so consult your interests, and don't be afraid to see them as skills—actual or potential. You've been skiing since you could walk—doesn't that sound like a lead-in to a part-time job as a beginners' instructor? You can dismantle your motorcycle and put it together again blindfolded—would you be interested in a summer's apprenticeship that would teach you to deal with other makes and models as a repairman? Even if those twins were devils, now that you're majoring in early childhood education wouldn't a few paid afternoons a week as a teacher's aide in the nearby nursery school help cement your academic interest into professional skill?

Build on what you have—talent, interests, experience—to acquire the skills you'll need.

The Broad Prospects—

In discussing how students can use certain skills—with the goal of giving you some idea of how to apply yours—it makes sense to identify what kinds of skills are in demand NOW.

The number of different skills demanded by today's sophisticated economy is great. Skilled men make their living at tasks ranging from neurosurgery to jet piloting, from automatic lathe set-up to computer systems analysis. The expanding technology of our society is creating demands for skills that a generation ago were not even in the science fiction novels. Where does the student fit into this boom? Surely there are not many summer jobs available to student brain surgeons? No, but the same growth that is creating so many jobs at top levels is providing thousands of new moderately skilled and semiskilled positions. This is the student's line of attack on the job market. If the advance of medicine has created the need for more doctors, it has also increased the demand for clinical lab technicians. If the startling growth in the popularity of air travel over the last decade has led to a shortage of airline pilots, it has also created new jobs for multilingual students leading European tours. The sheer increase in population (it has doubled in the last thirty-three years) has caused a construction boom that has sent building wages skyrocketing while the number of new craftsmen entering the trade has actually declined. In the summer (the peak building season) good construction jobs can be filled by skilled students.

Most specifically, the 1960's saw an increase in the service and distribution-of-goods industries, a trend that is expected to continue through the 1970's. The staggering number of machines that have been integrated into American life represent one reason for this development. Most families in the United States now own one or more automobiles and television sets, which will sooner or later demand the services of one or more repairmen, parts distributors, and the like. Add to the household a washing machine, a clothes dryer, a blender, a stereo system, and an electric toothbrush, and the explosion of jobs in the service industries becomes evident.

Service, of course, is a division of labor that includes more than sales and repair work. Dry cleaners perform a service, as do pharmacists, physicians, and elementary school teachers. Our country is experiencing a great demand for the services of those in the rehabilitation and health professions, as well as those engaged in providing transportation and recreational facilities and accommodations. Worldwide communications systems and jet travel have led to vastly expanded international investments. The distribution of men, materials, and data—over great distances and with efficiency and speed—has become a multimillion dollar effort. You will not necessarily end up with a job in these areas (and, given your particular skills, you might not even look there). Yet these are the spheres of the economy in which there are the most new openings and in which most of the hiring is done. The service and distribution industries do not by any means offer the most glamorous jobs available. Chances are that you will not be able to translate your job experience into training for a white collar job, although you might gain valuable background for later jobs after graduating. If you pack transistors in Cleveland for shipment to a radio assembly plant in Spokane, you are not necessarily in direct line for the vice-presidency in charge of distribution at your mammoth corporation. "Starting at the bottom" is becoming an obsolete training experience, precisely because of the specialization of skills needed in today's job market. Yet a college sophomore is far more likely to land summer work in the shipping department of Mammoth Manufacturing than he is to be appointed temporary assistant to the vice-president. You must be realistic about the existing job market.

The skill market was completely different in former years. Many large companies and industries had training programs and they were willing to hire students on the basis of their academic majors and place them in positions that provided preprofessional experience. These jobs helped to improve the company image with the community as well as to train young people who might be willing to work for the company after graduation. Although the resulting student research and activity were valuable, students' work often did not compensate the company for the effort that went into their training. When the job market tightened up in the early 1970's, these jobs were among the first to go, since the company's primary responsibility is to full-time employees who have to support themselves through their jobs. Very few of the preprofessional internships are now being run, although if the job market improves, they will probably be reinstated—so don't rule them out as a way of using or acquiring skills.

It is important to realize, as well, that there are no hard and fast rules in employment. Even though most jobs are in one area and most internships have been discontinued, you may be successful in one of the areas that statistics seem to rule out. One Brown sophomore was offered a high-paying summer internship with an insurance company. As an economics major, he was hired on the basis of his academic knowledge of statistics. The insurance company was willing to train him to use this knowledge in business, and it was eager to get him to join the company after graduation.

Skill Development—

Where do you fit into these categories? The early development of a skill will give you a wider choice of lucrative jobs than you would otherwise have—which increases your chances of finding a job you like. If you are not satisfied with the skills you have, or are interested in learning a new one, there are many sources of training available to you.

Depending upon the job market, the skills that you decide would be useful acquisitions may or may not be the same skills you will want to acquire for a career. The future lawyer will enjoy earning $4.40 an hour by bricklaying on summer construction jobs, but he won't be adding to his career skills. You should carefully consider which skills are most called for in your area. You may be studying astronomy, but if you live in a resort area and are interested in spending time outdoors, it makes more sense for you to learn how to repair outboard motors than it does for you to master key punching.

Because there is a difference between preprofessional skills and the skills used by most college students on-the-job, you should seize opportunities to acquire *marketable* skills that you would not otherwise consider. You may have little or no interest in a secretarial career, and may hesitate to learn shorthand for fear that it will make it that much easier for you to be shunted into a low-level position after graduation. You should remember, however, that a temporary job does *not* necessarily require the same skills that a professional career will. With this distinction in mind, you may feel free to learn the shorthand that will secure you high-paying summer jobs and finance your professional training.

Typing is the one essential skill; an invaluable investment. It will save you time and money to be able to type your own papers while you are in college, and a good typing skill can provide you with instant cash at a moment's notice; *someone* always needs a paper typed. Not only are the obvious clerical tasks open to you on a part-time or summer basis— many more interesting jobs simply require typing as a minor prerequisite. The gulf between the clerk-typist and the executive who commands his own private secretary is great and filled with fascinating jobs. Would you, majoring in urban studies, want to miss out on a position as chief assistant to the local city planner just because you couldn't type up memos? Your endocrinology professor may invite you to assist him in a research project that fits in perfectly with your biology thesis—will you have to say no because you can't type lab reports? Long after graduation, this basic skill will be a prerequisite for employment. A *summa cum laude* Columbia graduate was made a junior editor at the Columbia University Press evaluating manuscripts in his field. An ideal job? He would have been turned down, despite his intellectual qualifications, if he had not been able to type his comments and reviews, and replies to his own professional correspondence. You should acquire this skill as soon as possible.

If you have decided which skills you need, you can then look for learning opportunities.

Short Courses in School—

Both academic and nonacademic courses in high school and college can give you marketable skills. It is a good idea to plan ahead, taking a few of these courses in high school and perhaps working some into your college schedule. In high school you may be able to take advantage of typing, mechanical drawing, woodworking, home economics, or language courses. If you *elect* courses such as these in high school, with the incentive of earning $500 more than you would as an unskilled college freshman, you will probably retain more than you would if the courses were required and you did not realize their potential value. You can follow up on some of these courses in college; with a really good language background, for instance, you may be able to land one of the translating jobs that are often available in a college community. Even if you are acquiring technical skills in high school, you will be surprised how far your training takes you. Skilled technicians are in great demand in certain communities, and, once you have a head start, employers may be willing to let you learn on the job. With a basic high school course behind him, for example, a beginning welder can often get on-the-job training.

Computer skills command high salaries, and many high schools now offer courses in computers. In areas where they do not, local colleges may allow high school students to enroll in special training programs. One student took a course in programming at MIT in his junior year of high school. On the basis of that course, and a follow-up course that he took during his senior year, he was hired as a computer programmer by his university and given enough training to become a computer instructor. A steady source of income—and he was not even majoring in science or mathematics.

This example points up the fact that local and community colleges are a good source for learning skills, if you are still in high school. These schools often offer special night courses or specially scheduled day courses for high school students or the community at large, from which you can profit.

If you are in college, the options available to you widen. You may find that your college major will give you skills that can be used in jobs as an undergraduate. If you are a history major, this may not hold; if you are a home economics major, on the other hand, you may acquire enough credits to be a low-level dietician for a company or hospital.

Other sources, primarily for nonacademic skills, are adult education centers and night schools. Often a city or the local YMCA will offer courses in crafts, home repair, carpentry, clerical skills, lifesaving, and more either for free or at nominal rates.

You may want to consider taking courses at secretarial, art, or technical schools. There are problems with obtaining skills this way; the expense is greater and many such courses require more hours than a full-time college student can afford to give. Technical school training programs range from ten weeks (for training you how to install air-conditioning in a car) to two years (for training television repairmen). If you are interested in learning about technical schools, your local state employment service probably has a list of such schools in your area. Another source of information on technical schools is the National Association of Trade and Technical Schools, listed at the end of the chapter.

Some state governments run technical education centers, where you can get both short-term technical education and skilled crafts training for minimal fees. South Carolina, for instance, provides training in such diverse subjects as laboratory assistantship, welding, and electronics. Your state employment office can tell you whether your state has such a training program.

Apprenticeships—

If technical schools sound too formal for your purposes, you might consider learning a skill by apprenticing yourself to someone who will teach you while you work. The most advantageous apprenticeship arrangement for you is an informal one, although the terms of the agreement should be clearly understood from the beginning. Many state employment agencies run apprenticeship centers that will place you with a skilled master. Most of these formal training programs run for three to five years, however, and are not much help to a student whose interest in learning a skill is fairly casual. In such specialties as electronics and plumbing, it is difficult to obtain a job in a union shop without first having been a formal apprentice. On the other hand, if you can find a small nonunion contractor, he might be willing to train you while paying you low wages. Once you have learned carpentry, bricklaying, the operation of construction machines, and the like, you will be able to earn substantial amounts of money. One student mastered the art of pipeline welding, managed to join the union, and cleared $300 a week during his summer vacations. This arrangement can be applied to crafts—sandalmaking, silversmithing—as well as to technical skills.

In some fields, apprenticeships are an established means for inexperienced students to become involved. Summer theaters, for instance, often require little or no experience of applicants. The wages are low, ranging from $50 a week to the provision for a part-time job as a waitress or an usher that will cover your expenses. In other fields, you may have to create the apprenticeship by means of your own initiative. One Bennington student persuaded a local potter to let her work in his shop, hauling clay and doing simple work under his direction. She worked for $1.30 an hour, but at the end of the year she had enough experience to begin selling her own pots on commission. Another student apprenticed himself to a builder for low wages one summer and spent his next vacation avoiding union problems by hiring himself out as an independent contractor to do home repairs.

Making arrangements for apprenticeship does not mean that you need be the only student involved in the arrangement. A group of students at the University of Wisconsin got together and took a course in reupholstering at an adult-education school. Once they had got this basic background, they persuaded a retired upholsterer to supervise them for a small fee and set up an agency to market their skills. Their lack of experience was compensated for by the presence of someone who *was* experienced. If you and your friends are interested in learning secretarial skills, a group may be able to persuade someone connected with your college to teach you for less than the going rate at professional secretarial schools. Or you might convince a computer instructor to offer a short-term course in the basics of programming.

Another form of apprenticeship that should not be overlooked is volunteer work. People who would not pay to train you on the job will often gladly accept volunteer help. The experience and skills you gain doing volunteer work may enable you to get a more interesting and responsible paying job later on, perhaps with the same organization that has had an opportunity to see and appreciate your work. A Dartmouth freshman did part-time volunteer work during the school year for a community organization aiding delinquent boys; he was offered the same job, full-time and with pay, for the summer.

Volunteer work also provides you with valuable contacts. In the ecology field, for instance, it is virtually impossible to get a paying job unless you already have contacts and a specific skill to offer, plus a previous background in ecology work. Volunteer work can be your tool to break the frustrating circle of "no-job-without-experience, no-experience-without-employment." It can be your introduction to the organization, the employers, the necessary skills, and the field. One afternoon a week spent at a nearby day-care center might be a lead-in to a teaching assistantship at a nursery school. Schools, health care, and social service facilities are among the organizations that are most in need of your services but are unable to hire you as a trainee. Political parties pay many of their campaign personnel, but you must first prove your loyalty to the party or candidate by a certain amount of free labor.

Lest you associate volunteer work with candy-striped pinafores on upper-class matrons, remember that volunteer work is probably even *more* various than paid employment, and you are even more likely to find enjoyable work as an unpaid, rather than as a paid, trainee. You might assist the local veterinarian in farm country, do community organizing in a ghetto, or teach blind children. You might do a stint as an aide in a busy emergency room and confirm your ambition to become a doctor—or you might be a caseworker for a local service agency and decide that social work is not for you. A summer's volunteer work at an arts-and-crafts camp might give you the skills you need to be hired as an activities aide at a children's hospital. Aside from personal satisfaction, volunteer work may lead you to important employment and career skills.

Time vs. Skill vs. Interest

Any job you hold can serve as an apprenticeship of sorts. You will be able to learn some skills in class; others you will teach yourself in pursuit of a hobby or special interest. Some you could pay to learn in a commercial skill course. But the best way to develop marketable skills is through experience at a job. And while you are earning money at one job you can be learning skills that will enable you to advance to a better job.

This is why it is a good idea to plan into the future when you decide what jobs to accept. If you have to choose between $1.75 an hour as a soda jerk and $1.35 an hour as a messenger in the computer center, you might be best advised to take the latter, lower-paying job. Had you taken the first job, you might, by the time you are a senior, have advanced to $1.95 an hour as a soda jerk ($585 for 300 hours work); had you taken the second job, your salary as a senior would have risen to $4 an hour as a computer operator or programmer ($1,200 for 300 hours work).

If you have to earn $400, you will be able to earn it more quickly at a skilled job than at an unskilled job. There are two reasons why you may wind up spending *more* time at a *skilled* job than at any unskilled one. First, if you are earning really good money, you may be reluctant to sleep late when you could be earning $5 an hour. More important, skilled jobs are generally more interesting and satisfying than unskilled jobs.

Working fifteen hours a week, every week, behind a dishwasher for four years could become extremely unpleasant. Roughly one seventh of your waking hours at college would be spent at a boring job you disliked. Working twenty-five hours a week at your own business, drawing cartoons, writing programs, or aiding a professor could be your most meaningful college experience. If you plan to spend a thousand hours working at college during your four years, you should invest your time to learn skills, experiment with different jobs, and seek out the form of employment that will prove most satisfying to you—both personally and financially.

Translating Skills into Jobs

Academic Skills—

As a college student you are spending most of your time and money to acquire an education—why not make it work for you before graduation as well as afterwards? You can strengthen your academic skill as you apply it to earn money—and perhaps gain fringe benefits in professional academic contacts and experience.

A job as a faculty aide, research assistant, tutor, translator, or proofreader solves your unemployment problem right on campus, but there is one drawback. In an area saturated with students, the supply of academic talent is so plentiful that employers can afford to be highly selective. The best jobs go to the superior and highly superior students.

As we sometimes forget, though, the college campus is *not* the whole world. There are businesses beyond the ivory tower looking for students who are proficient in English or journalism, economics, accounting, foreign languages, math, physics, chemistry, biology, or, most prominently, engineering.

Don't overlook the possibility of trying out the other side of the professor's desk; the fact that you are a student qualifies you eminently to become a teacher. You may only be qualified to help out beginners with subjects in which you are an advanced student, such as elementary French, first-year Latin, calculus or physics. You may ease some underclassman or high-school senior over a real stumbling block, and earn some cash in addition. Specialized knowledge commands special prices—and an eager market. You may be one of the only people in town who can translate and tutor Serbo-Croation, and someone may want to learn this language. Europe-bound adults may appreciate individual or group tutoring in foreign-language conversation; students in your university's law and medical schools would probably sign up for a course in Spanish, when it was appropriate to their professional contact with the Spanish-speaking community.

Look beyond the campus. The adult-education center in your town might welcome a lecture or discussion course on modern art, Asian politics, contemporary music, theater arts, economics—whatever your expertise suggests. Could you lead a seminar in foreign affairs or regional architecture for the local men's or women's club? Opportunities may exist, as well, to prepare teen-agers or adults for Regents or high school equivalency examinations; to teach English as a second language to new citizens; or to instruct preschool children; retarded children; mentally, emotionally, or physically handicapped children; disadvantaged children; or gifted children. Recycle your education—and get paid for it.

Even if you cannot use specific skills from your major, you may be able to use general research skills that you have acquired in school—to work in a specialized library, for instance. If dozens of grade-A term papers have turned you into a good writer, try selling free-lance feature articles to the local paper or magazine.

Business-Clerical Skills—

The business world may not be as appealing to you as a job researching your favorite professor's next book. For every full professor that the university employs it has several secretaries and clerks who are engaged in communicating and transcribing data. Large firms demonstrate the same ratio of office help to engineers, chemists, and systems analysts. Many jobs are available in business, and for the student with solid business skills, steady employment is practically guaranteed—no matter what the area of the country or the state of the economy.

Certain business skills are almost mandatory for both men and women: you should be able to type forty-five to fifty words a minute and to take some form of shorthand or speedwriting. You can learn typing in a high school or commercial course, or teach yourself from a book, if you have a great deal of perseverance. There are many forms of speedwriting, a version of shorthand that uses abbreviated word forms, which you can also learn at home from a manual. Not only are these skills valuable for business employment but they will smooth out your student life, saving you time that you can invest elsewhere (perhaps even making money!).

Secretarial work may not be the most exciting or creative job in the world, but the market for such workers is universal. Every area of business, government, academia, and science is propelled forward in vast waves of forms, letters, reports, résumés, theses, journals, statements, and invoices—all requiring armies of diligent typists. The working conditions are generally good, and many people prefer to spend July and August laboring at easily available positions in air-conditioned offices, rather than negotiating all spring to grasp that once-in-a-lifetime opportunity to excavate under the withering Libyan sun. Remember, too, that secretarial work is not confined to steno pools in sprawling insurance firms. The work might suit you better if you were typing legal briefs, patients' charts, social-service reports, or government memos. You might find employment in an architectural or advertising firm, or work as a private secretary to the chairman of your department. From there, it might only be a step to helping him with research on his new book.

There are other clerical skills to be learned. Can you operate a switchboard, do statistical computation, or simple bookkeeping? Can you collate, catalogue, and file? Do you know how to run calculators, audiographs, copying machines, keypunchers, dictaphones, teletypes, postage meters, or machines that mimeograph, fold papers, or address envelopes? The more you know, the better are your chances of employment. These skills are fairly easy to acquire, especially once you are on the job. If you do land a clerical position, try to learn to use as many of the machines around the office as you can. It is simple to learn to use a dictaphone, but you are a more attractive applicant if you can put on your application that you have already used one, instead of trying to persuade a prospective employer that you can easily pick it up, if he will only hire you.

Technical Skills—

Together with business skills, technical skills are among the surest job guarantees. There is always a need for qualified, intelligent technical help; so if you have managed to pick up some technical skill, no matter how, it makes good sense to develop it. One student, for example, grew up tinkering with motorboats in his Great Lakes community. Years later, he found a summer job in a seacoast resort, helping to repair ailing yachts.

One of the most touted technical areas is the newly developed field of computer programming. The image of computer work is that of a highly specialized technology that only hardened science and math majors can crack. This image is far from the truth. Many different skills are involved in working with computers. These distinct levels of expertise generate jobs ranging from creators of sophisticated programs and supervisors of complex data-processing systems to ordinary messengers, who feed cards into machines or transfer them to other rooms in the building. Keypunchers are needed to make those little holes in the cards;

this task requires only the ability to type on a computer keyboard. Logical, experienced technicians are needed to wire circuit boards or to attend to the "soft-ware" surrounding every computer. Simple programs are written by knowledgeable people who have *not,* necessarily, had extensive training. Furthermore, computers are too expensive to be idle, and most of them are in use twenty-four hours a day—which means a demand for extra shifts of workers. The key, according to the manager of one campus computer-services agency, is for the aspiring student employee to *"get involved,* if only on a lower level—then advance according to ability." Don't let your lack of mathematical genius deter you from looking into the computer field. Once you have completed your elementary training, you will find that these jobs pay handsomely.

Other technical skills, such as welding, automobile repair, and upholstering are also much in demand. If you can repair small cars, motorcycles, bicycles, or stereo systems, you might provide your classmates with a valuable service and undersell professional shops. And you could get rich without ever leaving the campus. With rising prices and an increasingly higher standard of living, people have more possessions that need taking care of and are less willing to hire a high-priced professional repairman to take care of them. With a good command of a technical skill, you may be able to hire yourself out at wages lower than the going rate and do a booming business. Or you may be able to get a job with an established operation, especially one that is small and nonunionized. Otherwise you may run into problems about joining the union. Union regulations vary so much from industry to industry that it is difficult to make generalizations about them. If you manage to join a union you will find yourself in a position to earn much more than you otherwise could. Many unions are difficult for students to enter, however, given the amount of time that unions generally require in apprenticeships, and the professional technicians of a union will occasionally display hostility toward "amateur-technician" students.

Manual and Construction Skills—

The ability to work well with one's hands is among the oldest of skills, and is today among the most marketable. Every new house has been worked on by excavators, carpenters, bricklayers, electricians, plasterers, painters, driveway-pavers, and landscapers. Eventually, the outside of the house will need repainting. Perhaps the gutters will have to be cleaned, and the chimney swept. The brick walk may need new mortar; the flagstone terrace, fresh cement. Indoor rooms may require a change of paint, paper, or paneling. The homeowner may wish to plant a hedge, lay a linoleum floor or a soundproof ceiling, add a playroom or back porch, subtract a wall, or divide a room. Tools have become mechanized and materials sophisticated, but at every turn, a pair of skilled hands is required. Since this reliably high demand for construction skills reaches a peak in the summer season, it is well-suited to a student's employment needs.

The decisive factor is, of course, how well the student is suited to the needs of the construction industry. Construction jobs have not been easy to get recently, since so many people are available for such work. Although there is a continuing demand for experienced construction specialists (masons, painters, and the like), it is harder to get a job as a general, unskilled construction worker, and you will find that contacts in the construction industry are extremely helpful in landing such a job. Students have built independent businesses, however, around the skills they possessed. Lawnmowing, gardening, and greenskeeping may be familiar to you from your high school days, and snow shoveling has changed from a struggle of drifts against muscle to a sophisticated manipulation of snow-blowers and jeep-or-truck-mounted shovels. These chores, which must be performed at intervals over the course of the summer or winter, lend themselves to steady employment, and perhaps a seasonal contract arrangement with local families. Fee-for-service jobs, on a less predictable schedule, have provided cash for students who were accomplished at gasoline-engine repair, electrical appliance repair, humidifier installation, hedge trimming, tree pruning, driveway sealing, and wallpapering.

Manual skills are almost invariably acquired through experience. But don't let this deter you—last summer two college freshmen whose total experience amounted to painting their parents' houses (for free) made good money by contracting to paint other houses in town for as much as $300 a job, plus materials. (They made the serious mistake, however, of not insuring themselves against accidents—damage to person or property. A small special policy could have avoided a big gamble.)

Athletic and Recreational Skills—

There is a ready and growing market for men and women who can teach, organize, or oversee younger men and women in any of dozens of sports. The YMCA and YWCA need swimming instructors and life-guards. The local church baseball league needs coaches and umpires. Summer camps need waterfront directors and instructors in tennis, archery, and riding—and many pay extravagantly to get them. The town recreation department can be counted on to hire playground supervisors and pool or beach lifeguards, as well as coaches in all types of sports for municipal playgrounds and recreation programs. City programs and neighborhood youth organizations can not only give you the opportunity to brush up your basketball, but a chance to see city life and city kids in a new way. Physical fitness programs may involve teen-agers or kinder-garten children. Local ski resorts will need extra instructors for their ski schools and winter sports, as soon as the snow flies (or is manufac-tured). Almost any real athletic ability can be put to work to earn money.

Giving personal or group lessons in snow or water skiing, skating, golf, tennis, sailing, squash, bowling, archery, skin-diving, or horseback riding pays well—around $8 an hour, which is what you would earn tutoring Serbo-Croation. Run an ad in the school or local paper, or work through a nearby country club, which may let you use its tennis courts (pool, golf course, or stables) in return for a percentage of private lesson fees. Aside from the occasional trembling eight-year-old whose daddy wants to see him turned into another Pancho Gonzales, the working conditions should be excellent. Not the least of your rewards should be a general boost in your physical health, and you can often schedule your own working hours. If you can learn how to teach your skills effectively, an ability that you originally learned for fun can be turned to profit.

Hobby Skills—

It is unlikely that your hobby would be of interest to you alone. If it is potentially interesting to other people, you can probably figure out a way to be of service to them.

You collect butterflies. The National Science Foundation might offer you a grant for a summer's work catching and classifying the local specie or for putting the college collection back into shape.

You've been a fisherman ever since you could hold a pole. Teach the art of fly-casting or fly-tying; sell your fine hand-tied flies and lures.

You know all there is to know about motorcycles (or stereo com-ponents, foreign cars, or electronic rock instruments and sound sys-tems). Work where they are sold or repaired. You can instantly correlate a buyer's skill and affluence to come up with the ideally suited skis for him (or hunting equipment, or camera). Sell these goods. You can tell after a few bars whether a recording of Brahms' First Piano Concerto is by Artur Rubenstein or Rudolf Serkin. Some record store will value your expertise.

If the role of knowledge salesman leaves you cold, consider some more direct applications of your hobby skill. A scholarship student who mentioned his lens-grinding hobby on a college application found himself a job at the university observatory. Amateur photographers have built small businesses on their talents, taking passport photographs (get permission to place posters in travel agencies and at the school office that administrates group and charter flights). You might do portraits of fellow students or faculty children, or take formal and casual wedding shots. Most school papers pay for the action shots of football games and other college events that are written up; try the alumni magazine, as well, and perhaps the town newspaper.

Sewing can be turned into money—try an alterations service. Cooking can be turned into cash, and even into free room and board. Outdoor hobbies such as hunting, canoeing, cross-country skiing, and mountain climbing can lead to jobs as trip leaders or guides for camps, clubs, private resorts, and national parks.

And remember that, if your hobby involves a skill, you can probably earn money teaching the basics of it to young children or beginning enthusiasts.

Artistic and Creative Skills—

Skills related to the creative and performing arts are the hardest to acquire. Great cellists are not only born but spend years realizing their gifts. Such skills can therefore be among the most highly paid. Before deciding, however, that you are going to sculpt or tap-dance your way through college, you should make a realistic appraisal of what you have to offer; its character and quality.

If you plan to base your income on the direct "sales" of your artistic prowess, make sure it is exceptionally salable. Mozart died penniless; Van Gogh was unrecognized during his lifetime. *Starving artist* is a cliché in the language. Even if your talent approaches genius, your income may not approach the poverty level—particularly while you are still young and developing your style and technique. Some forms of art are simply more marketable than others, and in the America of the 1970's, the money drains in particular directions.

Performing artists are in demand, and if you are a musician, singer, comedian, actor, or mime, you may have a good chance at a job. Folk, rock, jazz, and popular musicians who are college students have prospered by performing at coffee houses, clubs, private parties, and dances sponsored by schools, fraternities, and community groups. Their amateur status, reflected in lower-than-professional rates, actually *helps* them to gain employment. String quartets, brass ensembles, and recorder quintets can often find work beautifying weddings. There have been concert pianists, violinists, and other superb musicians who have managed to pursue their professional careers while attending liberal arts colleges.

If you are an originating, rather than an interpretive, artist, the market dwindles. Three dozen actors and technicians may be employed to realize *one* playwright's effort. A symphony orchestra engages the talents of over 100 performers in order to play the works of one or two composers. A ballet created by one man may call for fifty dancers. Remember that the greater your potential audience, the higher is your potential income. Graphics are popular and relatively inexpensive: you can probably count on your etchings to sell better than your 300 pound cast-bronze sculptures. Journalism and volumes on student employment are likely to be published quicker than sonnet sequences. A topical musical is a better bet for financial gain, than a verse play on the Peloponnesian Wars. This by no means advises that you should channel your talents into sound cash crops—but you should evaluate your projected profits objectively.

If your artistic product is salable, it must still be of high quality. Your seascapes may not hang in the Museum of Modern Art, but they may hang in the living rooms of nostalgic summer beachcombers if they are quality work. Should you not feel that your work is of a mastery appropriate to direct sales, you can still market your talent in many motifs onto greeting cards, stationery, wrapping paper, calendars, or fabrics. Illustrate a book. Design posters for the summer theater or art museum. Compose window displays or brochures for local businessmen. Scatter a few sand dollars at the feet of your models and become a commercial artist for an advertising firm, newspaper, or school publication. Stir up a Danish sea beneath the cliffs of Elsinore for a local theater's *Hamlet*.

The same principle applies to other artistic skills. If you can't find a Broadway backer, consider accepting a job directing a high school production. You may spend your mornings composing twelve-tone music, but pick up a little cash in the afternoons as an accompanist for Tuesday dancing classes or a first-grade ballerina or a sing-along at the day-care center. Some artists paint murals-to-order on the walls of their friends' apartments—did Michelangelo get paid for painting the Sistine chapel ceiling by the hour or by the foot?

If you can't unload your skill directly and stay solvent, try teaching for fun and profit. While you are preparing to become the heir to Casals (or Jimi Hendrix), your aspiring artistic heir may pay you for beginning cello (or guitar) lessons. Many an accomplished ballet student has tided herself over with earnings from a class of youngsters or a course in the principles of modern dance for limber suburban wives. You can charge satisfying rates for private tuition, and in any case you will be able to make your own work schedule.

Recently this country has rediscovered its heritage of handcrafts. Knitting, crochet, embroidery, and needlepoint have enjoyed a renaissance, and the high cost of clothing has sent many women back to machines and patterns. Macrame and tie-dye have emerged as popular crafts, and serious pursuits such as weaving, batik, pottery, leather work, woodworking, and silversmithing have reemerged as hobbies and livelihoods.

If your designs are original and your products outstanding, by all means try to sell them. Crafts cooperatives may provide you with an outlet; also try museum shops, holiday bazaars, and local stores—or open your own studio sales desk. Student businesses have been built around the sale of fine crafts supplies and how-to books as well as finished objects. Some newcomers to hard work are willing to pay for professional designs, rather than struggle with their own. Students have made money marketing prestamped embroidery patterns and prepainted needlework designs. Include the proper wools and you are in the "kit" business. Could you adapt this service to your own craft?

Lessons, of course, are a profitable way of sharing your skill with others—beginners or advanced craftsmen.

Finally, you may possess a traditional skill or handcraft. Can you do blacksmithing or tinsmithing or make cane chairs, quilts, or dolls from cornstalks or dried apples? This type of skill is in demand by museums and restorations and by many private citizens interested in old houses and furniture. Whether you do the work or teach the skill, you can take a step to keep your art from vanishing.

Think about the new slants that your creative skill might take to help support you. If the women's club already has a crewel teacher, organize a sampler class for their daughters. Or introduce businessmen to the soothing art of needlepoint (many men practice it). Design stuffed-animal families, Victorian doll houses, or clothes for dolls and toddlers. Sell bikinis with separate-sized tops and bottoms so that a lady who is extra-small and medium (top and bottom or vice versa) can get an exact fit and not two unusable components. Plait hearth-brooms from straw. Create Christmas wreathes, dried-flower arrangements, pressed-flower pictures, or live-flower pots. Specialize in lovely Christmas-tree ornaments, wall hangings, or stained-glass plaques. Construct custom doorknockers, mailboxes, or birdbaths. Frame pictures. Design glazed tiles or ribbon lampshades. Hook rugs, shape mugs, or cast wedding rings. Hand-letter wedding announcements, hand-illustrate baby announcements, or hand-paint china dolls. But—it's *your* creative skill; use *your* imagination.

Sales Skills—

Enterprising students have sold newspaper and magazine subscriptions to their neighbors and fellow students for generations. Today, because of the high rates of pay to good salesmen ($3–$5 an hour or more, by commission), student salesmen are branching out into a multitude of other areas, from class rings, magazines, stationery, T-shirts, and beer mugs to European-delivered automobiles, mutual funds, cameras, and books. The best salesmen possess sales skills, and some are able to make enough money in the first few weeks of school to take the financial pressure off them for the rest of the year.

Often the organization that employs the salesman will teach him how to sell. Valuable sales training is offered by the Encyclopedia Britannica, the Fuller Brush Company, Alcoa's Kutco Division (aluminum kitchenware), the Electrolux vacuum cleaner company, and other firms who depend upon door-to-door solicitation for the major part of their business. Watch the want ads or check the telephone book (if you are in a city) and call the personnel manager of the company that interests you.

The key to successful selling, though, is not sales education but sales experience. The near-legendary Thomas Watson of I.B.M. told young men, "Don't spend too much time studying the science of salesmanship. Spend more time practicing the art of selling."

You may have worked in a resort gift shop, a hometown jewelry store, a pre-Christmas toy department, or your father's pharmacy. You have already discovered, then, how important a congenial and persuasive manner are to sales figures. Door-to-door or direct sales will require initiative, diligence, and perseverance on your part, but you will not necessarily have to resort to fast talk or strong-arm tactics. Making sales *without* these dubious resources is what the sales skill is about. If you possess it, or can master it, your financial worries are over.

Combination Skills—

Sometimes two skills are more than twice as valuable as one. A student who is both skillful in dealing with young people and well-versed in the history and language of Germany spent pleasant summer vacations leading bicycle tours through the Rhineland. A math major with a strong minor in pocket billiards invented a one-hole elliptical pool table and sold it to a manufacturer—the royalties paid his way through college.

Can you cook and sail? "Private yacht needs galley crew for Tahitian voyage." Can you do carpentry and juggle stereo components? One young man does a slow, steady, and lucrative business in hand-crafted, custom-assembled music systems.

Sometimes an exotic skill redeems a lowly one. Cataloguing books doesn't take long to master, but if your language skills allow you to deal with books in Urdu, Hindi, or Russian, you'll have sure employment plus a much higher wage.

Pooling your skills with others can make for increased marketability. One student group formed a house-repair cooperative that included people experienced in cleaning, upholstering, carpentry, painting, and plumbing. The group would rent itself out to completely overhaul a house. Not only was the enterprise a financial success but the people within the cooperative gained new skills by helping their fellow workers.

Skill in Finding a Job—"Connections"—

An old maxim floats around the frustrated lower echelons of business and industry: "It's not *what* you know, it's *who* you know" that determines what job you are able to get. Idealism and grammar aside, this is often true. A federal youth-employment director recently explained that the President's campaign for industrial employers to hire disadvantaged teen-agers had run seriously afoul of nepotism and "back-scratching" among employers (you hire my nephew and I'll hire your's). The surest way to get a job is to know someone who can get it for you. Your "connection" might be your father, a neighbor, a relative, a teacher, a municipal official, or anyone else who would like to help you find a job. One sophomore got a lucrative carpenter's job because his mother's church friend's cousin's friend was a union official in one town who knew another union official in a second town. The chain was long and tenuous, but it serves to illustrate that point that whereas it *does* matter *whom* you know, it does not necessarily matter much how well you know them.

Last summer a student got a construction job through a friend of his father. The base wage of $4.50 per hour was supplemented by plenty of overtime (at time and a half) and added up to well over $2,000 in only three months. Another, whose father works for a steel company, was able to find work relining blast furnaces and made $1,500. Such stories are commonplace, and would be even more so if each student extracted the highest mileage from his personal acquaintances. This is actually a skill. Remember, a man will generally welcome the chance to demonstrate his authority by exercising it on your behalf; if you can get him to catch the ball, he'll run with it.

On the other hand, you probably did not buy this book to read about working for your father. You have to make up your own mind as to the degree to which you are willing to ask for favors and get your jobs on "pull." You may decide to go to people who know you only for your good work and ability and to avoid relatives and friends of the family. Don't be shy, however, about extending your clientele through talking with your satisfied customers, or asking your professors for work, recommendations, or leads. Human beings are interdependent, and "connections" are not only unscrupulous bonds between back-scratchers but they also represent the links in the social fabric. You did not hesitate to ask for references when you applied to college; follow through on job prospects, as well, by means of associates and former employers. A word of positive feedback from your last boss may land you a new position, and you earned it, just as surely as you earned your wages. In looking for employment, remember that many jobs are never even advertised. World-of-mouth, particularly in a small community (such as your campus) usually does the trick. This method of hiring *counts* on you, the talented prospect, to keep your ears open, so let your friends, tutors, and department secretary know that you are seeking work. Someone else may have just explained to them that he is seeking a worker.

A touch of aggressiveness is not misplaced in your job search. Initiative and self-confidence reinforce your skills on the job and at personnel interviews, but they are skills in themselves when it comes to ferreting out employment opportunities. Urge yourself to make the most of these qualities. "Pushyness" may be obnoxious, but zeal and assertiveness are good for your personal economy—and the country's, too.

Skills in Demand

The two charts on the following pages were compiled on the basis of information from the personnel departments of many of the largest corporations in the nation. The first shows which skills are in demand in various industries; the second does the same for major fields of study. These figures support the conclusion that we live in an economic era of the skilled. Increasingly, distinctions of age, sex, and race, and even the time-honored advantage of personal connections are wavering before the cold utilitarian question: "Can you do the job?" The student who can answer "yes," the student who possesses marketable skills, will find more and better jobs opening to him with every step in the technological advance of our society. The unskilled man and woman will be relegated to the poorer jobs. Give your own skills thought and attention. Identify them, develop them, utilize them. Be adaptable: skilled scribes were out of luck when printing was invented. Invest in yourself, and your profit will be not merely money but interesting work and self-fulfillment.

Chart I

	Advertising	Banks	Chemical	Electronics	Food Products	Heavy Industry	Insurance	Light Industry	Printing	Railroads	Retail	Telephone
Technical Skills												
Accounting	√	√	√	√	√	√	√			√	√	
Chem. Engineering		√		√								
Computer Prog.	√	√	√	√	√	√	√	√		√	√	√
Drafting				√		√		√				
Engineering			√	√		√		√				
Journalism									√	√		
Law		√					√	√				
Statistics		√				√						
Systems Analysis						√	√					
Typography									√			
Other		1		2	3	4				5	6	7
Clerical and Mechanical Skills												
Business Machines		√					√	√		√		
Keypunch		√	√		√	√						
Steno		√	√		√	√				√		√
Typing	√	√	√		√	√	√			√		√
Other			8				9	10			11	12

1—Research knowledge, stocks and credit analysis
2—Dairy technician; food technician
3—Metallurgy
4—Finance actuaries
5—Transportation planning
6—Textiles
7—Practical electronics
8—Works with animals
9—Televoice operator
10—Manual dexterity
11—Comptometry
12—Teletype

Chart II

	Banks	Chemical	Consumer Goods	Electrical	Electronics	Food Products	Heavy Industry	Insurance	Light Industry	Printing & Publishing	Railroads	Retail Sales	Telephone Utilities
Anthropology													
Applied Math	Y	Y	I	I	Y	Y	Y	I	Y	Y	I	I	Y
Biology		I				I							I
Chemistry		Y	I	I	I	Y	Y		Y	I			I
Economics	Y	I	I	I	I	I		I	I	I	I		I
Engineering		Y	Y	Y	Y	Y	Y		Y	I	Y		Y
English	I	I		I	I		I	I	I	I		I	I
Government		I			I					I			
History	I									I			
Languages		I					1			I	I		
Physics		I		I	Y	I	Y		I	I			Y
Psychology	I	I	I		I	I		I		I			I
Pure Math	I	I		I	Y	I	Y	Y	I	Y		I	I

"I" indicates that the industry feels an applicant is strengthened by knowledge of this field.

"Y" indicates that industry is willing to offer the candidate a job on the basis of knowledge of this field alone.

Chapter Three

TERM-TIME EMPLOYMENT

The 1960's saw man reach the moon, and the 1970's have made it plain that the cost of your college education is not far behind. Soaring educational expenses have outstripped most family incomes and available scholarship aid. If you are not to slave while you study—if you are to study at all—you will probably have to take on a part of the burden of the skyscraping debts associated with your student status. You might seek out a benefactor: Daddy Warbucks, Sugar Daddy, John Beresford Tipton, or one of those patronizing captains of industry who always showed up in the nick of time for Horatio Alger's enterprising young heroes. You might win the Irish Sweepstakes, break into organized crime, or inherit a vein of uranium from Great-Uncle Scrooge. If these happy alternatives fail, the answer is *work*.

Student employment is being forced to assume an increasingly important role in helping to fill this financial gap for undergraduates and their parents. Never before have so many students earned so much—at so many different jobs, in every area of the country. This trend will continue, as necessity compels students to enter the labor pool and employers draw on the reservoir of student manpower and skills. With the growth of student employment has come its increased complexity. The student who is determined to get the best job for which he can qualify should view this complex situation with confidence. Upon examination, this complexity really represents diversity, and above all, opportunity. There is a good job for *you,* and your responsibility is to seek it out.

What can you anticipate in your search? Jobs are almost as various as the students who hold them, but here are the experiences of five undergraduates who tried their luck:

A prepossessing senior from Chicago, Frank earned $750 selling class rings during Freshman Orientation Week. He was a salesman for the type of student business organization described in Chapter Five, and after seven days of furious congeniality, he rested for the remainder of the fall term, free from work commitments. If you're motivated and a nice guy (or can impersonate one for a week), you're qualified for this style of employment. Tear yourself away from the beach: early arrival on campus is money in your pocket. Expect at least $100 for your week or two of lost sun and part-time selling at the beginning of the school year—but shoot for $750.

Sarah, an Oklahoma freshman earned $42 in a single afternoon, making telephone calls on a piece-rate basis as part of a research company's survey. You could be purple-and-green skinned, nursing a sprained ankle, disliked by practically everyone, unable to type or translate or program computers and *still* be highly successful at a job like this.

Greg, from Cincinnati, took home his basic wage of $8.00 plus a tip of $18.25, at the end of one evening bartending at a professor's party. The rudiments of this skill are quickly learned, and in most states you need not be twenty-one to serve liquor at private functions. You could have the worst grades in your dormitory and still pick up plenty of cash, working at college receptions or parties around town.

The earliest bird, Jason, earns $3 an hour delivering college and local newspapers to student rooms every day. It's an unspeakable hour, but Jason doesn't mind watching the dawn come up, as long as he's paid. There's no interference with dates or studies, and no experience required—no fluency in Japanese, no natural salesmanship, and no thought. Sleepwalk your way to $35 a week.

Dinah sings with a blues band. She and the three other students command $100 to $200 for an evening's performance (less the 15 per cent commission of the enterprising student who had set up an entertainment agency and finds them their jobs). Dinah is a sophomore, and she hopes that when her band has played together for another year or so, they will begin to get billing with groups who come to town on concert tours—fame *and* fortune.

Five examples; five different schedules, interests, and personal styles. The variety of these jobs reflects the current unprecedented student employment possibilities, and the level of income that students may anticipate. Inexperience, convenience, fascinating work, or hard economic times may dictate your wage at $2 an hour, but between your summer vacation job and your term-time work, you should be able to earn what you need. With luck and perseverance, you may also be able to gain more from your work experience than those vital wages alone.

Why Take A Term-Time Job?

September to June represents your school year and three-quarters of your employment year. Those students who are certain that summer vacation will provide them with time for all the work and wages they require can move on to the next chapter. Most college students will want to use at least part of that nine months for earning money and to exploit the job possibilities of their campus and college community. Before plunging into term-time employment, however, or even the discussion of the subject that follows, you should deal with a fundamental question: "What profiteth a man if he gaineth a plump wallet, but loseth his rank in class?" Your aim is to work your way *through* college, not out of it. Everyone has an uncle whose legendary roommate put in forty hours a week at the Post Office and sailed on to law school with his *cum laude* degree. Although this was possible and sometimes necessary during the Depression, it was never a standard effort and is now extremely rare. Few undergraduates, with the exception of dedicated entrepreneurs, hold "full-time" job commitments, and there is no reason why you have to risk flunking out over a forty-hour work schedule, even if you depend upon your earnings to finance your education. You are a *student,* first of all, and "making it" through college is more important right now than "making it" into a lofty tax bracket. Whether you are supplementing your scholarship or simply avoiding the necessity of economizing on records and beer, what you probably need is a part-time job that will leave you enough time to go to class, do some studying, enjoy your social life, and, on occasion, get some sleep.

Do you have time to work? Most educators agree that you do and insist that working will not affect grades if the student plans his time intelligently. The undergraduate who spends sixty hours a week building his catering company is likely to sacrifice something—his health, his A average, his girlfriend, or his ski weekends. But taking on a part-time job often compels a student to organize his time and studies more efficiently, and the intelligent utilization of time is the key to success in college, whether in an hour examination or a year-long course. Even when your job does mean the difference between an A and A−, there are compensating factors. Working closely with your biochemistry professor on a complex synthesis may dim your grades by a few points, but that same professor's enthusiastic recommendation could make all the difference to the medical schools.

But *do* you have time to work? Think of a typical day. A shower, breakfast, several hours of class, lunch. You may want to put in another block of time at the library or the language or science lab, and perhaps you have soccer practice, a play rehearsal, or another chapter of your novel to finish. Still, isn't much of your afternoon and evening free? And there's a whole weekend coming up! Few students can't spare two to fifteen hours a week for part-time work, if they want to. It's all a matter of priorities.

Why should you juggle your priorities to make room for work? For money, of course, but a part-time job can bring the student at least three advantages above and beyond the cash reward. Students who don't absolutely need the money often work, and in fact *all* students, regardless of their financial status, are well-advised to do so.

A term-time job can be an educational experience, allowing the student to learn a new skill or to perfect an existing one, to extend his knowledge of his own field or to come in contact with another. A sociology major may learn some relevant statistics while working on an experimental survey; a student tennis instructor may find that his serve improves as his students improve their game. A young man studying fine arts may find his career focus as a result of his part-time job in a graphics gallery; an undecided freshman might eventually choose to major in philosophy because of her introductory fascination with the research manuscript that she happened to work on as a part-time typist for the philosophy department.

Your job may offer you practical experience in the "real world" that is useful or at least refreshing. A premed student running errands in a community health clinic may be reinforced in his career choice by his satisfaction with the hospital environment, and his medical motivation will not be lost on the deans of admissions. Or he may be dismayed and disillusioned by the realities of "his" profession, and switch to pure science. In either case, his job has taught him something that college never could. Another student may change his political and social views because of a few months of night-shift factory labor and his resultant insight; another may find the friendship of the mechanics at the filling station where he pumps gas Tuesday evenings to be more satisfying than that of his cerebral roommates. Still another student, who never liked school much, may find his college days more tolerable when he begins part-time janitorial work and thinks about that alternative. First-year French may be a "drag," but it looks fine compared to a forty-five year vista of swabbing cellar floors.

A job that has little or nothing to do with schoolwork can be valuable as a sanity-saver; an escape valve that permits the harried undergraduate, heavy-laden with the abstruse and intangible problems of physics, metaphysics, or his own identity to forget it all for a while and concentrate on the more concrete challenge of getting supper served, a skillet scrubbed, or a plate-glass window shining. Applying yourself to the measurement of helpings of mashed potato, or the hefting of dozens of bulging laundry bags can be a great change of pace. Drop that pen; lift that bale.

Two final assets of part-time work should be mentioned, although they really apply to all student employment. The first is the sense of independence—from home, loan committee, scholarship board—which even minor earnings will bring you. If you've earned the money, there is every excuse for guiltless expenditure on a Harley Davidson, a pair of Head skis, a four-channel stereo system, or a trip to Florence. Secondly, you can't begin an employment record too soon or too minor. No matter how rich you are, you may want a job after graduation—one that interests you. The fact that you were lucky enough to be jobless and solvent in college will *not* now be in your favor. Even if your jobs have been pedestrian, a previous work record is an advantage in gaining employment. It impresses your potential boss with your industry, perseverance, and stability, and perhaps with your skills and experience, if they are relevant to the position he seeks to fill. Your own confidence will be greater if you meet him with some sort of résumé rather than a blank sheet of unseized opportunities. If there is a field that you know you hope to work in, start now—even as a volunteer. Your success in gaining future opportunities for work or graduate training in the field automatically increase.

If a term-time job can be educational and even relaxing, it can also be low-paying, soul-destroying drudgery, from which even studying can be a relief. Each person's temperament is different, and one man's drudgery is the next man's dream job. You may love long hours under the high-intensity lamp, gluing together shards of Attic pottery while your roommate would hurl down the tweezers in despair; he earns *his* pocket money moving furniture to ease out the kinks of those sedentary afternoons in the stacks. Down the hall lives a classmate who praises his computer job, because it "keeps me thinking," and across the hall is a part-time plate-scraper delighted with that chore because "you don't have to *think!*" In looking for a livelihood, consider your temperament and try to find a job that brings you something in addition to money—be it larger biceps, healthy fatigue, conversational French, or peace of mind.

Flexibility—

If you can find ten or twenty hours a week for a job, will you have them every week and at the same time each day? Probably not. There-fore, an important consideration in seeking a job is flexibility. Each student's own special situation may require a particular solution. If your academic load is very heavy, it will naturally be to your advantage to pick up spot employment during the weeks of the year when pressure is minimal (selling door-to-door during registration week; bartending over Christmas vacation; typing for others after your own term papers are finished). Or you may be able to find a position where you can study on the job (sitting behind a circulation desk at the library in the early morning when traffic is light, working as a night watchman, or handing out towels to classmates when they come into the gym). If labs take up your afternoons, then seek a job as an airline ticket agent or taxi-driver evenings and weekends. Or find work that can be done at home at your convenience—manuscript typing, translating, or proofreading. Tem-perament rules here, too. If you *must* sleep until 9 A.M. to insure your mental health, turn down the $3 an hour morning newspaper delivery job and keep looking.

Your odd schedule may be a disadvantage to you in going after many jobs. On the other hand, it can be very useful. Many employers cannot find help to work only an hour or two at lunch time or when the work load is heaviest. They either hire an extra employee full-time and try to find things for him to do most of the day or they operate under-staffed and irritate customers during the rush hours. Or *you* come along. Restaurants are especially prone to busy periods lasting an hour or two. A printing shop or boutique that needs overtime help in the evenings or on Saturdays will have to pay heavily for it—unless a student can be found to help out. The university mail office may need someone for just an hour a day, when you have a hole in your class schedule. The post office or local department store could certainly use your help around Christmas.

Your Earning Power—

How much money can a student reasonably expect to earn during the term? Senator Charles Percy earned $10,000 in his senior year at the University of Chicago. If you are seeking money like that, you are either reading the wrong chapter (start your own business, and good luck!) or you have extremely valuable skills, such as the abilíty to forge flawless Picassos or to spin straw into gold.

The typical (industrious) student spends from 300 to 600 hours working during the school year, earning at least $450 (300 hours at $1.50) and as much as $1,200 (600 hours at $2.00) or more. Once you determine the amount of time you want to spend working, estimate your level of skills, and correlate your anticipated hours with the going rate for that level. In this way you have predicted your year's earnings. Although you should not, with luck, have to choose your job on the basis of pay rate alone, don't underestimate the importance of that extra $.25 or $.50 an hour. Three hundred hours shelving books at $2.00 an hour would bring you $600 less than programming a computer at $4.00 an hour. But handling linen ($2.50 an hour) could have brought you $150 more than your library job, for the same number of hours—a significant gain.

Organizing Your Search—

The best place to begin looking for a job is your student employment office or its equivalent. Of the fifty colleges surveyed, only four reported that they had no such office. The kind of help your campus employment office provides will depend upon how it is organized. At some schools, it is simply a clearinghouse, where local employers post, list, or phone in descriptions of jobs for which they hope to hire students. Paid or volunteer personnel organize this information by job category, required skill, or duration of employment and make it available to you by means of bulletin boards, card files, or notebooks. Some schools provide such additional services as local daily papers, which have useful "Help Wanted" columns, and toll-free telephones so that you can contact potential employers immediately.

A number of colleges ally the student employment office with the office of financial aid, in a cooperative effort to solve the problems of financially needy students. These offices usually work hard, not merely accepting and distributing job offers but actively soliciting the community for employment for the undergraduates it serves. Often telephone or mail campaigns are mounted as each semester and the summer vacation approach, urging a wide range of potential employers, both on and off campus, to consider hiring students. This type of job search will undoubtedly benefit you, but if you are not on scholarship, you may find that student employment offices that are tied to financial-aid administration usually insist on placing the neediest students first.

The convenience of the student employment office is not its only advantage. Even if your office does not solicit student jobs, you will know that those employers who *have* called in definitely want to hire students; you won't waste time chasing dead-end newspaper leads. Furthermore, the office probably exists to serve only students from your school, and may actually demand identification before you raid its files. This protects you by eliminating some of your competition. Many jobs will be only available through the office—your college probably hires its library attendants and student porters in this way. The sociology professor who needs a research assistant, the faculty couple who want a live-in babysitter, the men's store that has had good luck with student salesmen in its University Shop will all think first of the student employment office. Likewise, you should make the student employment office your first stop, if you want to make your typing, translating, or piano-moving services available to the campus community, since most offices will offer your number to those employers who come in seeking someone with your particular skill.

If a visit to the student employment office turned up the job for you, stop reading and report to work. In the event that all you found were bare bulletin boards and files ravaged by 8,000 previous student visits, you're still unemployed. What next?

Walk over to your college's student business organization, if there is one; 30 per cent of the schools surveyed had some type of student business set up. These organizations are sometimes substantial corporations, employing hundreds of students in diverse agencies and enjoying a monopoly on the campus market, which they supply with everything from refrigerators to European charter flights. Small schools may support more modest operations, performing a limited function such as the sale of class rings and college stationery. These may employ only a handful of students. If your school has no type of student business agency, and if you are ambitious, your unemployed days are over: *start one.* (But first turn to Chapter Five, Student-Run Small Businesses, and pick up a few hints. These will serve you well even if some other campus entrepreneur beat you to the student agency idea: get him to hire you by passing on astute suggestions on how to expand or improve his business).

The student employment office and the student business agencies will present you with the bulk of the employment opportunities for undergraduates on your campus. To give you a sense of the wide range of jobs available through these channels, we will briefly discuss a case study of student employment on one campus: Princeton University in Princeton, New Jersey.

Princeton is an expensive private university, with an enrollment of over 4,000 and a yearly tuition/room-and-board charge of close to $4,000. Although about 40 per cent of the undergraduates receive loans or scholarship aid, more than 60 per cent engage in part-time work, and their combined total earnings run over half a million dollars every year.

The student employment office helps distribute the 700 jobs that students hold in campus dining halls, staff cafeterias, catering divisions, and other aspects of the University Food Service. One hundred and fifty upperclassmen in high academic standing hold jobs in the university's academic and administrative departments. Others play for rock bands or hold jobs in town. The student employment office provides leads in many of these cases.

Princeton has one of the oldest student business organizations in the country. Student agencies operated these organizations before World War I, and in the 1930's, business was brisk in peanuts, popcorn, and the restringing of tennis and squash rackets. By the late 1950's, a student Tailor Shop was bringing in $60,000 a year, taking advantage of the old rule that required the wearing of coats and ties during class. That profit-maker died with the coat rule, but the relaxation of the university prohibition on undergraduate cars brought a successful car-rental agency into being.

Princeton's student businesses fall into four categories. The service agencies provide baby-sitting, data-processing, rooms for weekend dates, thesis binding, furniture resale and moving, and laundering; the Student Laundry Service alone employs many scholarship freshmen. Five food agencies deal in birthday cakes, hamburgers, and late-night pizzas. Two publications have their own business organizations: a student telephone directory, and a photo book of the freshman class. Finally, there is the large group of sales agencies which sell such stand-bys as class rings, souvenirs, wall banners, and Princeton nighties, as well as skis, magazines, Christmas wreaths, and sweatshirts adorned with topical cult-figure photographs.

Could you make a circle out of spruce twigs, sell skis, rent a car, or load the dining hall dishwasher? Then the opportunities on this small-town campus would provide you with a job. If you're attending an urban college, you are even better off, and if your mountain-top college hasn't yet spawned a thriving student business organization, you have a fine opportunity to create your own corporate giant.

What can be done if you've exploited these sources and still haven't found a job, or a job you like? The last chapter of this book contains some more suggestions for your continuing job search. Take heart: any college student can land *some* job, and many, especially as upperclassmen, will find good term-time employment that they enjoy. When we conducted our survey of colleges, the American economy was shaky and the local ice-cream parlor was full of folks cooling off with their frothy "Wage-Price Freeze." Unemployment was high, yet numerous respondents noted that there *were* jobs available, if students would take them. The late 1960's were prosperous and gave some undergraduates employment ambitions that became unrealistic in a depressed economy. Research grants were cut off, with the result that research assistantships were eliminated. Payrolls were reduced, and many part-time jobs disappeared. The economy is now showing signs of improvement, but even in the worst months of the recession, students who were willing to lower their expectations were able to gain the wages they needed, if not pure job satisfaction.

One way of subdividing the great assortment of term-time job possibilities, and one that is employed by some student employment offices, is on the basis of skills involved and time investment required. Certainly the distinction between "skilled" and "unskilled" blurs, especially when "experience" rather than a particular "skill" is demanded. The difference between "casual" employment and "term-length" jobs is likewise flexible: you could turn a "casual" bartending business, where you took on parties whenever you needed cash, into a steady "term-length" operation simply by lining up a job for *every* Friday night. We maintain these expressions of time and skill for organizational purposes, to give order to our following discussion, but we have not gone to great lengths to sharpen the distinctions, and you certainly should not consider any of our categories absolute.

Casual/Unskilled

Casual refers to jobs that are not pursued continuously over a period of several months, approximately a semester. It may be an evening's work, a three-day project, or a spurt of employment over Christmas or spring vacation. A succession of these jobs may fit into your fluctuating schedule better than an all-Saturday, every-Saturday commitment, but remember that, financially, casual/unskilled jobs are the least exciting. They can bring you a few extra dollars, which will add up, but you can't rely on a steady income from this type of work. Nonetheless, the casual job is available throughout the year, and worth your investigation. The student employment office is your best source of casual job opportunities, as well as the classified section of your college paper.

The most obvious category of these jobs is manual labor. Leaves must be raked in the fall, snow shoveled or blown in the winter, and gardens spaded up and windows washed in the spring. You can expect to make $2.50 to $2.75 an hour for yard and chore work, and sometimes a tip, if your employer is impressed with your courtesy and efficiency. Your college community is undoubtedly filled with attics that need emptying and garages and basements that are desperate for a clean sweep. Behind many a shaggy hedge, overdue for a trim, rises a neat Colonial house, overdue for a paint job, not to mention the gutters, overflowing with last year's leaves. If you are willing to pitch in on indoor and outdoor cleaning jobs, you can "clean up." This sort of work often leads to further employment; if you satisfy a man with your lawn-mowing prowess, he may hire you to wash his car and recommend you to his next-door neighbor who needs a brush-lot thinned. These jobs are usually flexible; whether the lettuce is weeded this morning or tomorrow afternoon will not matter to most of your customers.

Institutions also have their cleaning problems. Your college probably hires some students to do janitorial work on a full-term basis. By remaining at school for a week after finals, you could pick up $3 an hour for eight hours (plus overtime) of hard work during the June clean-up in the dormitories. Most of the students who do this work have been student porters during the year and ask their dorm crew captains a month or so in advance about June work. You could start the summer with $150. Another end-of-term road to fast money is a job as a bellhop for your college's twenty-fifth reunion class. These men are at the height of their careers, and reunion is a jovial time and tips are high. A student who had worked for June clean-up the year before got a bellhop position only a day before the reunion. Although it is theoretically a week-long proposition, the work is concentrated in the arrival and departure days. When he had finished his work, the student was $75 richer in tips alone, plus his $2.75 an hour wages.

Temporary maid services will hire students; you'll start at $2 an hour and choose your own schedule, doing cleaning and perhaps serving food. Babysitting is a time-honored casual job, and if you are over twenty-one and can produce a physician's certificate verifying your good health (including a recent TB test), you can turn over all the arrangements to a babysitting agency. They will "train" you and pay you the minimum wage—again, you may get tips.

Another training course is your "open sesame" to the $25 an hour world of fashion modeling. The Barbizon Model Agency will hire *only* graduates of its own course, for which they charge $429. But if you have the cash, and look terrific in tights, you could recoup your investment and begin pure profits in your *eighteenth* hour of work.

If you lack a willowy figure (or $429), consider modeling for an artist or studio class. Walk dogs. Hawk underground papers on the street—300 per cent profit on every sale, and good people to meet, to compensate for the chill. Become a telephone interviewer; it's monotonous, but it pays you $2.50 to $3.00 an hour, and you don't even have to get out of bed. A student mover who loaded cabinet TV sets onto trucks reported an hourly wage of $3. He labeled the job *drudgery* and found himself too tired to study that night. His advice to his successors was, "Work slowly."

Within the campus gates there should be plenty of short-term, unskilled labor needed. If you live in a fraternity house or a cooperative, mention that you're seeking odd jobs. Work that might have gone to outside help—kitchen or yard work, painting the house—may come to you. Check out the student business agency again. Do they need short-term advertising or door-to-door salesmen, someone to put up posters, set up files, straighten out records; collaters, mimeographers, envelope stuffers, helpers with postage and address machines, or delivery men? If your job is "casual" but your attitude persistent, you may soon be hiring your own help as manager of the business—the turnover of personnel in college enterprises is understandably rapid. Proofreading is frustrating, and necessary; your college newspaper or magazine may pay for diligence at this chore. Many of the tasks facing student businesses are also problems for publications, and most will gladly pay you a commission on advertisement sales. College newspapers and alumni bulletins pay for sports or news photos that they print. Any of these jobs could win you a chance at reporting, as well as your pocket money.

Your own college is undoubtedly a source of casual unskilled jobs, since it is probably one of the largest employers, on all levels, in the community. Dartmouth is the second largest employer in the entire *state* of New Hampshire, outdone only by the state itself. In addition to the possibilities mentioned, there are numerous instances where the ubiquitous computer has not quite sewed up the problem of dealing with the vast composite of individuals known as the student body. People must shepherd registrants into the proper lines ("A–D, left and down; E–H, to your right and past the . . ."), and distribute ballpoint pens to the ill-prepared few. Course sectioning can require similar guidance, and exams demand proctors. Attendance lists may also need to be checked off at your school. All of these jobs pay about $2 an hour.

The most intriguing form of casual, unskilled labor available on campuses is the well-paid role of guinea pig, in psychological testing and sociology experiments. Want ads, bulletin boards in the Social Science building, or the student employment office may alert you to these jobs, but a friendly relationship with the secretary in the psychology department is your surest source of this type of work. The minimum for these experiments is $2 an hour; you often can get as much as $5 an hour, with opportunities in some game-theory tests to "win" (= earn) more, by playing well. But the real pay-off is usually the explanation of the experiment, after it is over.

You may race against time to sort many little wooden blocks by size, shape, and color—only to find out that the object of the study was your blink rate, or the effect that the test administrator had on your performance, by his prearranged comments that were either impatient or encouraging. The findings on such tests relate to the successes and failures of schoolchildren. One student sat down with four others to watch black bars projected on a slide screen. Each student in turn was to report his judgment as to which bar was the shortest. In the first instance, the fourth bar was definitely shorter, and all five students said so. In the next pictures, the short bar was equally obvious, and all the students agreed. Gradually the difference became subtler. On the next slide, four students declared the fifth bar to be the shortest one. Our student, the last person in the row, had been virtually convinced that the third bar was shortest, but he was embarrassed to say so, and went along with the others. The experiment had nothing to do with perception. The first four students had been coached in advance to choose the (wrong) fifth bar when the sixth picture appeared. What influence would this false consensus have on the lone dissenter? Be paid to learn lessons in sociology. Occasionally an experiment will involve harmless electrodes and other strange measures, but by and large, it is an interesting easy way to earn money.

Interesting to the tune of $2.44 an hour is a job with the Post Office during Christmas vacation. Some towns add extra deliveries during this period; in any case, there will be special deliveries, a deluge of packages, and innumerable holiday cards to be sorted and processed. Around December 1, local postmasters begin to call for help, and you should be on their list. This requires that you take a qualifying test administered by the Civil Service Commission every six weeks. Obtain an application form for the test at any Post Office, and plan ahead. If you expect to be home for Christmas, make sure to take the test early and to apply to your hometown Post Office. Western Union will need extra messengers at this time, and Railway Express and other parcel transport agencies may hire extra delivery men.

Holidays and vacations are an excellent time to pick up extra cash. Although such work seems to sidestep the issue of term-time employment, those students who don't want long-term employment will probably find vacations the most convenient time to earn needed funds. You could secure several hundred dollars in these weeks alone, if you worked hard at wisely chosen jobs.

The lucrative possibilities of the weeks just before and after the academic year have been mentioned. A sophomore worked as a waiter over one four-day Thanksgiving vacation, serving food at private parties. Posters in the dormitory tipped him off to the fact that a campus agency was arranging such employment. He applied about ten days in advance and made $3.05 an hour plus $5.00 a day in tips for part-time work. Thanksgiving is the time to talk to department- and specialty-store managers about Christmas sales work, either in your home or college town. Wages tend to be minimal ($1.65), but merchants invariably grant 10 to 20 per cent discounts on merchandise to their employees. This could be your big chance to buy a fur hat, a pair of snowshoes, or a floor lamp—or to do your Christmas shopping. The work is harried at this time of year, and the personnel interviewer will be looking for a cheerful manner and a sense of calm on your part.

One sophomore specializes in dishwashing for holiday parties. He makes $3 an hour, plus $5 a job in tips and plenty of good holiday food. The job is less work than you might expect—families who can afford your services usually have a dishwasher, which you simply load and empty. Make your specialty known at the student employment office and be courteous and prompt in calling potential employers. This work is available all year, but the demand is highest at Christmas. You might also weave wreathes or impersonate Santa at children's parties. Remember that Thanksgiving, Christmas, and Easter are the peak seasons at the florists, and if you don't get to deck the halls with boughs of holly, you may be able to deliver poinsettias.

Rural colleges are sometimes located in areas of agricultural production, where a different type of seasonal employment reigns. New England students, for example, may help to pick the fall crop of MacIntosh apples. Inquire at local farms and granges, or check the rural papers, but don't expect more than the minimum wage for your farm sojourn.

City-dwellers, on the other hand, should register with the nearest branch of the state unemployment office, who will call you when they get requests for short-term unskilled labor.

Our final suggestion is the most "unskilled" of offerings and really cannot be called a job at all. It is the sale of blood. Although we strongly urge that your blood be a *gift* to those who need it and that you donate through your campus blood drive, it is a fact that hospital blood banks pay $20 to $25 a pint, and someday you may be desperate enough for that sum to cash in on your lifeblood. Call a local hospital, which will give you an appointment and take a sample of your blood to test. If you do sell them a pint, remember that you can only sell two pints a year—this is not the route to your first, effortless million.

Causal/Skilled

If you have a skill that you can put to work or are willing to acquire one, you can probably land a more lucrative job than those in the casual/unskilled category, even if you don't want to commit yourself to working for the whole semester. There are, clearly, many levels of skill, and wages vary accordingly. Waiting on table is not difficult to learn and pays fairly well; translating a physics monograph from Russian into German pays better, but it takes longer to master. Both efforts fall into the casual/skilled class.

Typing is the most useful simple skill to have because it is always in demand. You might type news articles for the school paper, envelopes and invoices for a local business once a month, or term papers for your classmates at panic-time. The standard rate is $2 an hour, but if you have an electric machine, work neatly and accurately, and type faster than a speeding bullet, you may charge by the page ($.40 to $.75) and make more that way. Foreign-language typists are well-paid for their combination skill. Many jobs that are not *primarily* typing may require it nonetheless: a packaging job may involve typing labels, or the results of a library research assignment may have to be typed for presentation to your boss. Many enterprises, be they local merchants, campus publications, or student businesses, operate with an overload of letters to be typed. Between this material and all of those senior honors theses, you should be able to find all the occasional typing you want, without wasting much time searching for work.

Waiting on tables is a skill that is often in demand. Perhaps your college departs once in a while from cafeteria-style suppers of slung hash and could use your help to serve at a sit-down dinner or to pour sherry at the alumni reception or tea at a faculty meeting. Private parties also use student waiters. A freshman who worked one or two evenings a week as a busboy earned $2.60 an hour, whereas a student waitress cleared $2.50 to $3.00 per hour, plus $2.00 to $10.00 in tips each evening that she worked. Both students were put in contact with employers through a student catering agency at their school. They agreed that their jobs were easier than comparable work for commercial restaurants and they liked the variety of people whom they met. Free food is a bonus in this type of casual employment, although there are drawbacks as well; you may have to wear a uniform, and your social life might suffer from the fact that weekends are prime dinner-party time.

Bartending is another skill that lends itself to profitable evenings of free-lance employment. But what if you can't type and loathe parties? There are casual/skilled jobs within academia that you may prefer. If you let it be known in your departmental office that you are looking for work, the secretary who is told to "find someone" to check the accuracy of footnotes and bibliography in a new book—will find you. Perhaps you can get work grading exams and papers for high school teachers or at your own college, particularly if your school has no graduate program (graduate students tend to skim off this work in large universities). A senior in math, for example, is certainly competent to grade freshman problem sets, and an honor student in Romance Languages would make short work of the quizzes for first-year French. What might be unrewarding drudgery to an assistant professor may be interesting to you, and you would be paid to brush up on your fundamentals, whether of quadratics, conjugations, or the interpretation of dreams.

Who needs a physics major with a B average? A potential physics major with a C— average, a high school junior struggling with compulsory physics, or an undergraduate biologist who needs an introduction to new concepts as he begins a project in biophysics. There are probably subjects in which you are qualified to tutor less advanced students, and you need not be an outstanding student to be a good teacher. No commercial tutoring schools, we found, will hire students, but the student employment office or your school's special bureau of study counseling may have a set-up for matching tutors and tutees. Try bulletin-board notices and the college newspaper classifieds as well especially if your subject is one for general consumption; a Paris-bound vacationer may be as eager to brush up on his conversational French as a desperate sophomore anticipating his exam. Expect $3–$4 an hour for elementary tuition in common subjects and charge more if your approach is advanced or your subject obscure. Who else can your tutee turn to, on your central Montana campus, if he really wants to learn Tamil dialects?

Languages are a particularly valuable asset when you're looking for short-term employment. Your college may be a source of translating jobs, but commercial agencies such as Berlitz also hire students for this work. You will probably have to work against a deadline, but otherwise your schedule is your own. Such agencies, likewise, try to match a student's interests and professional vocabulary with the manuscripts assigned him: premed students will get the biology treatises, and history majors the medieval chronicles. The usual rate is $3 a page but naturally you will find a premium on Sanskrit and Icelandic.

Fine arts majors are subjected to a four-year barrage of color slides, and someone has to operate the projectors. You could pick up not only cash but culture. Can you operate a movie projector? Movie buffs may marvel that such a simple technique is considered a skill at all, but many a brilliant professor hasn't the faintest idea of how to thread the film, or how to deal with a jump in the "visual aid." Not only will they pay you for your help, but you can moonlight as the projectionist for the college cinema club or screen classics series. These jobs pay about $2.50 an hour, for dozing in the dark.

But you want *out*. Out of the classroom, lecture hall, and library. An off campus job. Start with your skill and consider how your community might buy it.

Can you drive? In many cities, students have become an important component of the cabbie corps. Taxi companies will probably welcome you if you have a safe driving record and some knowledge of the local highways and byways. You can pick virtually any hours—all night, Sunday dawn—and count on keeping about 50 per cent of what you take in. A hack license will probably be necessary, but the taxi fleet eager to hire you is eager to get you the license as well. If you can deal with the union, you might hire yourself out part-time to a trucking firm. A dapper alternative to these transportation jobs is a position as a chauffeur with an airport shuttle service. You'll clear about a quarter of the profits, but there's no dawdling and cruising or looking for fares, and the territory and hours probably hold fewer risks than the average cabbie's situation. Unlike the cabbie, however, you will have to sport short hair and a clean-shaven chin. A black suit and an establishment manner will help you to land this one.

Do you need only one try to drive a nail cleanly into a two-by-four? Carpenters will be in demand on a casual basis in local stores that need display racks built or shelves installed, in fraternity houses or dorms that want a bar constructed or a TV alcove built, and in student or commercial businesses that wish to avoid high professional costs for simple remodeling jobs. The college theater may need a supervisor for its set builders. Professors may hire you to repair a battered garage or to prove, with pickets or stone, that good fences make good neighbors. One student picked up $3 an hour one October for constructing a brick-and-sand patio. He had never worked with these materials before, but found that following the pattern was the whole job—sandbox crossed with paint-by-numbers.

Can you operate a key punch? If you type well, you can easily learn to keypunch, which is almost exactly the same, although a little more fun, taken in small doses. Keypunching pays better than typing, and, as businesses increasingly computerize their records, the demand for this skill races past the supply. Even more lucrative is computer programming. Far from abstruse, this is basically a mechanical operation, organizing data and rendering it into "computer language." Nearly any college will make it easy for you to learn this skill—perhaps for academic credit! The $5 to $10 an hour will later reward you for your diligence.

Can you play the piano? A fraternity might hire you to play at Saturday night dinner. Private parties will pay you to come and entertain (while other students serve the drinks), particularly if you know some straight dance music. Good restaurants may want live music in the lounge or at banquets held in their private dining rooms. A theater may need a rehearsal pianist. Other instruments are equally profitable. A Portland, Oregon, junior played the guitar in a downtown bar; he was given an enthusiastic and unsolicited mention in the local newspaper and played to large audiences all spring term. A coffee house in Philadelphia hired an undergraduate harpist to grace its evenings, and she picked up extra money playing at the weddings of lovers who had courted over espresso there. It is easier to transport a string quartet than a harp—so why not form one, and play for weddings yourselves. For an evening or afternoon of private entertainment, $25 to $100 is not an unreasonable charge. (Consider rehearsal time, number of players, and so forth in arranging your fees).

There are two lucrative alternatives for your musical talent if these possibilities don't appeal to you. One is instruction, which pays about $5 an hour, depending upon the instrument and your level of skill. This could, clearly, be considered a term-length job, since you are more likely to have regular lessons with steady pupils than to teach an isolated blues riff every few weeks. This type of work, however, is "casual" in that you hire yourself out when you like and without the rigidity of an employer's imposed structure. If your courses turn out to be a snap this term, or if a torn muscle keeps you off the squash court, advertise in the paper or bulletin board, and pick up an extra pupil. If group lessons suit you and your students, work things that way.

Glamour, fun, and risk combine in the musical undertaking that is potentially the most profitable: forming a band. The investment in equipment and instruments alone—not to mention managers, agents, road managers (if you're lucky enough to get bookings), electricians, and time spent rehearsing together and working up your material—is enormous. But the musical and financial rewards can be great, and many groups organized in college have gone on to professional success and recording contracts. Some are one-shot famous, whereas others made an impression only in their home city or area of the country. But the 1950's revival group Sha-Na-Na is a good example of nationwide success and fat bank accounts for a group of men who began singing together as Columbia undergraduates.

Graphics is the most profitable area for the amateur artist. A cinema or Shakespeare society may pay for a series of silk-screened posters; a Gilbert and Sullivan production might buy a rococo program design. Your talent has a market, whether it runs to the organizational (advertising design, brochure covers, layout and paste-up), the technical (cartography, engineering diagrams, medical illustration), or the creative (embroidery patterns, fashion drawings, stationery designs). You may find employment through want ads, or through friends who know of your skill. But if you are willing to take the initiative, mimeograph a brief statement of your ability and your willingness to work, together with a sample of your work (or, if this is impractical, an offer to provide samples on request). Drop off these résumés at appropriate local businesses, college departments, and student organizations. A junior with graphic arts skill applied in September to the assessor's office at his hometown courthouse and landed a full-time position as a tax assessor's assistant over Christmas vacation. This work consisted of measuring and sketching houses in the county, at $2.05 an hour. Not only did he meet many interesting people but he gained insight into court dynamics, local politics, and the mazes of the construction industry. This vacation employment turned into a full-time job the next summer.

If you can't draw a dissection in living watercolor, the science departments may still employ you. Washing test-tubes, feeding white mice, taking stockroom inventory, or dismantling superstructures of glassware in the wake of an organic chemist may not be skilled work, but a chemistry major can probably find casual jobs setting up apparatus or wielding a slide rule for a professor doing research. A sophomore earned $2.50 an hour and picked up a little biology on the side when he worked as a research assistant for the duration of an experimental project at a hospital in his city. The hiring was done through an ad in the college newspaper: first come, first served. Although the job itself tended to be tedious, a large metropolitan hospital proved to be an interesting place to work.

Craft skills can bring you a couple of dollars an hour for private lessons to children or adults, but the direct products of your hands may sell even better. Macramé chokers in pretty colors are completed in half an hour and sell for $3. Handmade candles are a feature of nearly every student's room, and those staple hand-thrown coffee mugs might as well come from you, instead of from Japan. Make up a batch some weekend and sell them through shops, craft fairs, or door-to-door. A student leather craftsman reports that his prices run about $25 for a pair of custom sandals and from $6 to $12 for belts. The most unusual and creative designs sell best, he adds, and emphasizes the variety of people he meets through his job. Because he sets his own hours and pace, the work is relaxing—he has never even bothered to figure out his profit-per-hour.

How much time did you spend on your car in high school or on your motorcycle last spring? Maybe you can make it pay. A good mechanic commands top wages and can work at odd hours. If you sign on with a local repair shop, filling station, or high-performance specialty garage, the job becomes steadier and less "casual," but if you can work without a pit and have your own tools, you might do private mechanic work and save your friends and classmates the possibility of rip-off repairs.

Photographers have an ideal free-lance skill. If you don't have a darkroom or the use of one, perhaps you could set one up with several photographer friends, and share work assignments. Portrait work is one source of income, and weddings, bar mitzvahs, and children's parties often demand photographers. Your college may hire occasional technicians for the science darkrooms or to work on public-relations and catalogue photography.

If your heart leaps up at the first white flakes, while all around you are shouldering their shovels in dismay, you may have the makings of a weekend ski instructor. Winter weekends and Christmas vacation are the times when the slopes are crowded with first-timers—and those are the times you're free. If you're just not good enough to teach ski school at Stowe or Aspen, one of the newly developed local areas might be grateful for your help. Or cash in on your skating, snowshoeing, or cross-country skiing prowess. Your $40 ski weekends will now be $50 ski weekends—profit instead of loss. If you're really proficient and can throw in a little French or German, try contacting a travel agency or the student charter-flight organization about chaperoning a group of classmates or lucky high school skiers to the Alps over Christmas.

When the snow melts, can you coach a baseball team or officiate at a high school swim meet? Can you teach swimming or water safety courses, or be a lifeguard at a YMCA or community pool? Can you give tennis lessons to teen-agers or teach karate to young women, or caddy, or help a businessman perfect his putts? Warm weather and recreation mean plenty of casual work for the skilled student-athlete.

Most of these casual/skilled jobs can clearly be turned into term-length employment simply by your initiative. By simply lining up more customers, or making long-term contracts with present employers, you insure yourself a steady income in return for a definite time commitment. If you want a job with these features built in, you are looking for term-length work suggestions.

Term-Length/Unskilled

If you need a substantial amount of money and are able to commit yourself to a regular work schedule, you should look for a term-length employer who will count on your reliable service and compensate you with a steady weekly wage. The casual jobs mentioned previously easily metamorphose into such positions: ten hours a week of caretaking and yard work may only regularize a patchwork of leaf raking and porch repair assignments. Term-length/unskilled jobs account for the vast majority of jobs, whether on or off campus, which are held by undergraduates.

On Campus—

Three mainstays of unskilled term-length work are offered by many colleges; dining hall jobs, janitorial jobs, and library jobs.

Your dining hall job may set you operating a dishwasher or potato masher, guarding the desserts against greedy seekers of seconds, doling out Swiss steaks, or standing at the end of a conveyor belt, trying to keep up with dirty trays. The pay for this work is about $2.50 an hour, and you will often get a free meal or, if your college meals are prepaid, a cash rebate. The big advantage of dining hall jobs is that they use up mealtime hours only; time that you would otherwise probably spend lounging over coffee. You don't lose a moment's study or activity time. Boredom may be a problem, as you pour gravy over your five-thousandth mound of mashed potato, but these jobs are routine and most students find them easy and harmless.

More equivocation occurs over janitorial jobs. As a freshman you will probably be delegated to do the "wet" chores; swabbing the shower floor and scrubbing porcelain in lavatories. One dorm crew worker described his skills as "an ability to clean Brooks House bathrooms." If you ever have a bathroom of your own in later years, it will probably betray your freshman job by its delightful sparkle. If we thought you would be satisfied with a job like this for more than one year, we wouldn't have bothered writing this book, and even the dorm crew hierarchy offers you greater things. The "dry" chores, which sophomores enjoy, including vacuuming, sweeping corridors, and emptying the trash. Wet or dry, you'll get about $3.25 an hour, and you will probably be responsible for a couple of hours work a day, which you may be allowed to work in whenever your free time dictates. Two hours a day means $32 a week—over $1,000 a year. If your school assigns you a certain *amount* of work, rather than time-period, you may perfect a system of speed sweeping.

Once you have mastered housekeeping, move up to a cushy supervisory position: dorm crew captain, at a raise of $.20 or $.30 an hour. These janitorial jobs can land you big tips or overtime pay when reunion or June clean-up time arrives, because experienced students will be hired first.

Library jobs may not offer much room for promotion, but they are often the best jobs around. Wages run from $2.00 to $2.50 and $2.75 an hour, and you may in effect be paid to study. You may work checking out books or checking out people to make sure *they* have checked out their books. Other tasks range from cataloguing to book-finding in the stacks, or pushing a cart quietly through the aisles, shelving returns. Someone may actually be required to oversee the reading room, answering questions and glaring at whisperers. If you work in the early evening you will be kept busy, but morning hours will probably be silent and sparsely populated in the library. Find out just what your hours and duties will be. Your library job may create or enforce a "compulsory" study time for you each day. If you spend four hours a day studying anyway, why not pick up a little added something for it?

Although some colleges use these three job categories to handle most of their student employment problems, other jobs may be offered to students by your school. Does the health service need orderlies, receptionists, or assistants in the records room? Who mans the phones when someone calls university information or the student directory? Probably students. The dormitory switchboard usually requires a student to answer the telephone; it pays $2 an hour and is strictly a push-button job, allowing you to study between calls, and you can get extra hours during vacation if you want them. It's convenient—you only have to step downstairs. If your dormitory or house is large enough to have a library, you might find equally handy employment. The wage will be lower than at the college library, but the silence is deeper and the study time is uninterrupted. The university mail service may need regular student help. A film courier, who carried film cans from place to place for classes in his university's law school, earned $2 an hour and described his work as "the easiest job in the world." Perhaps sitting in the college information office, answering tourists' questions, appeals to you, or clicking switches in the language lab. The athletic department needs personnel to hand out towels at the pool, handle the tennis court sign-up sheets, and take attendance at compulsory phys-ed classes.

Student businesses are the other obvious on-campus employers. Sell rings, hawk banners, or deliver birthday cakes. Help out with the bookkeeping (the adding machine can be mastered in ten minutes), or sweat in the linen depots. Many jobs that the college distributes may go to scholarship students, preferentially or exclusively. The most helpful work possibilities for students, those of the Federal Work-Study program, discussed in Chapter One, are limited to students receiving financial aid. If your financial need is more personal than vital to your continued study, the student agencies may be a richer source of job possibilities. A well-heeled economics major who was willing to plod the corridors from 6 to 8 A.M. earned $3 an hour making dormitory deliveries of the student newspaper, hot off the press. It was hard, dull, sleepy work, but it led to his employment as circulation manager of the paper, one of the country's largest college dailies.

Another student landed a summer job at the university theater after a term of working at ticket sales in the box office. This work pays $2.00 an hour, plus free tickets to the shows. You're likely to have to deal with irate patrons if the play is a sellout, but the work is usually in blocks of an hour or two and is always finished by 8:30 P.M., so that you still have time to date, on weekends.

Off Campus—

Numerous jobs are available off-campus, if there is *anything* off-campus—that is, if your college is not the sole feature of an oasis or a mountain crag.

There is little point in trying to name every part-time unskilled job possibility in the "outside world" since thousands exist. The ones that are most frequently held by students are mentioned because of their suitability and availability to undergraduates. Some of these jobs may be brought to your attention by a look at the classified newspaper ads, the supermarket bulletin board, or the student employment office file. If you don't find a job this way, go to the various businesses and merchants you think you would like to work for, ask to see the owner or personnel manager, explain your schedule, and ask for a job. Government agencies, hospitals, hotels, museums, and restaurants are worth a try.

Assertiveness is an asset here: if you need a job, go after one. A previous edition of this book, circa 1968, caroled, "Particularly when the economy is booming, the need for bright young part-time help is great. It should not take you long to find a job this way." Times change. As this edition goes to press, the American economy is moving toward recovery, but "booming" is still an epithet of nostalgia. Senior employees, fathers of families, men with skills and experience remain without jobs. You have plenty of competition in your search for work. But youth is on your side, and the fact that you are not supporting a family means that you can work for lower wages. Nor are you "overqualified" by your education or experience for unskilled jobs. Whatever the level of skill, remember that the businessman, particularly in a sluggish economy, is frequently faced with the problem of needing "half an employee": there is too much work for his present complement of salesgirls, draftsmen, or computer programmers, but not enough to justify hiring any employee to work forty hours a week. You are his answer. Don't let the newspaper unemployment reports discourage you; student labor is in part a special segment of the work force, and persistence and assertiveness should get you the job you need.

Restaurants and hotels employ both skilled and unskilled workers. Into the latter category fall bellhops, chambermaids, dishwashers, busboys, and fry-cooks. A bellhop at a Holiday Inn makes $1.75 hourly, plus tips averaging $.25 a bag. Two to three nights a week, or a whole weekend, will be your usual schedule. Chambermaids earn about the same, although their tips are less; their work week is eight to ten hours. Small restaurants and hamburger chains pay their dishwashers $2 an hour for a similar time commitment. You will be loading, rather than scrubbing, most of the time. A freshman worked as grill man at a diner for $2.50 an hour plus $1.00 or $2.00 a day in uncertain tips. If you can fry an egg, you might land this one. This student's term-time schedule was two weeknights; the next summer, and during vacations, he worked full-time since he went to college in his home town.

If you have your license and can drive a stick shift, you can be a parking-lot attendant, making $1.75 to $2.25 an hour plus the occasional tip. Delivery men and messengers for commercial firms make $2.25 an hour. You can get the same wage for making change at outdoor newsstands—but it's mighty chilly, come December. All of these jobs feature flexible hours.

If your classmates beat you to the soft jobs at the college library, you might try shelving and stacks work for the local public library, at around $2.25 an hour for a ten to fifteen hour commitment per week. Perhaps they will permit you to do special displays or lead the children's story hour.

One job for which only enthusiasm is required is that of companion to an elderly person. You may do a little cooking, cleaning, shopping, reading aloud—but your real job is just to be cheerful and *present*. Sometimes you may be able to study on the job. Young children, particularly if they are retarded or handicapped, may also require a paid companion. Newspaper ads and hospitals are your main sources of these jobs. You'll earn $2 per hour and deep satisfaction.

If you're over eighteen and a night owl, you might try working as a night watchman for a factory or business, either directly or as an employee of a large agency such as Pinkerton's. You will probably work sixteen hours a week (two eight-hour night shifts), at $2.50 to $3.00 an hour with periodic raises. Your duties will primarily involve pacing around the premises, punching a time clock according to a schedule. Those who tire easily will lose study time the next day, but perhaps you can pick it up during the long silent nights. Some watchmen have had to withstand cries of "pig" from passing teen-agers; don't take this job unless you feel comfortable in uniform.

Film buffs may be willing to don a scarlet usher's jacket at a local theater. Four hours a week is the minimum time commitment to this job; just long enough for the double feature. A plush theater specializing in long-run popular films may compensate you for the lack of variety with $3 an hour. A college-town cinema where the programs change every four days pays only $1.50 an hour to its ushers, but offers free tickets to ushers and their friends—not only at *that* cinema, but at its three affiliates in town, all with different programs. Your entertainment budget could disappear. Be prepared, however, to chase away small boys without tickets and the occasional exhibitionist in the balcony.

If your brain needs a vacation, your brawn could get you a job as a mover. A junior who did this tiring work for a while made $3 an hour, with long hours at overtime pay on his energetic days. His moving crew had a labor pool arrangement. The principal requirement was to hustle (or appear to) whenever in plain view.

You may never have considered your living arrangements as a job, but they could become one, if your college allows you to live off-campus. Professional parents, or wives who are attending schools, will often supplement the room and board of a live-in babysitter with a small salary. A senior who moved into a student cooperative figured that he saved $400 a semester in living costs. But shared tasks can mean a lot of work—supper for forty is no snap preparation. You may not mind the idea of preparing gallons of spaghetti or bathing three squirming faculty daughters every night, in September—but January and exam period may find you longing for your quiet dorm room. On the other hand, a home atmosphere may be invaluable after a few months in the rabbit warren of identical dormitory cubicles.

More term-length unskilled student jobs involve sales than any other field. Whether you're pumping gas at midnight or selling cupcakes in the corner bakery at noon, you're technically a salesman. Many local merchants will take on student salesclerks, particularly if their merchandise appeals to students. A sophisticated dress shop whose imported print fabrics appeal to university women finds that it does its biggest business in the afternoons and on Saturdays, so it hires students as part-time sales help, specifically for those hours.

A job with a stationery store may provide you with the steady income you need and is a perfectly good way to work your way through college. But a job selling dictionaries, encyclopedias, or kitchenware door-to-door can be a gold mine for you, if you are outgoing and ambitious. Even selling ads for the school newspaper can be, over the year, a profitable proposition if you work at it. Perhaps this type of work should be termed *skilled,* since good salesmanship is certainly an art. You will learn on the job, however, and you will probably need no experience to be given a chance. You will be paid by commission (20 per cent or so with ads, much more on other items) and if selling does not agree with you, you can quit quickly, earning little but losing nothing. If you are a real salesman—and you may not know until you try—your financial worries are over.

Crowded shopping-center parking lots and the shortage of baby-sitters has made American homemakers more and more prone to buying at home. Many people enjoy watching a salesman go through his spiel and appreciate ordering and receiving merchandise without leaving their living rooms. Student salesmen capitalize on this tendency and many average $200 or more for a fifteen to twenty hour week. Of course, your hours are your own, and your work schedule bends effortlessly with your exams and term paper assignments. This is no employment for the easily discouraged or for those who prefer a highly structured work situation. But successful students in direct sales earn more money than in almost any other type of employment.

Most of these jobs will be advertised in newspaper columns. If you are interested in direct sales as a possibility for term-time employment, you should be selective. Shop around for a company that has a well-known name; this will help sell the product and guarantees both you and your customers against fly-by-night merchandisers. The Stanley Home Products Company, Tupperware, Aristo Craft, and Vita Craft Corporation, all of which market pots, pans, and other household products, have well-developed student representative programs. Avon cosmetics and Fuller brushes are so well-known as to be clichés of the stand-up comic—but they *sell*. Beehive Fashions specializes in housedresses. If skillets and vegetable brushes bore you, the World Book Encyclopedia will be happy to send you out with examples of its superior encyclopedias, dictionaries, and atlases.

In each case, the student salesman works alone or with a partner; he is set up with samples of merchandise, order forms, catalogues, and any other selling aids designed to do the job. Each of the companies has long experience in this field and should provide a complete training program to help you succeed. Never take on sales of a product if you aren't "sold" on it when you see it demonstrated. Remember that, in most employment interviews, the product will be presented to you in the same manner that you will be trained to use with customers. If the demonstration doesn't excite you, how can you hope to make a housewife enthusiastic about the product? Try not to be turned off by rousing sales meetings. You may be subjected to nauseating doses of *esprit de corps,* but keep in mind that the men you work for make nothing if *you* make nothing; whatever they do or say is designed to help you in your efforts, which are in their interest as well as your own. Finally, and most important, make sure that you are thoroughly trained in your sales presentation. This is your profit-making tool. You should be trained "in the field," so that you can see, in advance, customer reaction to your product and to salesmen in general.

Not all students have great success with direct sales. You should look into selling because it *can* be fun, honorable, and lucrative; it offers you valuable experience, and may lead to employment after graduation. But there are many more companies than the ones presented here, and although most are honest, some are less candid than others. Few will suggest practical or ethical cautions to you, and the unscrupulous company knows that, if you have a bad experience, there will be another prospective salesman right behind you. Term-time sales work, however, virtually guarantees the industrious student a steady income ranging from modest profit (like the salary at the dorm crew drudgery you're fleeing from) to spectacular earnings that can be matched only by going into business for yourself and succeeding handsomely.

Term-Length/Skilled

You don't fancy hawking hosiery and you don't aspire to corporate status. But you still dream of a high and reliable income. Skilled term-length employment is your answer. Although you will probably not be able to qualify for or land a highly skilled, long-term job when you first enter college, by the time you are an upperclassman you may well have met a number of influential people and acquired useful skills that will help you secure such a job.

Many such job possibilities have already been described implicitly in the earlier discussion of casual/skilled employment. Consider how those examples would apply to a year-long situation. Instead of taking on individual term papers, find a steady typing job with a business or university department. Rather than snapping an occasional portrait, apply for a salaried position as a photographer for the Alumni Bulletin or College News Office.

If you are planning to profit from your skills in a long-term job commitment, make the effort to locate work that dovetails with your personal interests or enables you to gain experience in your anticipated career. A university student and film-maker took a scriptwriting job with a local educational television station. He was promoted to making documentaries, one of which he was paid to research in Eastern Europe during summer vacation, and after graduation he continued his work full-time. A future lawyer found a job as a small claims manager for his college newspaper through the student employment office. He averaged about $30 a month (10 per cent of the ads that he collected) and found his inside view of business and the court system fascinating. His chief skill was the nerve to write threatening letters.

Two premed students found that their hospital jobs were not only interesting but excellent references for medical school applications. One made $2.50 an hour as a hematology lab technician, and although drawing blood turned out to be more difficult than he had expected, the hospital trained him thoroughly. He applied several months in advance, and found that most hospital laboratories need workers. A sophomore saw an advertisement for a laboratory research assistantship and landed it on the strength of her interview only three days in advance. She received $2.75 an hour and, like her fellow premed student, worked about eight hours a week. She learned so much that she was eventually able to expand her time commitment to the job by arranging it as part employment and part independent study (learning the science involved).

Faculty aide programs, which employ large numbers of students on most campuses, are worth special attention. Some of these jobs are filled through the student employment office; check there first. Call up friends on the faculty—a professor whom you got to know in a seminar, your advisor, your tutor, or a section man. Tell them the kind of work you are looking for and ask them for suggestions. At the very least, they may be able to give you the names of others to call. You may talk with a string of sixteen people before you are through, but landing a job makes it all worthwhile. In a couple of hours of telephoning you will have penetrated the inner circle of your department and notified a lot of people of your availability. Your reward for taking this extra initiative may be interesting work in your field rather than dishing out fruit compote in the cafeteria with the unskilled and unassertive. Never forget that a departmental secretary can be the crucial factor in your search for work; she is probably the nerve center of the whole operation, and she has the perception and pull to find you what you need.

Even these jobs vary in wages and satisfaction. A secretary who typed a professor's letters, at $2 an hour, found her work tedious and time-consuming, although she felt that her employer's influence might help with graduate schools. A clerical assistant working on another professor's book discovered that her job entailed mostly xeroxing, and was bored despite a salary of $2.25 an hour and an interest in the topic of the study. An economics major with a background in computer work was invited by one of his teachers to work for him as a researcher. This job paid $2.50 an hour, and was academically stimulating as well as promising pull for graduate school. A transcriber of tape recordings for the Institute for the Study of Families made $2.75 an hour, and reports that his employers went out of their way to enliven his rather repetitive task by explaining to him the interpretations of the tapes. He is convinced that his experience gained him admission, as a junior, to a graduate psychology course. A research assistant ($2 an hour) in sociology was hired because of her persistence, but once on the job she grew to resent her role as a "deceptive experimenter" and ended up with a distrust of sociological data and a sense of the "vague immorality" of some research techniques.

Not all skilled academic work is for professors. A tutor at the Russian Research Center of a large university got a senior, with a background in Russian language and history, a job in the library there. She works two full days a week and has classes on the three remaining days. For her work she receives $5 an hour—$80 a week, *part-time,* not to mention the contact with the higher-ups in her field. A prelaw student earns $4 an hour doing computer work for the *Law Review* at his university's law school and considers it a learning experience.

Clerical skills are in perpetual demand. An office boy who works full-time in the summers and part-time during the term makes $3.25 an hour. A bookkeeper, whose hours are completely at his own disposal, makes $2.50 an hour. The local public library pays about $2.25 an hour to students who are typists.

Athletes over eighteen who hold a Water Safety Instructor's Certificate may be hired as lifeguards at country club pools, at around $2 an hour. The YMCA requires a degree in physical education from its assistant athletic instructors, but if you are working for such a degree, they may hire you. The city recreation department in one college town was willing to hire students for the following jobs and wages: bath attendants ($2.40), lifeguards ($2.60), and assistant recreation leaders ($2.20) for adolescent centers. Apply to the recreation office directly or get on the list at the local Civil Service Office.

Restaurants and private parties need service personnel. Waiters and busboys at a hotel dining room work from 5 to 9 P.M., the dinner hour, several nights a week. Between tips and their union wages, they clear around $2.45 an hour. Waitresses in an inexpensive coffee shop with a high turnover of customers make $1 an hour, plus their tips. Short-order cooks in the same establishment get around $2.25 an hour, with wages increasing as they become more skilled. A sophomore, who waited on table at parties assigned him by a student catering service, earned only $2.25 an hour, with few tips, but he praised the flexibility of the hours and the dates he met through his job. Happiest of the student party-personnel are the bartenders—could it be the free liquor? They are usually trained in a short course given by the student bartending agency that then employs them and enjoy a chance to escape briefly from the student community into the homes of faculty and alumni. The work is hard, but the conversation memorable, and sometimes a reception or exhibit opening will take the student bartenders to local theaters, museums, and art centers—even city hall. Student bartenders get about $2.90 an hour, and can count on $5.00 in tips per job.

Some sales jobs require a skill in addition to salesmanship. Students who work for apartment rental agencies as brokers must learn enough to pass an exam that is frequently administered by the state government. If you have the initiative to sell yourself to a local apartment rental agency, a staff member will probably be anxious to train you for the exam and put you to work (the material for the exam can be mastered in a few days). Many university towns have a rapid turnover of faculty, off-campus students, and summer school students—so that business booms. An able student who has chosen a good firm to work for will earn healthy commissions in his spring term and $1,000–$3,000 during the summer. Be sure to ask your prospective employer for the names of other students who have worked for him in the past; when you talk with them, remember that they were undoubtedly the most successful salesmen.

For the first time, student salesmen are becoming involved in the mutual funds industry. On commission sales, you may earn 2 to 4 per cent of each investment, so that a sale of $10,000 to a rich uncle who wants to start his retirement fund will pay the student over $200 in commission. Write to the National Association of Securities Dealers (888 Seventeenth Street, N.W., Washington, D.C., 20006) for the name of a good mutual funds firm in your area and for their study pamphlet. Again, you should be able to learn enough to pass the requisite exam in a short time. There is also a registration and examination fee. Once you become a mutual fund salesman, however, you will be able to "talk up" sales whenever you happen to meet a family acquaintance or personal friend who wants to make a good investment. Some students have had spectacular success following up leads given to them by their company or selling to friends of the family; one student earned $1,000 in the last two weeks of his summer (which he spent as a sailing instructor); less successful students still report an overall hourly wage above $2.50 an hour.

Consult your neighborhood stockbroker to learn more about this job. You could also write to the Horne Investments Company (1430

Massachusetts Avenue, Cambridge, Massachusetts 02138), since it was started by an enterprising student who has trained fifty other students to sell for him.

Working for a consulting firm is another skilled job that is lucrative, if you can land it. In various university towns, particularly on the East and West coasts, clusters of small firms specialize in developing educational curriculum, designing transportation systems, city planning, organizing health care delivery, and setting up cooperative farms in the Deep South. Whatever the project, a student with an analytical mind, relevant academic experience, *and* a few contacts may find himself doing exciting intellectual work with concrete applications. Professors are often involved in such operations and may be willing to help you get a job if they have been favorably impressed with your intelligence and energy. Consulting and research-and-development firms pay students around $5 an hour.

The most intriguing skilled, term-length jobs that we discovered, although the skill required is not exactly run-of-the-mill, involved a junior majoring in biology who called up a doctor after seeing his ad in her college paper. She assured him that she had both experience and guts, and went on his research payroll at $2.50 an hour. This job occupied her Saturday mornings and she described it as "intriguing at first, but tedious eventually." The mystery task was dissecting chicken embyros.

Volunteer Jobs: A Footnote

Our last word on the subject of term-time employment is really a footnote to the chapter. If money is your object, you will not "make it" by volunteering your services. A few of the many rewards to be gained by part-time volunteer work while you are an undergraduate are reviewed here.

Volunteer work can directly influence your career plans and provide you with experience that may test or reinforce your vocational goals. A future surgeon felt that he had seized a "great opportunity" in volunteering for work in the emergency room of a sprawling city hospital. Although there was more errand-running and less blood than he expected, the experience impressed him with its diversity and continuing interest. A teaching assistant who worked with third graders in a school volunteer project in her college town was likewise pleased with the variety of her work. In addition to assisting slower pupils with their lessons, she supervised recess, made a bulletin board, taught crafts, and learned about the city school system from the inside. But this experience, gained by answering a radio appeal for teacher aides, convinced this child-development major that teaching was not for her, and she has since gone on to work professionally in the field of planning for day-care centers.

A volunteer job can provide academic research and fieldwork material. One sociology student gathered information for the "little city hall" in a poverty area of a large city that was trying to encourage neighborhood government. He was also gathering information for his senior honors thesis—although that had never occurred to him, when he originally volunteered. But the opportunity to work with this inside knowledge of the interactions of various political influences in a circumscribed community seemed too rich for him to pass up. This student found his "profitable" position through a student-run clearinghouse for social service projects. This type of organization is, on many campuses, the volunteer's equivalent of the student employment office.

Finally—and most pertinent to the aims of this book—volunteer employment can lead to a paying job. A young woman majoring in early childhood education took on an unpaid job as a teacher in a kindergarten for children suffering from cerebral palsy. She found the work difficult, but so worthwhile that she didn't mind when it began to dominate her other school activities. That summer she continued her work full-time; at $3.50 an hour. When the fall term began, she returned to a part-time schedule at a salary of $4.05 an hour.

Without taking the edge off the financial potential of volunteer work, we must conclude with the fact that although these jobs bring concrete returns in experience, new skills, and contacts, their basic advantage is the obvious: satisfaction. All of the student volunteers described were agreed on the point that their work was unpaid only in a monetary sense, and that the deepest reward that they received was the satisfaction of accomplishing necessary and priceless work, some of which would go undone, leaving desperate gaps, if there were no student volunteers.

Chapter Four

SUMMER EMPLOYMENT

Spring thaw in the college community brings a trickle of consciousness to undergraduates who remember that the coming summer demands employment. The job hunt begins. Soaring temperatures and the advent of exams step up the urgency. If your search reaches peak intensity in the glare of June, you can probably look forward to days of pounding baked pavements—unless you fall back on the underground papers: "Hip octogenarian seeks liberal, nubile female companion; room, board, $100 a week plus mutual satisfaction." The end of the spring term will find the student employment office devoid of listings, the classifieds picked bare. Even Uncle Pete, the steel magnate, may have been forced to fill his quota of $7.75-an-hour construction workers with the scions of mere second cousins, since his own day-dreaming nephew failed to ask him for a job. If this has ever happened to you, try to profit next year from your sadder-but-wiser summer spent shining shoes. The students who land lucrative and/or interesting jobs usually plan ahead, laying the groundwork for their success while the snowdrifts are still deep.

One freshman, who worked for a large business firm, began hatching plans for his dream job two years in advance. He created a theoretical position of management consultant, tailor-made to the firm's needs, and proceeded, of course, to fill it himself. As a junior, he finished his exams and stepped into his shiny new office, pulling down a graduate school reference and $15 an hour. A sophomore steelworker who cleared almost $8 an hour at his summer job reported that he had applied for the position four months in advance. "But realistically," he added, "I applied when I was born." His employer was his father. This type of advance planning is probably superior to all others for its efficiency in landing high-paying employment. Although the Pop-jobs are discussed later, we sympathize with your predicament if poor planning, on the part of the Fates, has provided you with a Pop who lacks the pull you need for that certain job. Not all preparations for summer employment must be made decades or years in advance. Several months will probably do nicely, and if you make some inquiries in December or February, you can probably forget about that typical late-May scramble.

Summer employment is worth considering early and approaching deliberately and persistently. The three-month vacation is the longest period of potential employment that you have to count on, a time to escape from those thin paychecks representing eight or ten hours a week, and to receive a wage padded by your full-time effort. It is your chance to land jobs that were denied you during the term, because they demanded a forty-hour commitment. Summer employment is, moreover, critical to financing a college education. It can be your single largest source of income and as such, can make or break your budget. Without the pressures and obligations of your academic work, you are free to pursue money-making full-time—which may make it possible for you to return to the trials of your senior thesis free from the pressures and obligations of a dwindling bank account and able to pursue learning full-time. At the very least, an extra dollar an hour all summer may mean the difference between study dates and dinners out, that 1954 Ford or a near-new VW, an orgy of new records or reliance on your tinny transistor radio.

Starting early is important—but how will you go about looking for a summer job? Thousands of students approach this problem by sending out dozens of letters, making a hundred telephone calls, and arranging personal appearances before as many potential employers as possible. Some find the work they want, but most are rewarded with discouraging piles of form letters. This haphazard approach to summer employment is not really much more efficient than the catch-as-catch-can method of the student who dawdles through April, muttering "something will turn up." Whereas "trying harder" may be part of the answer, it will not guarantee a job. You need to channel your determination into something better than mass canvassing of employers. You need a plan, a systematic approach to job hunting. Begin by assessing the facts of your job search realistically.

You will need to consider both your personal requirements and those of the job market; your task will then be to match these two sets of factors. To assemble your data, ask the following questions.

How much money do you need to make? If you need $1,100 to pay your tuition in September, there is no point in investigating day camps that pay $65 a week. If your continued scholarship depends upon a $500 contribution from you, be sure that you make it, even if it means sweeping streets. If a job that simply pays your summer expenses is adequate, the possibilities open up—perhaps you could even work in Europe.

Where do you want to work? If you must make a lot of money, living at home is best, because you save on room and board. But don't limit yourself; if there are no jobs at home, be prepared to relocate. A number of jobs, provided by summer camps and resort hotels, will board you free as part of the employment arrangement. If this is not possible, be realistic about counting up your profits and weigh a distant job's potential salary against the living and travel costs involved. Personal preference demands attention here, as well as sheer profit-mindedness. If you feel smothered at home, or can't bear the idea of another three months in your college town, try to arrange your job accordingly. If your girlfriend's going to summer school, and you *must* be around, plan your job search around that area.

What are your skills? Not only does a skill generally insure a higher salary but it makes your job hunt easier. Skilled positions are not necessarily easier to obtain, but if you know what marketable talents you have to exploit, your search has direction and you can concentrate on appropriate areas and employers. There are a myriad of unskilled jobs—if you simply offer an extra pair of hands, you have a vast undifferentiated job market to tackle. But it's simpler to take hold of the problem by focusing on a salable skill. Did you take water-safety instruction? Check out the beaches, pools, and country clubs for lifeguard positions. Can you program a computer? Take your choice of positions, and start toting up your profits. Can you bartend, mount insects, operate heavy machinery, or give tennis lessons? Any skill is in demand somewhere: search to find out where. A skill may help you obliquely, as well as directly. You'd like to do group work with children, but you have had no experience. However, you speak Spanish. This may earn you the chance to work at an agency serving Spanish-speaking people in your community. It may pay you to brush up your skills before trying to sell them: fifty words per minute looks better than forty on your typing test, and that musty high-school shorthand may prove to be an asset, once it is polished.

What are your interests? Academic interest may lead you to a job possibility. A history major with a background in political science landed a job as a library researcher in this field. He earned $3 an hour the first summer, and the next year his wages rose on the basis of his experience. Transforming a hobby into a money-maker is not unusual. Two New York City undergraduates began designing posters for drama groups at their school. By the second summer they had become so well known that they were commissioned by summer arts festivals and campus theaters all over the East Coast at more than $100 per design. Your interests may not secure you a job, but they might direct your search. A premed junior with a knowledge of organic chemistry and lab techniques worked as a research assistant at a metropolitan hospital for $2.15 an hour, and valued the "inside" experience with medical research that his job provided. At the same hospital, a senior was earning $2.80 as an orderly in the operating room, watching surgery all day; in addition, he received a medical school recommendation from his supervisor. An economics major with some statistical knowledge took a summer job, at $400 a month, with a bank, as an economic investigator. He traveled, interviewed, and wrote up reports—and was so impressed with the interest and responsibility of his work that his experiment with working in industry has led him to a permanent career choice. These students, guided by their interests, selected summer employment that tied in with their anticipated or potential professions.

What if you're unskilled? Probably more unskilled jobs exist than any others, but how excited do you get at the thought of working as a part-time library attendant in Oxford, Mississippi ($1.65 an hour), a filling station attendant in Phoenix, Arizona ($2.00 an hour), or a janitor at the beach kiosks in Atlantic City, New Jersey ($2.60 an hour)? You may need more effort to get an unskilled job; no businessman will probably approach you with an invitation to become his all-night stockroom clerk and inventory-worker ($2.40 an hour), although your biology professor might offer you a research assistantship, if you are his star pupil. But the jobs are there, if you uncover them—and can tolerate them. There will be plenty of competition, however, and you will have an edge if you apply for unusual or out-of-the-way positions. For example, an Ohio State junior spent his summer researching the derivations of words for a forthcoming dictionary. In a more exhausting job, a Berkeley student earned $3.25 per hour digging and blasting in an Arizona copper mine. One stalwart sophomore taking a less popular position rerouted sewer pipes for three months in Dayton, Ohio. And in probably the least popular job, an unsuperstitious New Hampshire student received $3,500 for moving the residents of a small town's cemetery 300 yards up a hill.

How does the job market look? Evaluate the possibilities in the employment field and geographical locale that you have selected. Write to the state employment office for that area, and check the want ads in the local papers. See if your student employment office has any possibilities. Get leads from friends and pull from relatives. The Chambers of Commerce, particularly in the cities, will send you a book-length dictionary of employers in their town. A number of books with employer listings are noted at the end of this chapter. Get all of the information you can. You want to find out *who* the employers are and *whom* (or *whether*) they are hiring.

What about the specific employer? If you're preparing to apply to a particular company, organization, or program that interests you, do a little research as preparation *before* applying. This is especially important if you plan to be working far from home. Occasionally that job that you were promised in March, at $3.50 an hour, disappears when you fly out to the West Coast in June to claim it: "unforeseeable circumstances" have forced the employer to withdraw his offer. This happens rarely, but why should it happen to you? A contract will protect you, but so will foresight. There is no point in working for a known sweatshop, a stingy merchant, a slipshod day camp, or a notoriously autocratic professor.

In addition to helping you avoid pitfalls, a knowledge of a potential employer will also make you a stronger candidate for the job. In your letters, interviews, and telephone conversations, you will seem more attractive to the employer if you can speak intelligently about his activities. The company's or organization's pamphlets and material may give you some leads. If you can, snoop around your prospective employer's business before your interview. Sometimes the pressure to land a job, any job, is enough to obscure the fact that the setup at *this particular* job is not for you. A girl who was hired as an administrative assistant at the American Heart Association looked forward to her promised contacts with the research and educational aspect of the organization's activities. Instead, she ended up straightening out the files and was exiled to an office full of chattering middle-aged typists. In contrast, a young man who was hired to park cars at a resort marina, found to his delighted surprise that his primary responsibility was for docking and maintaining yachts.

Are you limiting yourself? Don't. If you restrict your applications to jobs that you are sure to get (accountant for your brother-in-law) or are dead sure you can handle (just how can you fail at loading a dishwasher?), you are not only diminishing your potential reward from a job but narrowing your employment possibilities as well. Don't insist that you can type if you can't, but don't shy away from the possibility of being trained to use office machines that you've never tackled before. The spectrophotometer in the biochemistry lab may look forbidding, but if the research supervisor is impressed with your organic chemistry grade, he may take you on and teach you how to use it—if you don't demur. Although you must be confident that you are giving your employer his money's worth, there is no reason why you must endlessly repeat your employment experiences, doing bookkeeping or waitressing summer after summer. Perhaps you can be hired as a trainee. In this case, it will be helpful if you have some other skill to offer: many people break into publishing while typing, learn about law while doing case research, or gain theater experience as extras in the productions they build sets for.

Be willing to learn instead of earn. A sophomore who got the minimum wage as a workman in his city's public service clean-up campaign returned the next summer, at $2.50 an hour, to supervise the project— and he also got an inside look at the politics in the mayor's office. Another student started his summer stoically sweeping up scraps in a butcher's shop. Little by little he was able to learn the art of meat-cutting, and now earns $4.50 an hour as a part-time butcher.

These then, are the crucial factors: wage, location, skills—or the lack of them—interests, the job market in general and with reference to specific employers, and flexibility. Your search for a summer job should begin with a review of your answers to these questions and a fair consideration of your own priorities. If high earnings dominate your concerns, sacrifice the $2 an hour traineeship at a social service agency for $190 per six-day week as an auto mechanic. If what you're looking for is really a free vacation, try a job as a companion, mother's helper, or camp counselor; you won't earn much money but you'll get some sun. The salary of $1.89 an hour, in return for exercise, fun, and a fine tan may be reasonable if you can live free at home, but it is out of the question if you had to find room and board in ·a resort town. Juggle these priorities and come up with your own personal strategy. Apply early—and correctly. (Be sure to look at Making It, the last chapter, which deals with the fine points of nailing a job.) You may need to take a Civil Service Examination, provide references, or arrange an interview, so be sure you organize your applications well in advance.

Now you have a system, a "how" of summer job-finding. Your next consideration is "where." A number of areas are available in which to look, and in fact any area of the economy, with the possible exceptions of neurosurgery and guided-missile testing, offers you some hope of summer employment.

Government Jobs

The United States Civil Service is the nation's largest employer, and although most federal jobs are of the permanent, year-round variety, summer jobs are also available in many fields. Some of these positions are less drably bureaucratic than they are popularly conceived to be. Each year, over 20,000 undergraduates find summer jobs with the federal government, the largest single summer employer of college students. Although the number seems large, don't jump to the conclusion that your employment worries are over. Uncle Sam wants you, but there are usually 150,000 eligible applicants for U.S. government positions every year—the competition for these jobs is fierce. State and city governments, however, employ three times as many permanent workers as the federal government, and you will discover many state and municipal summer openings.

Jobs with the Federal Government—

Summer jobs with the U.S. government fall basically into four groups.

Group I, office and science assistant jobs, is by far the most common employment category for which the government hires students. Group I covers a wide range of actual jobs: typist, office machine operator, stenographer, clerk, biological technician, library assistant, mathematics assistant, engineering draftsman, meteorological technician, and dental assistant. The position of Post Office clerk-carrier, PFS-8, also falls into this category. Many students have held this temporary Post Office job, which may place you returning packages, delivering mail, or selling stamps. The pay is excellent ($3.95 an hour), future job possibilities in the Post Office are assured, and the working conditions are generally excellent—the summer postman deals with very little rain, snow, or sleet.

Another student earned a high salary as a Group I employee by landing a temporary position as an "enumerator" in a Property Value Survey, an operation that is carried out every five years as an activity of the Census Bureau. He was hired after an interview, a short written test, and the completion of an application for federal employment, including a Civil Service Examination. All of these procedures were carried out at his regional office of the Census Bureau (Boston). His job involved traveling all over New England, in his own car, while the bureau reimbursed him at the rate of $.09 a mile, and provided a daily expense stipend of $12–$20. This student cleared almost $3 an hour and found his work and contacts fascinating.

The government labels its pay scale by grades, and Group I jobs are in grades GS-1 to GS-4. In 1971, GS-1 paid $79.20 a week, whereas GS-4 paid $112.40. Overtime pay can give the federal employee an excellent income, as one Stanford student learned during two summers as a clerk in a New York City Post Office, working a lucrative sixty-hour week—at $2.78 an hour, plus time-and-a-half for overtime. Your salary grade depends upon both the type of job you hold and on your score on the Civil Service Summer Employment Examination, which you must take in order to qualify for Group I employment.

This examination is a one and one-half hour test of your vocabulary, reading comprehension, abstract reasoning, and ability to interpret charts and tables. Don't underestimate it: the level of difficulty is almost equal to that of the S.A.T.'s. Most students who are veterans of this examination, however, don't worry too much about it. You might look at a brochure on the examination and brush up on your long division. Because of the great number of summer applicants, a score of 90 or better on the examination is usually required for employment.

To apply for this exam, use Form 5000-AB, which may be obtained from your college placement office or your local post office. The form can also be obtained by writing to the U.S. Civil Service Commission. You should make every effort to apply by early December to take the test, and in no case later than February, which is the last time it is given. In general, application must be made eight weeks before the actual testing date. The examination is free.

With brilliance or diligence on your side, however, you may not have to take the Summer Employment Exam at all. If you have completed at least two years of college (or will have completed two years at the time you accept your appointment) and have a cumulative grade point average of 3.5 or above, you qualify as an "outstanding student" in the eyes of the United States Civil Service. To top off the prestige, you are exempted from the test, and will be given a "score" according to your grade point average: 4.0 = 100, 3.99 = 99, 3.8−3.88 = 98, and so on.

If you apply for a Goup I position as a typist or stenographer, it is required that you present *either* a notice of skill rating from a Civil Service typist-stenographer examination (which can be taken at your local Civil Service office), *or* a certificate of proficiency from your typing or shorthand teacher. These verifications of clerical skill are presented in addition to the Civil Service Summer Employment Examination.

Group II jobs have the same pay range as Group I jobs, but they require no examination. Some jobs in this category are available with the Department of State as a typist or stenographer. Jobs are also available with the Veteran's Administration in health care and related fields. You should contact the V.A. hospital where you want to work directly to see if they are taking on summer help. The largest number of Group II jobs are with the Forest Service, the National Park Service and the Bureau of Land Management. These jobs are discussed in the section Outdoor Work.

Group III jobs are specialized, involve a wide range of responsibilities, and are offered in a number of agencies. These jobs require at least a bachelor's degree, however, so they probably will not be open to you, unless you are a graduating senior.

Jobs in Group IV fall into the category of trade and labor jobs. You should apply directly to the local federal agencies in which you wish to work by April 15. Laborers are paid in accordance with the prevailing local rates. There are very few jobs in Group IV.

Beyond these groupings there are, of course, other government positions. Various federal agencies have Vacation Work-Study Programs (not to be confused with the Cooperative Work-Study Programs for which there is a maximum family income cut-off point). These jobs aim at potential career employees of the federal government and provide preprofessional training and experience in specialized areas on that basis. A good example is the Vacation Work-Study Program in Engineering and the Physical Sciences. Successful applicants receive on-the-job training in scientific agencies, with a GS-3 or GS-4 salary for the summer. They are then expected to return to school and pursue a normal academic program as a part of their training. Upon graduation the student is given a GS-5 professional appointment. Inquiries about this and similar programs should be addressed to the local area office of the U.S. Civil Service Commission.

The federal government also runs programs to provide jobs for students from low-income families. Students interested in the details of these jobs should apply to their local state employment office. Government-sponsored jobs involving social service are described under that heading, in a later section.

The most glamorous of the summer jobs that the federal government offers to students are its 1,500 positions as government interns in the offices of congressmen, senators, and various federal departments. These internships are open primarily to college juniors, and the work varies from office to office. Some students spend their Washington summers addressing envelopes and answering correspondence; others may be asked to research legislation or to do the actual drafting of a bill for Congress. You may be able to lobby for your particular interest—anti-pollution or consumer-protection laws—and work toward them, if your legislator-employer is sympathetic. One intern was pleased to be loaned out by "his" congressman to the policy committee of the Republican Party, where he did research on topics including NATO and the draft, and met with State Department officials and Senators.

Even those students who are utilized as clerical help usually praise their Washington sojourn as a learning experience, and the student internships are extremely competitive. You should apply as early in the year as possible to the congressman of your interest; he need not be your local congressman, but if he is a national figure, your chances of appointment are slim.

Salaries for the students accepted are usually from $75 to $85 a week, over a ten-week period, but some student assistantships with congressmen and senators pay only an honorarium. Check your finances to see whether you can afford the glamour of a summer in the capitol.

Although the Washington Seminar Program is not administered by the government, it is of interest in this context. Run by the Y.W.C.A., it provides paid employment in both government and nongovernment jobs. Applicants, however, must take the Federal Civil Service Employment Examination. Application forms and further information about the program can be obtained from the National Y.W.C.A.

Whatever government job tempts you, bear several points in mind. Apply early. The government makes an effort to offer equal employment opportunities to all citizens of the United States and it receives thousands of applications. The processing of applications and examination results takes time, and application deadlines as early as January 15 are set for some jobs, to allow for this ponderous selection process. If you are considering summer employment with the government, it is wise to visit or write to your local United States Civil Service Commission Office in the fall.

Don't be afraid of the red tape. Because the government hires large numbers of people through its regional offices throughout the country, the application forms are necessarily somewhat involved. A standard form is used for most government jobs. Don't be put off by the dotted lines and boxes; it's petty and detailed, but straightforward. Remember that this form can lead you to many jobs that are quite remote from the central stream of bureaucratic trivia.

Consider the government's part-time jobs. The federal government hires part-time employees for the same reason that industry does. The Post Office has a peak season at Christmas and takes on extra help accordingly, but many federal agencies must plan on replacing vacationing employees during the summertime. In order to be hired for any of these government jobs, however, you must first take the requisite examinations, even if the work is only part-time.

Finally, a discouraging word: don't count exclusively on getting a government job. Since federal agencies often do not notify you as to whether you have been hired until May, it's a good idea to keep other work possibilities on tap, so that you are not both disappointed and unemployed in June.

Useful Addresses

U.S. Civil Service Commission:

Summer Employment Examination
U.S. Civil Service Commission
1900 E Street, N.W.
Washington, D.C. 20415

Washington Area Office
U.S. Civil Service Commission
1900 E Street, N.W.
Washington, D.C. 20415

Civil Service Commission Announcement #414, free from the U.S. Civil Service Commission, discusses summer jobs with federal agencies and how to apply for them. Information on the Summer Employment Examination is available from the same source. You may also obtain the booklet, *Directory of Federal Job Information Centers,* which is a state-by-state listing of such offices.

Washington Seminar Program:

Ms. Barbara Taggart
National Student Y.W.C.A.
600 Lexington Avenue
New York, New York 10022

Jobs with State and City Governments

State Governments—

Summer jobs with state governments are similar to those offered by
the federal government and are often easier to get. The state Civil
Service Commission is a good starting place for finding a summer job.
Some state governments require summer employees to take a state civil
service examination, which is often given in the early fall. Be forewarned, and apply early. Some jobs, however, are open to applicants
with the required skills on a first-come, first-served basis. These jobs are
usually posted with the State Employment Security Division. The State
Employment Office maintains statewide information about jobs. You
can find out about the best procedure to follow in order to get a job with
a particular department by calling the department directly. Salaries for
summer jobs with state agencies range from $50 to $140 a week.

In many states, the governor's office has established a summer intern
program for college juniors and seniors. Some interns stay in the executive office whereas others are assigned to various state departments.
Interns answer mail, investigate complaints, do research on legislative
proposals, and act as general administrative assistants. They may learn
about such issues as unemployment compensation, mental health facilities, education, commerce relations, and business development. These
jobs offer good experience, and students compete for them. Because
some states regard summer internships as extremely desirable positions,
they may give these students only nominal salaries. For information on
the summer intern program in your state, you should write directly to
the governor's office.

State legislatures also have summer job openings for students. Legis-
lators sometimes have positions in their offices for students who want to
do research; others may have a large enough campaign budget to hire
part-time help, although most rely upon volunteers. Even if a state
legislator does not have a job opening in his own office, he has access to
information about employment opportunities with state government
departments. He may even be able to arrange a job interview for you or
recommend you to a particular executive officer for a summer position.

One junior met with his state representative at Christmas vacation and explained that he was an economics major interested in a career in politics. He was hired as a state budget assistant, at $80 per week. Direct contact with your legislator is the way to approach the job possibilities that he, or his connections, may offer.

Other areas of state government also provide summer employment to students. There is, of course, no lack of positions for typists and stenographers. The State Department of Public Works and the Highway Department of many states hire students for construction work and other unskilled labor. The salaries for these jobs are usually high. The wages offered by the state park and conservation departments, on the other hand, tend to be very low—often the minimum wage. If you would rather use your mind than your muscles, you might look for a state job as an administrative assistant, clerical worker, lab technician, or social worker. The salaries for these white-collar jobs usually fall between the highly paid highway-construction jobs and the low paying park jobs; you can expect to make $75 to $100 a week.

There are four chief steps in obtaining state employment. Register and take any civil service examinations required in your state, register with your local state employment office, persist in your inquiries about summer openings with all of those state agencies that interest you and pursue your hometown legislator, and get him to use his influence on your behalf.

City Governments—

A survey of one large metropolitan area recently showed that the city had at least 700 summer jobs open to students. Like state jobs, city jobs are usually distributed through politicians or through individual agencies. You should call the department in which you would like to work directly or contact your city councilman.

Local boards of education often operate summer remedial and enrichment programs and Head Start programs for preschool children. Such jobs are usually given to neighborhood residents and often to personal friends of people in the department. If you have no connections in the board of education, you should apply early and remain in contact—a periodic telephone call to learn what has become of your application is a good idea. Summer jobs with educational programs are rewarding, but they are rarely full-time, since the programs only operate for a few hours a day, on a day-care schedule. Most of the available positions are called "teacher's aides," an ambiguous term that may mask a reality of washing coffee cups and watching someone else teach. Many programs, however, delegate real responsibility to aides with initiative. You should investigate the program before you apply, and expect a salary of approximately $2 an hour.

Although children's programs have suffered in recent years from the lack of federal money, such issues as the drug epidemic have prompted many large cities to invest heavily in different types of adolescent services. These may range from runaway houses to free medical clinics and special series presentations of outdoor concerts, plays, and recreational events. Call City Hall to see what your town has to offer, what jobs might be available, and what departments these activities fall under. You might end up running a youth hostel, organizing a rock festival, helping high school students organize a recycling project, or leading a finger-paint free-for-all in a public park.

More traditional summer jobs that are often available are lifeguards at public pools, ponds, and beaches, playground supervisors in urban areas, medical or clerical assistants in city hospitals, and waterfront personnel, if your city hires out sailboats or rowboats on its lakes and rivers. The department of public works may need summer help: one Columbia student with an insensitive nose cleaned sewers for the City of Chicago at $3.50 an hour, and there are still apocryphal reports of exorbitant wages paid to those trusty souls willing to shotgun the alligators scuttling in the sewers under Manhattan. As always, typing is in demand, but the student who earns $2.50 an hour as a secretary in the mayor's office will doubtlessly have a more exciting summer than her roommate, who gets the same $2.50 for typing invoices in a furniture warehouse.

One interesting example of employment that is available with both a city and a state government is the internship program of the Port of New York Authority. Each year this mammoth and powerful organization hires students as interns in one of three categories: administration, accounting, and engineering. Like most programs run by cities and states, this one is used to identify students who might be offered full-time employment after graduation. It is a unique opportunity to study city and state politics and power flow, and to focus on the commercial and transportation structures of a vast urban area.

Outdoor Jobs

After dividing the school year between the brick dormitory, the fieldstone library, the granite classrooms, and the reinforced-concrete science labs, many undergraduates are more than ready for the great outdoors. You can be paid to sleep in a tent under the stars; summertime is outdoors time, and as America moves outside, so do the jobs. Your main areas of search for employment should be with the National Park Service and other federal agencies, and with summer camps.

Jobs in National Parks

You will find beautiful surroundings and a congenial group of fellow-workers if you obtain a summer position with the National Park Service. This federal department operates and maintains the nation's 200 national parks, seashores, monuments, memorials, cemeteries, battle-fields, and historical sites, and as such it preserves and presides over some of the loveliest and most moving countryside in the world. Another significant aspect of Park Service activities is its supervision of this national property for seasonal use as playground of the American public. For better or worse, most parks are an integral part of the summer tourist trade, and most of the thousands of college students that the Park Service hires each summer are primarily engaged in shepherding and restraining the thousands of middle-class campers who pour into the parks every June, July, and August. The campers require motel beds, mountainside rest rooms, restaurant meals, souvenirs, postcards, chewing gum, gasoline, and miles of film. As a National Park employee, you are less likely to spend your summer days pathfinding than to dedicate them to finding wandering ten-year-olds, and although your Daniel Boone fantasy pictures you taming a grizzly, you are far more likely to spend hours convincing balding businessmen to abandon their own attempts to be a pal to a bear. But in the shadow of the sequoias or under the Cape Cod blaze of sky even pedestrian chores are ennobled, and you may be able to improve the rapport between tourist and scenery, between man and nature, as a summer employee in a national park.

If you are considering summer work in a national park, your imagination probably conjures up Yosemite or Yellowstone. In addition to these popular and highly developed tourist attractions, remember the dozens of other national park preserves. The type of area or monument determines the kinds of jobs that are available, and whereas the Cape Cod National Seashore may require lifeguards, an undergraduate anthropologist may find relevant work at a site of Indian cliff dwellings. Local climate and volume of tourist travel influence the number of jobs that are available at a given season. Acadia National Park, on a cold bay in northern Maine, opens only for a few midsummer months, but the Mesa Verde National Park, in southern Colorado, welcomes visitors from April 1 through November 15. Although most college students cannot work for this entire period, many are hired for that portion of the season when the influx of tourists is greatest. If your school is near such a park, you may be able to extend your employment into the term. In addition, job competition is probably eased slightly when you apply to the less famous resort parks.

If the official dates of your park's season are June 15 through Labor Day, employees may still have to work before and after this period. Trails must be cleared of winter debris and camp sites prepared before the tourists arrive; their departure is followed by fall clean-up. Opening and closing seasonal hotels and park facilities take time. Summer employees may be expected to help with these pre- and post-seasonal operations; in your inquiry about jobs in these areas, be sure to indicate the exact dates when you will be available and do not simply mention that you will be free for "the season."

The variety of summer employment that is possible with the National Park Service is great. Seasonal park rangers are the summer employees with the greatest responsibility. General rangers supervise visitor services, park management, fire suppression, rescue activities, and law enforcement. Rangers may also work as specialists in the areas of history, archeology, or natural history. Seasonal technicians collect fees, fight fires, and assist in providing visitor information and in conservation and restoration activities. Seasonal aides work with technicians but at a more elementary level. Unskilled seasonal laborers work at trail-building, forestry projects, and park maintenance, whereas seasonal employees in skilled and semiskilled trades and crafts provide the parks with cooks and maintenance supervisors and services in carpentry, auto mechanics, building, and motor-vehicle operation. Fire-control aides are hired by many parks, and seasonal lifeguards, who must take the Civil Service Summer Employment Exam to gain eligibility, carry on lifesaving and rescue work. Park guides, who lead special tours of the geological formations, are needed at Carlsbad Caverns, New Mexico, and Mammoth Cave, Kentucky. As always, clerical help is in demand everywhere.

A specific academic background is generally required for those jobs that relate directly to the full-time occupation of the professional park rangers. Ranger-naturalists, ranger-historians, and ranger-archeologists fall into this category, and students who work at these jobs may have the opportunity to do research in their fields. Employment is also available to student architects, landscape architects, and engineers, who work on the planning and construction related to park management. Any of these positions requires academic experience in the particular field and may specify up to two and one-half years of study as a prerequisite. Information about these jobs is most often distributed to the placement offices of colleges that conduct programs in forestry, conservation, and related fields, since these summer positions are partly oriented toward identifying those students who might seek full-time employment with the National Park Service after graduation. Anyone can obtain application information, however. It is worth noting that since these jobs are related not only to the tourist trade but also to the maintenance and study of the parks—such jobs may be held for periods up to six months, and many require you to work for a longer period of time than the summer season.

Students without these specialized academic credentials will probably be most often hired to fill the substantial number of salary grade 1–4 positions that are available in public relations and administration. Guides, guards, tour conductors, bus drivers, publicity directors, and information and reception center assistants may all be needed. The skilled jobs, mentioned previously, complete the listing, together with the unskilled laborer positions, which require only willingness, a strong back and a minimum age of eighteen.

Applying to the National Park Service is straightforward, but it *must* be done *early*. You should make your job inquiries in the fall, to either the national or closest regional office of the National Park Service or directly to the superintendent of the park or area in which you want to work. Addresses will be found at the end of this subsection. Application for these positions is made on standard form 171, which is available from post offices, U.S. Civil Service Commission Area offices, and the personnel offices of federal agencies. Together with your letter of application, this form should be sent to the specific park where you wish to apply. All applications should be made after January 1 but before January 15; this is the only way to insure your consideration among the great number of competitors. No examinations are required, except for positions as seasonal lifeguards and as student architects, engineers, and landscape architecture assistants; applicants for all of these jobs must take Civil Service Exams, and their application deadline is waived until April 15, except in the case of lifeguards.

Outdoor work is also available in two other federal agencies, the Bureau of Land Management and the Forest Service. The latter hires students to work during the summer as fire lookouts and aides in the areas of forestry, fire control, range management, recreation, and biology. Application should be made to the director of the national forest that interests you, between January 1 and February 15. The Bureau of Land Management offers emergency and seasonal assignments of uncertain or temporary duration to applicants with training in forestry, conservation, range soil and water management, and related fields. Positions offered include lookout, in addition to aides in recreation, conservation of resources, forestry, and fire control. Applicants should write, as early in the year as possible, to the offices of the bureau in those states in which hiring will take place. A listing of such states is available from the Bureau of Land Management's national director.

It is important to remember that the National Park Service supervises as much tourism and recreation as it does science and research. Although the service itself does not operate the hotels, restaurants, and concessions within or adjacent to the boundaries of the park areas, the employment possibilities of these tourist services are great. Run by private companies who are granted the concessions by the Park Service, these businesses provide tourists with food, lodging, flash cubes, souvenirs, and postcards of Old Faithful. They may also supply other products and services. Gas stations may be allowed within the park boundaries or, in lieu of internal combustion, concessioners may rent out mules or pack horses and hire out guides, for they maintain the pack trips that are popular at some parks. Concessioners sometimes run sightseeing buses and other intrapark transportation.

Although the jobs vary with the concession, the following are some possibilities: bellboy, chambermaid, waiter and waitress, short-order cook, busboy, room clerk, sales clerk, kitchen help, and service-station attendant. The salaries tend to be lower than those of government jobs, but these jobs offer a prime opportunity for making tips. Inquire directly of each concessioner to find out his job openings, wages, and desired qualifications.

Helpful Addresses

For a map of the national parks, and for more information about specific job openings, write to The National Park Service, either at its central office or at the regional office closest to your home or in the area in which you want to work. All can supply you with the free booklets *Seasonal Employment with the National Park Service* and *Employment Opportunities with National Park Concessioners.*

Personnel Officer (National office)	Regional Director, Southwest Region
National Park Service	National Park Service
Department of the Interior	P.O. Box 728
Washington, D.C. 20240	Santa Fe, New Mexico 87501

Regional Director, Southeast Region
National Park Service
Federal Building, P.O. Box 10008
Richmond, Virginia 23240

Regional Director, Western Region
National Park Service
450 Golden Gate Avenue
P.O. Box 36063
San Francisco, California 94102

Regional Director, Midwest Region
National Park Service
1709 Jackson St.
Omaha, Nebraska 68102

Regional Director, Northeast Region
National Park Service
143 South Third St.
Philadelphia, Pennsylvania 19106

Camps

You won't get rich quick as a camp counselor, but if working out-doors is high on your list of priorities, it may be profitable to you in other ways. While your college roommate is withering under the fluorescent lights in his air-conditioned office you will be out experiencing the summer. Early to bed, early to rise should at least gain you strong muscles and a healthy tan. If you're prepared to deal with irrationality, it can be great fun to work with kids, and at those camps that specialize in fresh-air experiences for emotionally and environmentally deprived children, you will also have the opportunity to perform vital human service. Recreation can be re-creation, and you are perhaps more likely to find it so if your summer is spent among frogs, ferns, and vacationing kids than in the shiny resorts of the adults.

Perhaps you picture the camp counselor as a classical body, clad in a T-shirt with a pine tree on it, blowing his whistle authoritatively from the dock. Not every counselor is a waterfront director (although those who are are paid handsomely), and not every counselor is an athlete. There are shop counselors to help kids make sailboats out of wood and crafts counselors to teach them to weave lanyards and shape pottery ashtrays on rainy days. There may be a drama counselor for the Parents' Day Pageant, or a music counselor to lead camp sings. Skill in camping and woodcraft may land you a job overseeing hikes and overnight sleep-outs. And there is always a nature counselor to watch over salamanders in mason jars and the netting of moths and dragonflies. There are even counselors entrusted with putting the kids to bed at night and keeping them from mauling each other.

Skill in athletics and games is, nonetheless, usually part of the counselor's role. If you can head a sailing program, you can expect to earn over $1,000 a summer. An ability to play and teach another sport—archery, tennis, riding, swimming, baseball, and so forth—may gain you a job.

Although many counselors start out at camps that they attended as a child, this is not the only way to gain such employment. There are hundreds of summer camps, and if you are willing to take *any* job, you will certainly land work as a camp counselor *somewhere*. The good jobs and the good camps fill up first, of course. Your chances for these are slim unless you arrange a personal interview; written applications are too numerous to be effective. You will be wise to make your initial inquiries and applications in the fall, unless the camps that interest you are nearby, because many camp directors do their interviewing over Christmas vacation and have their staff hired by early spring. Even if the camp itself is near your school or home, its director may spend his winters in a distant city. If a personal interview proves to be impossible, at least follow up your written application with a telephone call.

Many camps advertise during the winter in college and big-city newspapers, such as the Sunday edition of the *New York Times.* You can find the names and addresses of all registered summer camps in the *Directory of Accredited Camps for Boys and Girls* ($2), which is available from the American Camping Association, Martinsville, Indiana. Another good source of information is *Sargent's Guide to Summer Camps and Summer Schools,* which lists the camp director, his winter address, and the camp addresses for most summer camps in the United States. Particularly useful is the section on unusual program emphasis (for example, science-oriented, work programs, music camps, and so forth), which should prove helpful to you in marketing your particular skill.

If you are baffled by the selection of camps to which to make direct application, you can apply, alternatively, through a counselor placement bureau. Such an organization will attempt to match you with a suitable camp. To obtain a list of counselor placement bureaus, write to the American Camping Association, enclosing a self-addressed, stamped envelope.

If you have decided to experiment for a summer with this civilized version of life in the woods, you should investigate each particular camping situation before accepting employment. Ask questions at your interview. Visit the camp, if possible, and contact other counselors with past experience, and former campers, if you know any. A camp with a highly stable population—where campers return year after year, followed by their little brothers and sisters, and eventually graduate to counselorships—is likely to be excellent, because such loyalty is based on repeated experiences of fun and companionship. Such a staff is obviously harder to join than that of a fly-by-night lakeside enterprise, but it is worth your effort to pursue such a position.

The following are some of the questions that you should keep in mind.

Exactly where is the camp located? In its brochure, *every* camp is "in a beautiful pine forest by a sparkling blue lake," but once you get there you may discover broken-down buildings in the wilderness. How far is the camp from civilization? When you're sick of campfire sings and mosquitoes, will you be able to escape? And will a car be necessary to do so or an aquaplane?

What duties will you be expected to perform? If you sign on as kitchen help, you may expect to peel potatoes—but is this also expected of the tennis counselor? How much free time will you be allowed? Can you expect any weekends free? This could be a problem if your boy-friend is working in a city, 200 miles away from the camp. How many children will be assigned to you? Will you be working with another counselor or will you be all alone with your group of children? Working in pairs gives you someone to talk to and the chance to take breaks during the day. How much supervision will you get? This is important if this is your first camp experience or if you resent having a camp director constantly checking up on you.

What is the social policy of the camp concerning its counselors? One junior earned $400 a month as a boating instructor at a camp but he had to keep his hair in a crew-cut for the duration of the summer. Another cheerfully accepted only $20 a week because he discovered that his camp had the advantage not only of Blue Ridge Mountain scenery but of four women counselors to every male counselor. Some camps are strictly opposed to counselor-dating, so try to get a feel for the flexibility of the social atmosphere, unless you intend to concentrate completely on sports and children for three months.

What is the philosophy of the camp? A young man once described how his parents had sent him off to camp at the age of four. A listener exclaimed, "I didn't know there *were* camps for kids that young!" "There shouldn't be," he replied. It is not likely that you will be asked to contribute your services to such an enterprise, but you should try to find out the general goals of the organizations for which you might work. "Camp philosophy" tends to be somewhat romanticized at best, but from the exaggerated words that the camp director throws at you, you may be able to find out why parents send their kids to his camp—re-member, he said the same things to them. Is the camp out to produce

America's Cup yachtsmen or Olympic riders? Does it engage in highly competitive intercamp or intercabin sports programs? This can be fine, or it can be frantic. Is the camp just supposed to give the kids a good time or does it purport to help them lose weight, build athletic prowess, or resolve their emotional problems? If so, are there professional staff members who are prepared to deal with problem children?

What kind of children does the camp attract? This is important to the satisfaction that you get from your summer. At a fresh-air camp for city children, you may find great appreciation from the campers, as well as challenges to discipline. Handicapped or disturbed children may give you a summer of exhaustion, frustration, and enormous reward. If the camp is a luxury retreat for wealthy children, you may primarily be helping rich parents who abandon their kids to you and jet off to the Aegean. These children may be spoiled—or their awareness of being dumped may make them as needy as any ghetto child. Most camps, of course, simply provide normal middle-class kids with a summer of exercise, natural surroundings, and social experience. Chances are that the references in the brochure to "character-building" mean exactly this combination of rural delights.

What is your salary? Will you be paid weekly or monthly? Pay scales vary widely—from a $100 honorarium per summer to a healthy $1,200 per season for an experienced waterfront director at an expensive camp. The highly paid camp jobs often require skill and/or experience. Waterfront counselors must have American Red Cross Senior Lifesaving certificates. In order to qualify to give out the Red Cross swimming badges, which usually go along with swimming programs, they must have the Water Safety Instructor's certificate. Information about obtaining these papers can be obtained by contacting your local Red Cross office. Each summer of counseling experience usually nets a pay increase for the counselor who sticks it out.

Can you expect tipping? At some camps, tipping is the rule and may increase the counselor's summer earnings by as much as 50 per cent in a windfall at the end of the summer. This is especially true of luxury camps. At other camps, tipping is forbidden. Be sure you know where your camp stands on this issue, in order to enable you to properly evaluate your salary. At nearly every camp, you can figure that your room and board will be paid for, when you calculate your potential summer earnings, and insurance may also be provided. Remember to count in travel and clothing expenses before you add up your profits, and consider the pocket money that you may want to squander on civilized pleasures on your rare days off.

Most of our remarks have centered around counseling experiences at private general camps. Although they are applicable to most camping situations, you should remember that organizations also run camps and may provide you with employment.

Both private and organizational camps may be centered on a special activity or goal, including baseball camps, basketball camps, tennis camps, riding camps, and sailing camps. There are work camps and travel camps, camps for young musicians, and camps for young biologists. There are camps that work on emotional, environmental, physical, and learning disabilities, camps with emphasis on the religion of the church that sponsors them and nondenominational camps that are operated under religious auspices.

Several national organizations maintain systems of general summer camps across the country. Their addresses appear at the end of this subsection, and their programs are discussed briefly here.

The Boy Scouts of America runs one of the most famous camping operations in the world. The Scouts tend to have openings for counselors experienced in administration, archery, accounting, first aid, aquatics, natural history, conservation, crafts, or youth work, and although a background in scouting is helpful, it is not required. Boy Scout Camps provide a short salaried period of precamp training and prefer to receive applications in December so that interviews may be arranged for the Christmas vacation.

The Girl Scouts of America operate over 600 camps in the nation and their counselor requirements are similar to those of the Boy Scouts. Folk and square dancing join the usual camping skills at Camp Fire Girls Camps. The YMCA and YWCA offer students employment at their many local resident and day camps, emphasizing swimming and other group activities.

Helpful Addresses

Professional Recruiting Director
Boy Scouts of America
North Brunswick, New Jersey 08902
or the director of your local Boy Scout Council

Personnel Department
Camp Fire Girls
1740 Broadway
New York, New York 10019

Recruitment and Referral Division
Girl Scouts of the USA

830 Third Avenue
New York, New York 10022
for camping brochure

National Council of YMCA's
291 Broadway
New York, New York 10007

For information on YWCA camps, contact the Executive Director or
Camp Director of the YWCA in the area where you wish to work; a
telephone directory should list the address.

Resorts and Hotels

Although resorts and hotels offer their adult clientele many of the
same advantages that camps provide for the children, resort work is a
world away from camp work for the summer employee. Above all,
resorts are far more lucrative than camps. Even those students who take
nontipping positions such as cashiers and switchboard operators can
expect to make at least $80 a week, probably with paid living expenses.
The BIG resort money, as everyone knows, is in tips. Waiters and
waitresses who work at restaurants and hotels with good food and a
large turnover of customers generally earn superb money. A waiter
whose nominal wage was $.37 an hour found that he could count on
$200 per week in stable tips. A waitress in a large seafood restaurant
reports that she cleared $120 in a five-night working week, plus the
small basic salary that the management provided.

The second major difference between resort and camp work is that
resort employees are not generally expected to share the delights of the
vacation atmosphere with the paying guests. You should not set your
heart on three months of partying at the bars and beaches that attract the
tourists. Most resort jobs involve working at night; if you get off at
10:30, after an exhausting evening of juggling trays, you may pass up
the party and the next morning's sun as well. Being a bellhop or a
waitress is hard work, and you may spend your free time quietly asleep
by the pool. One large hotel in the Catskills even bars employees from
the "customer beach," apparently for fear that contact with the working
class will contaminate the bourgeois sands. You should anticipate your
summer of resort work as a change of pace or a financial bonanza, but
don't count on three months of paid, tanned relaxation.

On the other hand, the amount of fun you can expect depends
largely upon your stamina. A thesis-weary senior may not be quite as
ready as his freshman coworker to dance in the sand all night after a full
working day. One college junior worked as head waiter in a gourmet

restaurant, which provided its help with a sumptuous dinner (the blue plate special) every afternoon before work. Stuffed with prime ribs or crab imperial, he would work steadily from 4:30 to 12:00 P.M., making as much as $100 *a night,* on the weekends. Then he would find out which one of his friends was having the evening's party; at midnight, the night was still young. The next morning he would be off early, to his full-time job (8–4) as a lifeguard on the large public beach. On his day off, he would get in some extra surfing, or hold a party himself. If you're looking for a tan and a fortune, this is the way—if you, too, have an iron constitution.

Summer resorts are the original setting of the summer romance. Most big hotels and vacation towns are swarming with student employees, and the scene after work sometimes resembles a Fort Lauderdale beach-blanket movie. There are plenty of people, and plenty to do—the surf, the movie houses, and the clubs are all yours, once your work shift is over. Not for you is the frustration of the camp counselors whose big biweekly thrill is a lift in a borrowed camp truck to a third-run film fourteen miles down the pike. Sometimes the starlight pays off for more than a vacation romance; this editor's brother met his wife in a seacoast town in Maine, where he waited on tables with the moonlighting lifeguard mentioned previously while she sold sweaters to lady tourists in a sportswear shop. So don't be too discouraged by the crushing work load assigned by your resort-town taskmaster. Generations of students have staffed these holiday spots and had a good time doing so

If this sounds like the vacation employment for you, you have several options for particular jobs.

Nontipping positions are the lowest on the ladder. Motels pay chambermaids about $12 a day, plus room, and sometimes, board. If you do get room and board, you can expect something more like a camp cabin or a dormitory than the plush accommodations that the guests enjoy. Cleaning hotel rooms is hard, fussy work, and you may be expected to work six days a week (standard resort practice for almost all jobs). Your working hours will fall during the day, so you may not see much of high noon at the beach. Although chambermaids may receive some tips, this job is generally classed with desk clerk and switchboard operator as a nontipping position; so don't expect much. Unless your hotel is enormously housy, however, these last two jobs will be more tedious than difficult. Lifeguards and beach maintenance jobs are likewise nontipping jobs. Restaurants will need assistant cooks, salad girls, hostesses, and clean-up personnel.

Tipping jobs usually require skills and/or experience. With the exception of the unskilled busboy and bellhop, which are usually positions for men under twenty-one, most of these positions are distributed by the seniority system: this year's waitress was last year's chambermaid at the same hotel, and last year's grill man is now a waiter. High school students can take advantage of this situation and get training at the same time by working as busboys. Try to pick a restaurant you enjoy and know to be profitable, so that your time investment will pay you back if you return the next year. Students who work to the top of the profit ladder often return right through graduate school. A college student can learn waiting in a skill course offered by his college or state employment service. Every dining room has its own serving system, so you will pick up variations with each job.

Men can also qualify for lucrative positions if they have some experience tending bar and are old enough to serve liquor legally (twenty-one in most states). Cocktail waitresses must also meet this age requirement, but take home plenty of tips. If you are willing to don a scanty uniform and show off your undergraduate figure, you can earn better-than-waitress' money without ever lifting anything heavier than a couple of dry martinis. The ability to play the piano in a hotel lounge will also bring you tips and high wages.

Remember that tips are a gamble. If you are going to be a waiter or waitress, be sure to ask someone who worked in the same dining room—not just the same area—how much he or she cleared in tips. As with camps, the presence of many of last summer's staff is a good sign. Tips are highest at dinner, much lower at lunchtime, and almost nonexistent at breakfast; they rise with the turnover of customers, but level off (how fast can you eat a hamburger?) and never, in a quick-meal establishment, approach the level of tips in excellent, expensive eating places. If liquor is served, tips soar—partly because the cost of drinks pads the total bill and partly because bourbon and wine tend to make the well-fed diner more generous. A restaurant that has a lot of parties and "night-out" couples is likewise a rich lode: the epithet "host" makes a man liberal with his tips. You should check that the restaurant for which you expect to work really does attract dinner customers and that your schedule ensures you dinner as well as breakfast shifts. A waiter's or waitress' basic wage is so low that tips are no luxury, but a necessity of financial life.

Even hiring for these jobs may be a gamble. Beware of a common practice of resort restaurants: namely, overhiring. These establishments take on more help than they need or intend to keep, and after a week's observation, they quietly give notice to the least efficient workers. This is a shady practice—ask veteran summer employees in the area whether your potential employer ever does this.

A final job possibility in resorts is that of sales clerk or cashier in one of the many dress shops and gift shops that spring up like mushrooms in the fertile summer seasonal atmosphere of the vacation town. These merchants sell everything from Italian dinnerware to iridescent Frisbees, and exist to urge the housewife to take home with her slippers, lamps, and bureau scarves with seashell motifs. Some of these stores sell elegant gifts and sportswear; others concentrate on doormats with the woven legend "Welcome, Y'all" or "Souvenir of your Seaside Sojourn." Whatever the quality of the merchandise, all of these stores will need sales help. Such jobs offer little chance for advancement, and the basic salary will run around $80 per week. If you return a second year or work for a particularly classy store, the salary may rise. Although there are no tips, many resort shops use a bonus system as a selling incentive. For example, a swimwear boutique might offer its girls 10 per cent commission on their individual weekly sales totaling over $200, or an automatic $10 bonus if their sales rise over the $150 mark. Often this bonus is accumulated and withheld until the end of the summer, in order to prevent the salesgirls from leaving before the season closes. Beware of the bonus system; it may work for you if you are aggressive and self-confident, but it makes for a highly competitive atmosphere among the workers, and you may be dismayed to find that pleasant coworker to be a shark when it comes to absconding with "your" customers at the point of sale. Shops that have a relaxed sales policy are easier to survive in than those where the manager is always pushing his sales stuff. You may find yourself torn between high wages and a yearning to discard your manipulative supersalesgirl pose. On the other hand, these jobs carry the usual discounts on merchandise and often have flexible hours, allowing you to spend some time in that summer sun. Sales jobs are also the resort jobs with the most human contact—a waiter cannot chat with his clientele, get to know steady customers, or meet many types of people in the way that a store clerk can, given the browsing atmosphere of most resort shops.

Once you have determined the type of work you wish to do and the resort area in which you want to work, your best bet is to apply *in person* to likely looking hotels, shops, and restaurants in that area. Written applications are often left unopened by resort managers, who frequently judge applicants primarily by their looks, personal manner, and appearance of competence and responsibility. If you would like to limit the possibilities by writing before you visit, include information about your age, your skills, and the dates that you will be available. The final chapter contains advice on applications.

You will actually do best by applying at the end of the summer *before* you wish to work, since at this time you can "case the joint" and get information from present workers that will help you decide whether to apply to a specific establishment at all. Many summer employers do not live in the resort area year-round and may not arrive there until soon before the season opens. Much hiring is done then, in May and early June, but you may not want your summer employment prospects to be in suspense that long. If you cannot apply in person, you are at a considerable disadvantage, but a letter, followed up by a telephone call, is the best procedure.

One point must be made in concluding our discussion of resort employment. These areas trade on nostalgia for childhood summers and on traditional notions of privilege and service: they are extremely conservative in their employment concepts. Such common resort job designations as sales*girl* and bus*boy* incorporate this conservatism, which maintains strict distinctions between male and female job categories. Just as the National Parks Service piously cites the rigors of physical labor and law enforcement as reason enough for their rigid limitations on jobs for women, so the mind of the resort manager and the resort patron tend to narrow the field on employment types open to each sex. It is also true that, in comparable jobs, women invariably earn less. A waiter will always clear more than a waitress, and it is the bias of the customers that they have to thank for this. These economic facts, and the atmosphere that cherishes them, will be part of your resort summer, so you should keep this information in mind if you want a resort job.

Helpful Addresses

In addition to the general directories of summer employers listed at the end of the chapter, the following publication, which appears annually in June, contains geographical listings of all the hotels and motels in the country (state-by-state and city-by-city, within states) and Canada, plus international listings. These entries mention the address, facilities, and manager of each establishment.

Hotel–Motel Directory and Facilities Guide
  published by and available from the
Hotel Sales Management Association
Suite A21
55 East 43rd Street
New York, New York 10012

Private Clubs

Private clubs often combine the advantages of camps and resorts. Two types of employment are available at private clubs during the summer. One group of jobs is connected with the primary club activities, such as golf, tennis, swimming, and sailing. The other group of jobs relates to the everyday maintenance of the club and the provision of collateral services for club members—gardeners and ground crews, restaurant help, parking attendants, and employees who safeguard clothes and valuables. The former group offers extremely lucrative jobs for the student who can teach a sport.

A sports instructor at a private club can expect to receive a base salary, some of his meals, and the opportunity to earn a considerable amount of money from private lessons. One student director of a junior sailing program at a yacht club in Texas earned $700 for the summer plus lesson fees. Tennis instructors can usually expect a minimum of $50 per week plus $3 to $5 per hour from lesson fees. Swimming instructors at private clubs usually get a minimum of $75 per week plus $2 to $4 per hour for swimming and diving lessons. Lesson fees for golf instructors range from $2 to $5 per hour. For the student with a sports skill, private clubs offer some of the best-paid summer jobs.

You should be able to get leads for jobs at private clubs from your college employment office, the college newspaper, personal contacts, organizations such as fraternities and sororities—which often keep job files—or, occasionally, from the help-wanted section of your city newspaper. Local private clubs are listed in the telephone directory, so you should be able to get information about hiring practices with a telephone call. If you are offered a job, find out whether or not lesson fees are a part of your basic salary, and make sure that you will be available for the entire season for which you are hired.

Teaching

If you are reluctant to leave the halls of ivy, even for a few months, and are interested in teaching, you have a chance to explore that profession merely by switching campuses temporarily and working as a "teaching fellow" at any one of the numerous private schools across the country that runs a summer program for secondary-school age students. Teaching fellows can be hired in any subject from astronomy to zoology, and the classes they teach are often not merely standard fare (such as modern European history or physics) but challenging courses dealing in seminar fashion with such topics as Far Eastern history, comparative economic theory, or modern psychological drama. Generally, the teaching fellow works under the supervision of a master teacher during the summer program, preparing lessons, grading assignments and, occasionally, actually giving lectures and presentations. A teaching fellow's activities also include dormitory supervision and the overseeing of one or more athletic activities. The schedule is demanding, leaving little free time. Pay is between $400 and $600 for the summer, plus your room, board, and laundry. A list of schools offering these programs and giving the director's name, address, and further information can be found in *Sargent's Guide*.

These positions provide you with an opportunity to practice teach under an experienced educator. This teaching experience is often free, because of its high school orientation, from the parochial professionalism and hyperspecialization of so much college instruction. Your pupils may be bright students seeking the challenge of college-level work or disadvantaged students who are identified and subsidized by the private program in order that they may be offered precollege training. In any case, you will probably find the campus green and patrician, the intellectual level high, the fellow workers ideal, and the students among the most exciting you will ever get. Summer teaching fellowships may, as a by-product, gain you a useful reference for later teaching, fellowship, and graduate school applications. These positions are usually open primarily to juniors, and application should be made shortly after the first of the year.

All summer teaching positions are not strictly academic. You might be able to get a job teaching sports in a baseball or basketball camp. Two students from California started their own baseball camp when they found out that the neighborhood children were dissatisfied with the one they were attending. The students contacted the parents of each of the children, and promised to pick up the children each day and provide them with a full day of instruction and activities. When "school" was over, the students had $1,000 apiece for their efforts, and the kids were looking forward to another summer of batting practice.

Social Service Jobs

Those involved in working out alternative vocations for social change, and students who are simply interested in helping other people in a direct and organized manner will find that their summer is best spent in social service. The financial reward will not be high and the work is usually demanding, but in addition to the satisfaction you receive will come a realistic, practical sense of the challenge and frustration involved in "the helping professions." Whether your struggles are over the funding of a street theater project or the freeing of an emotionally disturbed adolescent, the experiences of a summer of social service are invariably eye-opening. The wide range of possibilities in this field means that you may find work that trains you for whatever service career you have in mind.

Essentially, there are three ways of becoming involved in social service work during the summer: through private agencies, through the government, and on your own.

Many private agencies operate interesting and valuable summer programs in hospitals, settlement houses, community centers, and professional counseling services. The salary range is about the same as for federal programs, although these jobs tend to be underpaid. Employment with private agencies often involves less "busy work" and administrative trivia than government jobs do—probably because the top man on the program is usually right there within calling distance. A typical summer job with a private agency is recreation work at a settlement house, which usually involves creating and executing programs for children, who are often overwhelmingly grateful for your attention. One student, who spent a summer working with elementary schoolchildren, reports that she was the guest of honor at a summer-long string of birthday parties and that, since she lived in the neighborhood, "her" children often visited her after class.

Summer workers in service agencies are often utilized to ease the work load of professionals by easing their clerical burden. A summer typist for a large vocational service agency spent her working day with a dictaphone, not a client. But a case-aid worker for a social-work organization refused to stick with the errand-running that greeted her when her job began. She made it known to her superiors that her employment agreement was not being fulfilled, and she ended up working with children, as she had anticipated. Make sure that you are hired for satisfying work, and insist on the realization of your arrangement with the agency.

The largest source of summer employment in the field of social service is the United States government. An unstable national economy and a profound confusion of priorities in federal spending have closed down many of the programs that were begun so idealistically under the banner, "War on Poverty." But many programs still survive, and one may provide you with a summer job. The best known of the programs administered with federal money through the Office of Economic Opportunity are Head Start, the Job Corps, Upward Bound, Adult Basic Education, VISTA, Legal Service, and Community Action. In addition, hundreds of programs are designed to tackle specific regional problems.

Federal administrators usually hire residents of affected communities, not only for community organization but for all other jobs as well. Individual programs are operated on the neighborhood level by neighborhood planning-action councils or social centers. Neighborhood administration can have a positive effect on the spirit in which communities can accept federal aid: the programs belong to the communities themselves and are run by them, whereas the federal programs create new jobs for people who need them. If you are a resident of a community that receives federal aid, and particularly if you are from a low-income family, you may be able to get a job on such a program in your neighborhood. Likewise if you are on work-study, you should ask your financial-aid counselor about social-service opportunities in federal and private programs.

If you fall into neither of these categories, securing a job on a federal program will be much more difficult. The Washington Office of Economic Opportunity does little direct hiring, but it can give you the names of poverty agencies in your area. These agencies hire students for several types of summer work: administrative jobs (which are usually the best paid—up to $110 per week), secretarial work (which is a gargantuan operation in most federal programs), and some community organization posts (recreation work or tutoring, for example). If you want to work directly with people on the neighborhood level, you will probably have to go through program directors. The central agency should be able to give you descriptions of openings—or at least a list of places to apply. Write to the Office of Economic Opportunity, Washington, D.C.

Through its various bureaus, the Department of Health, Education, and Welfare also administers various social service organizations. Two of the most prominent programs are Upward Bound, a program designed to interest lower-income students in attending college and Adult Basic Education, a program designed to upgrade the learning skills of lower-income adults. Both of these programs hire college students but only through specific regional offices. To obtain a list of these local offices, write to the national director of the programs that interest you. As in the case of Office of Economic Opportunity-sponsored programs, you must apply directly to the head of the local office for which you want to work.

Salaries in federal social service jobs vary widely, not according to the type of work but according to the amount of money that the government has allotted to the program for that particular position. The salary range for these jobs is usually from $50 to $110 a week. Although finding a federal job is exhausting, the jobs themselves are usually worth it, particularly if you can work on a community level rather than in a central office. You should begin looking for these jobs early, but be prepared for delays: programs cannot hire until they are assured of funds, and funds often do not come through until long after the proposed program should have been under way. For the same reason, if you are hired early, make sure that you have not been hired *tentatively,* pending receipt of federal funds. Despite its statements to the contrary, the government is spending less on programs for social change every year, and many programs that really expect funds for summer employees find themselves without money in June—if you depend too heavily upon these programs, you may find yourself without a job.

City and state governments sometimes become involved in summer social-service activities, some of which were mentioned in the section on government jobs. Some city boards of education sponsor full or part-time summer schools and after-school programs that create paid positions for student interns. Juniors and seniors at teacher's colleges may be preferred, but usually any undergraduate who is committed to teaching as a career may be appointed. The beneficiaries of such programs may in some cases be required to be permanent city residents. Wages may be as high as $4.50 an hour. A student who has the ability to speak Spanish spent a summer deepening her social and cultural awareness while working with the Puerto Rican Forum at a salary of $90 a week in a program sponsored by the Ford Foundation of New York, in cooperation with the city.

Some colleges also run counseling, tutoring, and recreational programs for the community. An East Coast student has returned for three summers to the campus of Ohio State University, where he serves as a math tutor in a National Science Foundation program in which he had participated while a high school student. He earns $125 a week, and, because his on-campus room was arranged through the math department, his living costs are only $135 for the eight-week program. In addition, he is free to audit courses in the university's summer school. In Massachusetts, a student teacher-counselor who had volunteered for a tutoring program throughout the term was able to continue his work with the children on a full-time basis during the summer because his college provided him with a free room (no board) and a stipend of $75 a week.

This type of two-step approach to a paying job in social service is a common one. You may progress from volunteer to full-fledged employee or you may graduate from a dull routine position to a responsible one. A student who worked as a laborer during the Public Service Clean-Up that his city sponsors every summer found himself in the mayor's office the next year, supervising the entire project. He was paid $2.50 an hour for his efforts, and a good look at municipal politics and economic activities.

Many of the advantages of volunteer jobs were discussed in the chapter on Term-Time Employment. The big *dis*advantage is, of course, the fact that this sort of work will bring you no closer to the $600 that your financial-aid office may expect you to bring in every summer. If money is not a vital consideration, or if you have time free from your money-making activities, you will find that volunteer work, in addition to its intrinsic satisfaction, is your best introduction to the field of social service—both in terms of gaining skills and experience and in terms of the important contacts and "previous work" record that will be demanded in this poorly funded area in which every salaried employee must count. Private agencies have frequently established programs in which they utilize volunteer help. If you do volunteer, try to make a prior arrangement with your employer to do a specific job without pay; if you offer him no concrete expectations, the inertia of the organization may propel you toward errand-running and minor typing, the most menial work in the agency. This is no doubt worthwhile, but if you're going to be bored, you might as well be paid for it. Even salaried students sometimes have to speak out in order to break out of the bureaucratic labyrinth in these organizations, although you may find that by holding out for the payment of a token salary, you will attract the attention of the agency and encourage it to redeem its investment in you by providing you with useful work.

The federal agency ACTION now oversees the government's volunteer programs, such as VISTA. This work often proves to be a break-even experience financially, since you may receive room and board plus an honorarium to cover your out-of-pocket expenses. As in most federal social service efforts, regional programs do their own hiring. For a list of these programs, contact the Washington office of ACTION.

Your one reliable and unique source of social service jobs is your own willingness to get out and help. Perhaps you can organize a food co-op in your neighborhood or join others to run a small day-care center.

One student in Houston ran his own educational project. Funds for this work were obtained from local businessmen and from a local community service organization. He taught his pupils, who ranged in age from nine to twelve, reading skills, and felt it was the most rewarding summer he had ever had. Social service is well worth your time, both for others and for yourself—is this the summer you give it a try?

Helpful Addresses

Director, Upward Bound
Division of Student Special Services
Bureau of Higher Education
Department of Health, Education, and Welfare
400 Maryland Avenue, S.W.
Washington, D.C.

Director, Adult Vocation Programs
Bureau of Adult Vocational and Technical Education
Department of Health, Education, and Welfare
400 Maryland Avenue, S.W.
Washington, D.C.

Director
ACTION
806 Connecticut Avenue, N.W.
Washington, D.C. 20525

A list of volunteer projects and private social service agencies, some of which may take on summer help, is available from the

American Friends Service Committee
Personnel Office
160 N. 15th Street
Philadelphia, Pennsylvania 19102

The most comprehensive guide to volunteer and subsistence social service work is the book *Invest Yourself: A Catalogue of Service Opportunities.* For $1, you are provided with listings of summer and winter projects in community action, intercultural exchange, conscientious-objector alternative service, and such enterprises as work camps, in addition to traditional service programs. The range of coverage is international, with emphasis on American, Canadian, and U.N.-sponsored projects. This book is available from its publisher,

The Commission on Voluntary Service and Action
475 Riverside Drive
Room 830
New York, New York 10027

Sales Jobs

The range of employment opportunities in the sales field is a wide
one. Whether you are selling magazines, computer time, or chocolate-
covered ice cream bars, you will undoubtedly be able to make a profit if
you join the thousands of other undergraduates who sell their way
through the summer.

The most secure—and the lowest paid—sales work involves selling
in a store. Although this can be a high pressure chore in some resort
shops, as mentioned in the subsection on hotel and resort employment,
it tends to be more conducive to the maintenance of integrity and mental
health than are most door-to-door selling jobs. In addition, you can
probably count on a base salary of at least $75 a week, with a possible
bonus in the form of small commissions that may be added on as an
incentive. Your wage will, therefore, not depend directly upon how
much you hustle. A sophomore landed a job in a jewelry store on the
basis of her trustworthy reputation and honest face. At a salary of $2.25
an hour, she spent her summer selling trinkets that cost a hundred times
that much, enjoying the air-conditioning, and playing with the bright
baubles.

Clothing stores are likely to pay you less and force you to depend
more on commissions. Unless you have worked in a particular store
before, it is sometimes difficult to find a salesclerk job that lasts through
the summer; many stores take on extra help only in late July when, by
the vagaries of the fashion calendar, it is already time for the new fall
styles, despite the soaring temperatures. You might consider taking
some other short-term work for the beginning of the season, or treating
yourself to a vacation in June, and then working right up until the
beginning of the school fall term.

Sales jobs are sex-linked; women sell to women, and men sell to
men, with the sole exception that men may sell shoes to women. Master
this sexual distinction and you will see where you fit into the great
scheme of summer sales employment. If you are a college girl, you have
one more unique option; you may sell to high school girls, as a member
of the "college board" at a large department store. Nationwide fashion
magazines for young adolescents promote this selling gimmick for back-
to-school clothes, and most good-sized towns have at least one store that
participates. A group of girls from various colleges is hired to sell and
model the new fall styles and to advise customers how they can best

emulate the "campus look," as promulgated annually by the magazines in scrupulous detail.

In return for your mastery of the fall styles scene, the department store gives you its college board member, free training in buying, modeling, and store management, plus free clothes to wear on the job and to keep at summer's end, so that your "campus look" will not lapse. Any other clothes that a board member buys while working are hers at a discount, a policy that is true for almost all sales positions, not merely college boards. These sales jobs usually run for about six weeks, from late July through early September. Although the salaries are only about $70 a week, the fringe benefits are considerable and the work is much more varied than that of ordinary sales clerks. You should apply early for these jobs and arrange an interview during your spring vacation, if possible. Girls are selected, in general, from local residents or from the students at local colleges in order to aid customers in their identification with the models. You have a head start if you look nice in this year's styles, but fashion experience and poise are also important in hiring.

The most lucrative and most available sales positions open to students during the summer are of the door-to-door variety. The mechanics of this type of employment were discussed in the chapter on term-time employment, but summertime provides you with a full-time base on which to build your first million. You may make it legitimately in direct sales, but you should remember to look carefully into the product and its market before committing yourself to a sample case and order book. Take a long look, as well, at your own stamina. Trudging from door to door in July, lugging a valise full of face cream is an exhausting business, and the high-pressure sales procedure—whether it is illegal or merely intense—can wear out the sensitive and the sympathetic. There is no question but that you can earn well over $100 a week (twice that, if you are aggressive and lucky) in direct sales. It is also a fact, however, that the vast majority of student comments on this work experience were negative. Three examples are sufficient.

A junior at an Eastern women's college described her experience graphically:

> Remember the circus barker's cry, "Come one, come all!" that lured crowds into "the greatest show on earth?" Well, the barker is fading now, but his come-on still lives: commission sales agencies are using it every day.
> Prime target of the new circus, as I quickly discovered, is the college student on summer leave from the groves of academe. He (or

she) is frequently eager (did someone say desperate?) for a job. The newspaper leads are designed to catch the eye of the unwary: Interesting, Lucrative, Summer Employment for Qualified College Students.

Of course, everyone qualifies. Answering one such ad I found it promised to be as interesting as the big show ever was. Certainly, most of the other applicants (all promptly dubbed "sales trainees") were friendly, pleasant people.

As for the product we were selling, a collection of forty-odd books scaled from preschool through high school, it was excellent. And it was associated with a large, respected national company with a name to uphold. There was no hangup here; all of us were genuinely enthusiastic about the value of the program.

Problems then? For the first few days, there were none. Mainly, I guess, because for the first few days we were in the air-conditioned Boston office, learning the barker's trade ourselves.

Then we were sent out into the field, each of us with an old hand, we went through a regular selling, or, in my teacher's case, non-selling day, while we watched and learned. Even this, at the peak of an old-fashioned Boston heat wave, didn't daunt me; a bad day could happen to anyone, and I was filled with missionary zeal. So, the next day, I tried it on my own.

I might add, at this point, that more than zeal was goading me. Part of the office-manager-barker's lure was the $30.00 per sale that we received for commission. We were assured that one out of four presentations of the program led to a sale, and since we could "easily make four presentations a day," we were guaranteed $150.00 per week—more if we worked Saturdays. Great! Great!

Great?

Realism reared its ugly head only when I went out into the field alone. For the first time, I realized that the job was not as stated, to present and sell the program; the job was to get into the house. This is infinitely more difficult than it seems, for the barriers are high and many. One of the greatest being that, in the heat of summer, young mothers do not stay home waiting for the educational opportunity of a lifetime; they pile the children into a car at dawn and spend the entire day at the beach. As one nice, elderly lady explained over lemonade and cookies (for we were free to take breaks pretty much as we liked), all the young mothers in her neighborhood had formed car caravans, and regularly every morning, like departing armies, the station wagons rolled away to the sea.

That was one barrier; another was the fact that an amazing number of people will slam the door in a salesman's face as soon as they see his (her) kit. For this reason, I was advised to put the kit to one side of the door until I was admitted.

And how did I gain admittance? The standard procedure was to ring the bell and, when asked who it was, to call out "Area Check!" which sounded both official and mysterious and was the best way of getting the door opened. Immediately, with a greeting and a smile, I plunged into the spiel. Area check of all families with children under the age of twelve, and may I come in, please? This was a crucial point —if admitted, I could usually make a presentation, for which I received credit (ninety presentations a month guaranteed $300, regardless of sales; however, if anyone had made ninety presentations without making ten sales, he probably would have been fired; it was safer to count on commission!). A presentation meant a possible sale.

Frequently, the mother simply wouldn't admit me, which ended that. However, sometimes she would, and then the qualification began. Company policy dictated that the prospective buyer have a telephone (the better to dun you, my dear?) and some prospects were lost there. If the prospect did qualify, I went into the real spiel, demonstrating the illustrated broadsides—descriptive literature. This part of the program I really liked, and most of the mothers liked it too and agreed that it was wonderful but . . .

But.

Part of the program was an activity card for the children, and as I finished describing the entire program, I would whip out the contract (called a guarantee until signed on the dotted line) and say, ". . . and I can enroll Johnny in the club right now. How old did you say he was?"

Then the fight began.

Whether the mother wants to buy it or not (and I personally began to doubt that any of them did), she is not going to surrender "all that money" without a fight. It's a point of honor for any red-blooded American housewife. The struggle would go something like this:

"Oh—I have to ask my husband."

I would only be in the area for a day, and not in the evening, so I couldn't wait; I had to get her to sign then and there.

"Look," I'd say, "does your husband believe in education?"

"Well, sure, but—"

"Then there's nothing to worry about. Just sign here."

"But all that money—"

"That's why we have the quarter bank, just a quarter a day, sign right here."

"No."

Our office manager had said, "Let them say 'no' five times." The idea was that they gave in before the fifth "no." Unfortunately, they didn't.

It is here that character plays a vital part—here that the salesmen are separated from the mere "college kids." I soon realized that I was irredeemably a college kid, and having had time to analyze the causes of my failure, I have managed to come up with the following:

I was soft. When I met a mother with six children, I bled for her, having been raised in a large family myself. This was very bad, however, since I couldn't, then, press her very hard.

I was sensitive. When doors slammed in my face, I tended to take

it personally; ditto the snarled "no." Consequently, after the fifth no,
I was more than ready to give in.

I was tired. Walking from house to house in the heat wore me out.

All of these things, together with the fact that I made only one
fluke sale (husband was home and wanted it; no selling involved) during my time there, prompted me to resign and seek salaried work.

Don't mistake me; there were some salesmen who averaged five
and six sales a week; average sales run to two or three. The determined, aggressive, strong individual can—and did—make excellent
money in commission sales. It is interesting work; if I were an heiress,
I might do it for fun. But I needed money and decided I would never
make it through commission sales.

I turned in my sales kit and left the Big Show to others.

The experience of this student points out some of the tribulations of
a door-to-door sales job, particularly for a person whose temperament
balks at customer manipulation and ambiguous ethics.

A sophomore who sold brushes in two rural towns and the surrounding farm country recalls that she began work just a week after answering
a newspaper advertisement for the company. Although she was promised a 40 per cent commission on her sales, this amounted to only about
$20 a week in wages since, after her initial week of training, she was
sent to cover a territory where another of the company's salesmen had
canvassed only four weeks previously. Unfortunately for her, her company was reputable—the brushes did not wear out *that* fast! She did not
find much of a market, but she did discover that "the farm people told
me everything about themselves—things they never would have dreamed
of telling their families—because they figured they'd never see me
again." Even this by-product did not distract her from a nagging feeling
of earning her living by exploiting others. When she quit at the end of
the summer, she reported the following qualifications to be necessary for
success at direct sales: "guile, lack of conscience, the ability to sell your
soul, and a capacity for living with guilt."

A black student in California had a more complicated experience
with a commission sales company, which demonstrates how important it
is that you judge the ethical-legal standards of your employer before you
accept a job. He explains:

> In the course of my summer employment as a researcher and
> investigator for California Rural Legal Assistance, I had the oppor-
> tunity to engage the nefarious forces of social injustice as an under-
> cover investigator. CRLA is an Office-of-Economic-Opportunity spon-
> sored legal services program for rural poor people in California.
> For this particular assignment I got myself hired as a camera sales-
> man for a company that one of our lawyers was intending to use for

consumer fraud. One of the salesmen of the company had visited a cleaning woman at 10:30 in the evening and "sold" her a "photographic program" for $500, despite the fact that she earned $35 a week, had no husband, supported three children, and was on welfare.

On the basis of the sales training program I took part in and observations of a few of the salesmen out in the field, I gathered enough information to provide a strong case against the camera company.

The staff trainer began his lesson by stressing the importance of presenting yourself as an advertising researcher, not a salesman, when you came to the door. One of the entries we were taught was: "Excuse me, Madame—are you in the middle of dinner, or may I come in?" If she says "yes," you say "thank you," and walk in. If she says "no," you say "good," and walk in.

In demonstrating the camera, we were instructed to stress its light weight "I want you to feel how light this camera is." You hand them the camera, pressing it down into the customer's hand firmly with your thumb, and then, gently slip your thumb off the top of the camera so that it and the customer's hand rise, involuntarily. "See— isn't it light?" But, we were not selling just a camera. We were selling a "photographic program," which included $700 worth of discount stamps for developing rolls of film. With these stamps, a roll of film could be developed (only by the company selling the program) for $3.95 instead of $4.95. The whole package sold for only the cost of a Class A daily newspaper bought for ten years. But, if the customer elected to buy the package over a ten-year period, there was a small $240 service charge added to the basic price of the program.

As if to add insult to injury, we were instructed not to accept the orders of any customer unless they could furnish us with the names of five people to whom they would be willing to recommend this camera. Every lead that paid off for a salesman brought a $100 commission with it, and many of the salesmen did quite well. In showing the camera to the most reputable retailers in Los Angeles, I found that its real value was appraised at anything from $0 to $79. I also found that neither the Federal Trade Commission nor the Better Business Bureau had approved the program's sales brochure, as we had been told.

If I had been working for this company and not against it, I would have made a very substantial weekly salary; but, I don't think that I will ever find myself working for a company with such low ethical standards. The company is being brought to court for consumer fraud on the basis of what I learned. My summer job with the CRLA paid $75 a week plus expenses and has gotten me excited about law school.

These stories indicate a skepticism of selling, although in fact, many students have made more than $3,000 during a summer selling cutlery or dictionaries or apartment rentals. If you decide to try your luck at commission sales, you should be able to find a worthwhile product to sell from your student employment office or from the classified ads in any city newspaper. Encyclopedias and cosmetics are popular items for student salesmen. Often overlooked but especially lucrative are positions as ice cream vendors or milkmen. You should try to find a reputable firm with a reasonably useful product. It is hard enough to sell brooms and mops, which people *need;* your chances of selling enough hideous plastic figurines to make a living wage are infinitely small.

In most door-to-door sales work the salesman covers a large residential area to make a small number of sales. The salesman who shows a product to large businesses covers a selected market; he should be able to make a sale at almost every presentation. Office machines and supplies, new items of interest to doctors and dentists, and computer-related products all have large markets to service and require trained salesmen to contact their business and professional clientele. These highly sophisticated sales jobs are, of course, harder to find than ordinary door-to-door work. You will have a much better chance of getting one if you apply to a company in a field where you already have some technical knowledge—knowing how a photocopier works is obviously the best way to get a job selling photocopiers. Salaries for this type of sales work tend to be higher and more secure than for door-to-door sales.

Jobs in Business

Although most businesses are permanent, year-round enterprises with permanent employees, some establishments hire temporary student help in the summers to replace those employees who are on vacation. In some industries—construction, European travel, and popsicles, for instance—the market is increased during the summer. A few businesses still hire students with a basic interest in encouraging them to enter the field after college, but the recent state of the economy has not left many salaries begging, nor much executive funding for public-relations hiring programs.

The most predictable summer jobs are the clerical ones. No matter how it fluctuates, the ebbs and flows of the economy always seem to involve a flood of typists, file clerks, receptionists, key punch operators, and people to preside over office machines. Even if a company is holding its Giant Going-Out-Of-Business Sale, it is probably hiring typists to get out the bankruptcy notices. Counter clerks to take orders and distribute services are also in demand at travel agencies, laundries, banks, and assorted small businesses.

In theory, business offers a wide variety of summer jobs, ranging from white-collar trainee to production-line worker. These jobs are still available in isolated instances, although widespread unemployment has wiped out many positions that were once filled by students. If you apply for unskilled or semiskilled jobs, you should saturate the market with applications in the hope of finding one or two leads. During periods of economic growth, students have found work plentiful in retail outlets, chemical and heavy manufacturing industries, railroads, and food-packing companies. The number of these summer positions may rise again as economic times improve. One junior with some past experience in railroad work did obtain a summer job as a train conductor in New Jersey at a salary of $4.25 an hour. Although his work week ran to sixty hours or more, he enjoyed his job and the variety of people he met through it enormously.

Some small businesses will hire you for your manual skill. A freshman with experience in simple wiring and electromechanics earned $2.10 as an electrician's assistant for a contractor—however, the wiring to be done was in greenhouses, which were steamy and suffocating in late August. A junior who could run an adding machine landed a job on a day's notice, when the accountant for a small insurance agent was taken ill. This job paid $3 an hour in an air-conditioned office. Skills involved in manufacturing and building trades may only benefit you if you join the relevant union. Don't hesitate to do so, if you can. Union shops generally pay higher wages, and the dues are recouped in wage benefits, even in a single summer's employment.

Academic skills will assist you in your job-finding only to a limited extent. If your major in science or sociology has led you to a knowledge of computer programming, you can undoubtedly market this skill to private companies. One student worked for a securities firm during the term and continued as a computer programmer full-time in the summer at a salary of $12.79 an hour. A psychology major found that his computer skills could secure him a $3.50 an hour position as a systems analyst, and the experience of this summer job led, in turn, to a term-time job with a law school computer center. Engineers and mathematicians may also find their skills to be of direct use in industry. English and economics majors, on the other hand, are assured of few jobs, but most employers in business feel that experience in either of these areas is a valuable asset, and will count it in your favor. If you can combine such a background with a more specific skill, you will have a better chance at the low echelon, "white-collar" jobs. An English major with secretarial skills worked as a reader for a New York literary magazine, screening manuscripts and typing up her comments. One sophomore combined the knowledge he had gained from an elementary course in economics with his writing ability to land a job writing stockholders' pamphlets concerning the financial plans and status of a large manufacturing concern.

The nature of many industries is such that they are interested not in any particular skill or academic major, but rather in a variety of personal characteristics. Advertising agencies seek imagination, nonconformity, and artistic and writing skills. A legal office may hire its researchers on the basis of their diligence and respect for detail. Erratic brilliance may appeal to a design firm, but not to an accounting service. If you can anticipate the qualities, skills, or experience that your potential employer is seeking, you should by all means emphasize them in your interviews and résumé—but only to the extent that you actually possess them.

In addition to the clerical, manual, and technical positions, business offers a limited number of openings in management training programs. These are scattered and difficult to enter; their existence depends more upon the size and philosophy of the business than on the type of the industry, and all such programs have suffered during the recent economic decline. The financial sector—banking, insurance, brokerage houses, the Federal Reserve System—offers the largest number of possibilities. Juniors are preferred for these positions, and personnel managers tend to emphasize personal qualities, rather than academic distinction, in the chosen few. Motivation, intelligence, interest in the company or field (as evidenced by courses, hobbies, and previous summer jobs), and *proven* leadership ability (as demonstrated in college activities) are the factors that are often cited as influencing their hiring. You certainly have a better chance to be hired if you can demonstrate an acquaintance with the company during your interview.

Management traineeships may currently be mainly memories, but they are likely to be widely reinstated during the economic upswing, particularly since fewer college graduates are seeking jobs in industry. Should you land a traineeship, you can expect around $125 for a long week of more than eight hours a day. Your work will probably be interesting and may include travel—management wants to lure you toward permanent employment. You can, at any rate, count on a position of insight into a company, an industry, and perhaps the American capitalist system.

Despite the bleak general outlook of U.S. business and the dwindling number of summer job opportunities that it offers, there is always one business that has a place for you—the one that you run yourself. If you operate an enterprise during the school year, you should consider plying your trade with the summer school students. They, too, will rent refrigeraters, need help in moving their accumulated possessions, and wolf down hamburgers at your student grill. You might even start up a business directed toward the summer-school market; a fan rental agency, a bus service to the nearest beach, or even an extra cold drink machine.

Students who worked for college or student agencies during the term can often continue their jobs through the summer, although these are usually part-time positions and are best combined with another job or a summer school program. A freshman, who had learned bartending at a student agency-sponsored course in November, worked on summer weekends, clearing $2.80 an hour in wages, plus $5.00 a night in reliable tips. He found his job pleasant, with large supplies of good times, free liquor, and interesting people. A student who worked on the dorm crew during his first year kept his job, at $3 an hour throughout the summer session. He found the work far easier than it had been during the winter and that he had a great deal of free time after his assigned areas were cleaned each morning.

Even if you don't wish to stay on campus all summer, you can make a personal business work for you. In an earlier section, we mentioned students who had created a baseball camp to meet the needs of neighborhood kids. Another student, with some capital, simply *bought* himself an established baseball camp and ran it for the summer. He had previously been a counselor there, and took up an option on the establishment when the previous owner decided to sell. Although he worked long hours, seven days a week, this student had his room and board paid for and, when he resold the camp at the summer's end, he had a tidy profit of $2,000 to show for his vacation of speculation and sport.

One sophomore and his brother combined in a summer-long business partnership as asphalt driveway sealers. They had past experience as employees of a professional firm and were confident that they could do an excellent job at low rates. They distributed leaflets to advertise their services and even made door-to-door requests for jobs. As they accumulated a few customers, these references and the customers' own recommendations to their friends netted the brothers enough work to keep them busy until mid-September. They each made close to $500 a month—more if business was good and the weather stayed on their side—and each figured his average hourly salary, based on his profit-share, to be at least $4.

A business begun in the summer may go back to school with you. A California student started a local flea market and rummage exchange, starting with the disused contents of his own attic and garage. The market caught on, becoming a sales outlet for sandals, candles, jewelry, and other products of neighborhood artisans. When he went to college in the fall, he took the idea with him—an idea whose profits ended up putting him through school.

Creative Jobs

If you have a special interest or skill, you may be paid to develop it over the summer. If your specialty is artistic or academic, this section may give you some ideas of how to market it. Creative jobs are harder to find and often pay less than less interesting jobs. But you may be willing to make the sacrifice in order to win a job you like, a chance to learn, and experience toward a future career.

Summer theaters need stage hands, lighting assistants, costume designers, make-up artists, assistant directors and producers, extras, box-office assistants, and publicity directors. These jobs usually don't pay well, but for the student who is interested in the theater, they are an exciting and invaluable experience. Some college theaters rely exclusively on students for their summer staff, giving students the more exciting jobs that usually go to guest stars, designers, and other professionals in commercial summer theaters. Theaters in resort towns pay about $50 a week to their summer help plus room, board, and the chance to step into stardom as an understudy to an ailing Camille or Stanley Kowalski. One student started her own summer theater. She recruited a company of twenty-five at her university and appointed a reading committee, which proposed four plays, including one by Aristophanes and one by Tennessee Williams. Her productions played to full houses, and the reviews were full of praise. Backed originally by local businesses, she finished the summer with a financial gain and in an excellent position to qualify for a highly skilled job the following summer.

If you are interested in drama but need a more secure income, you should try the local radio or television station. A student with assertiveness and a third-class radio license can often find a job as a summer disc jockey. One girl announced the news, engineered her own shows, played pop records, worked in a few commercials each hour—and earned $95 a week.

Newspapers need good reporters, but they usually expect you to establish your credentials before they hire you. You can prove your worth by demonstrating service on your high-school or college newspaper, or by submitting one or two published articles. If you have no experience whatever, you can submit a short piece to the editor. A junior who had done occasional free-lance work for a local newspaper got a full-time summer position as a reporter, at $2.50 an hour, on the strength of these examples of his work.

A student who was one of eight summer trainees at a Boston newspaper said that he began his summer at the Day City Desk, where he sat behind a typewriter, took calls from correspondents, and rewrote their reports into stories. Occasionally he was allowed to research his own articles. Later in the summer, he covered the beat with reporters and photographers at City Hall, the State House, Municipal Court, Police headquarters, and other focal points of the city. He was paid between $75 and $85 a week, depending upon whether he worked the day shift or the night shift.

Other jobs in journalism are available to the beginner. Some reporters are paid by the article rather than by time spent in the office. One student in North Carolina added to his regular summer earnings by writing interviews for the local newspaper. He spent only four or five hours on this job each week, but he was paid $5 to $15 per article and received good writing experience.

Another way to break into journalism is to take a job as a copy boy for the editorial board of a large city newspaper. These jobs pay between $50 and $80 per week, and the enterprising student can use the opportunity to cover minor stories, particularly when more important news is drawing the attention of the reporters.

If you are quick with phrases—and particularly if you can combine your writing skill with an ability to use photographs and create attractive layouts—you should consider becoming a summer ad man. The best way to get the necessary skills for this job is probably to survive a part-time apprenticeship with an advertising agency during the school year.

Advertising agencies also hire commercial artists, as do magazines, department stores, and many businesses. This kind of job may not strike you as "real art," but unless you are an established artist, people are much more likely to pay you for drawing what they need—for example, fashion sketches, technical drawings, or advertising posters—than for creating what you want. A delightful summer art job is teaching art to schoolchildren. Unlike candidates for most summer teaching jobs, full-fledged art teachers often don't have to be college graduates. If you can qualify as a teacher, rather than an aide, you will be able to do whatever you want with your class, and you will probably have enough time left over to pursue your own interests as well. Likewise many books are being written at your college or university. You may be able to work with a professor or local author as his illustrator. You should also check publishing houses.

If your interests are primarily academic, you may never have to leave the ivory tower at all during the summer. Faculty members with government or private foundation grants often hire students as research assistants. This means that you will spend your summer in the library, in an office analyzing data, out in the field collecting material, or, particularly if you are in the natural sciences, in a laboratory. Although many research jobs require research experience and knowledge of a particular field, even the inexperienced student should not despair; often the material with which the student will have to deal is so specialized that the professor doesn't expect to find anyone who knows about it. He will hire a student who seems bright and interested, and then train him. This practice is especially common in fields where competing theories are being investigated. The professor would rather indoctrinate a completely ignorant student than work against the preconceptions of the "mistrained" assistant.

Research jobs are often listed with the student employment office. If you really know what you are looking for, you should approach the faculty member or department head of your choice. Your chances will be much better if you have worked for the department or professor during the term. Finally, an imaginative advertisement placed in the college newspaper may attract a faculty member who is looking for summer help but has not yet advertised himself.

A senior with a background of sociology, history, and political science worked as a library researcher on a professor's book for two summers. His initial wage was $3 an hour, but it went up as his familiarity with the material—and usefulness to the professor—increased. But a research job does not necessarily condemn you to the stacks. A sophomore who had been hired to research day-care schemes for a social service agency in Philadelphia found herself assisting with the setting up of actual centers, as a summer project. In addition to her library work, she hired staff, consulted child-care specialists, and worked with children once the centers were established. Her summer experience provided her with material for an independent study thesis the next fall.

Research jobs need not necessarily be relevant to your own background or interests. A psychology major at a California college returned to her home town on the East Coast for summer vacation. A friend, who was a graduate student at the university in that Eastern town, heard about an opening for a lab assistant on the staff of a Nobel Prize-winning biochemist. She arrived for her interview looking pretty in a peasant blouse (as advised by the graduate student), and prepared to slightly exaggerate the extent of her laboratory and science experience. The job was hers—at $2.50 an hour, with long tea breaks and the flexibility to put in her working time whenever she wished (for example, 9–5, or 10–6, or 8–4, and so forth). Since her primary interest was not biology, she found the work rather monotonous, but she still picked up some interesting facts, shared news of forthcoming parties with the entire biology department, and guaranteed herself a steady wage in air-conditioned laboratories. A premed student might have been in seventh heaven—but it didn't take premed training to secure the job. Private institutes also present opportunities for paid research. The American Cancer Society, for example, runs a junior fellowship program through its Massachusetts Division, in which students work with senior investigators on problems in cancer research. A peasant blouse alone will not land you this job.

Casual Jobs

If you are reluctant to commit yourself to a permanent position— because of claustrophobia, boredom, the desire to travel, or a short attention span—and still need to earn money, a series of casual jobs is your compromise solution. There are thousands of job possibilities in this category, since a casual summer job is almost anything that an employer is willing to pay someone else to do for him on a one-shot basis. You may take over as a garage mechanic for a week while the regular employee is on a camping trip. You may mow a suburban lawn, tend an urban terrace, or weed a rural radish crop. You might be a substitute lifeguard in Oregon one week, wash cars in northern California the next week, and lead a fishing expedition in the state of Washington the following week. You might scare crows off a cornfield in British Columbia. Short-term jobs are easy to pick up on and easy to get out of. The employer hires you because you're there, and he won't take the time to search for someone better qualified. Some casual job possibilities were mentioned in the term-time employment chapter—but your actual range of potential short-term jobs is limited only by your skills, your stamina, your contacts, and your willingness to work.

The student employment office at your college probably operates throughout the summer session; you should try it if you are looking for employment cleaning, painting, typing, tutoring, or moving furniture. Manpower, Inc., is another dependable source of short-term jobs. Each morning the unemployed gather at the break of day at the local Manpower office, to be assigned to eight hours worth of clerical or unskilled labor. The wage is not much more than the legal minimum, but the jobs are there when you need them. If the work is hard, console yourself with the thought that you won't be doing it for long. One Manpower employee spent a day knocking the roots off old potatoes to make them look young, and packing the renaissance spuds in new bags. Another employee found himself with a full week's assignment milking scorpions.

If you have sound clerical skills, Kelly Girls and similar local temporary help agencies will place you in more stable casual jobs at higher salaries. In the summer, these clerical agencies specialize in substituting their clients for vacationing secretaries. Sex is no object—men as well as women are hired, without discrimination. Those who have tried this service report that you can spend the summer moving from job to job, quitting when you're bored, and making fairly high wages—over $100 a week. The money varies with the secretary's experience and the job to which he/she is assigned, but you should remember that these placement agencies are generally interested only in skilled persons, who can accurately type at least 50 words per minute and, preferably, take shorthand.

Jobs, Jobs, Jobs

In our research for this chapter, hundreds of students from all parts of the country were asked about their summer employment experiences. They reported on the types of jobs they had held, the locations, and the duties involved. They provided us with information on wages, tips, and hours, job requirements, and advantages. They let us know how they heard about jobs, how they landed them, and whether they led to future employment.

Much of this material has been incorporated into the specific discussions of employment areas, presented earlier. Similar research contributed to earlier chapters of this book, and some of the job-finding hints will be passed on in "Making It," the final chapter. A wide selection of material, however, seemed unclassifiable within the area that was previously discussed and is presented in this subsection and the two that follow. These are, in a sense, the central portions of this book, for they best reflect the actual experience of students looking for summer work in the present economy. For the most part, the student reports will speak for themselves. In this subsection, we will try to bring you the good news.

Satisfying summer jobs are as various as the needs and tastes of the people who hold them. A junior with shipboard yearnings packed his copy of *Moby Dick* and spent a summer sailing the North Atlantic as a seaman on a large freighter. He received room and board, plus $100 a month in wages, and praised the asceticism of the sailor life—although he had not expected air-conditioning in the galley. A freshman, describing her $2.42 an hour position as a dime-store cashier, seemed to be referring to a monotonous change-making chore—but to her, it was fun and easy, with rich opportunities for meeting people. A student who had once bagged groceries for a supermarket chain worked for a summer wrapping meats in one of their stores for $2.02 an hour—not enough to purchase many of those prime porterhouse steaks. But the company had a scholarship program for its employees, and his summer's work led him to several hundred dollars extra in benefits toward his tuition expenses.

A student who was majoring in psychology and looking for practical experience in counseling found his career plans crystallizing around clinical psychology when he took a $3 an hour position as a psychiatric aide in a South Carolina hospital. He found the system of patient care and therapy everywhere deficient, and the shock of his eye-opening contact with the realities of hospital administration was balanced only by the rewards of his success in working with individual patients.

Priding himself on his ability to talk fast, a junior answered a newspaper ad for telephone solicitors and wheedled his way into a $3 an hour job, at the interview. He was shocked at first by the company's sales techniques, which seemed to him unethical and which he later learned were illegal. "Be prepared for your worst dreams about telephone soliciting to come true," he advises other students applying for similar positions. But he maintains that his employment was an invaluable lesson in "the evil of putting monetary considerations before human ones." Although this attitude soon got him fired, he recalls this job warmly as "a great radicalizing experience."

A sophomore worked on a Montana farm for $1 an hour, plus a bed in the hayloft, over the cows, and all the country food he could eat. He worked outdoors all day and lived as a part of the farm family. When he returned to his Chicago college in the fall, he was not much richer but he was healthy, relaxed, and content.

By passing by every day until the company needed help, a senior landed a job in an Alaskan salmon cannery. The wage was $2.50 an hour, and he reports that the only requirements for the job were that an applicant be "crazy and have a bad nose." Aside from the smell of the fish, this job was ideal for him, since he could work his own hours and live in Alaska, a state he had always wanted to visit but would have been forced to leave had he not found work. He had expected to stand on an assembly line as thousands of tins passed by, but in fact he ended up with a variety of tasks including unloading boats, loading freezers, driving and repairing trucks, and sorting and boxing fish. His earnings financed his Alaskan stay and travels, and he even cleared a little pocket money for the fall.

A freshman, bumming his way along the East Coast, found a seaside town where he thought he'd like to spend some time. He cleaned sail-boats part-time, at $2 an hour, to finance a summer of loafing in the sand.

You, too, may be lucky enough to find a job that dovetails with your personal requirements—be they stimulation or lack of it, travel, money, or novelty. For every student who settles down to satisfying work in June, however, there are five who are stoically prepared for a summer of typing or making change, and a couple of luckless classmates whose every effort has, despite themselves, landed them with three months of anticipated drudgery.

Jobs?

A Minnesota sophomore, frustrated in his month-long attempt to secure summer work, applied to an employment agency in his home town. A day later, he was pumping gas for the service station they had sent him to (at a 10 per cent commission). This student's wage was $1.60 an hour, and he describes his required skill for the job: "I wasn't blind." Although slow moments allowed him the consolation of working on his own car and the occasional theft of gas or oil, he advises students considering this type of work to "pass it up—unless they're desperate."

House painting was the summer job which fell to a Louisiana junior, who had also begun his employment search late in the season. He was paid $3.25 an hour for a long, hard work day, and his suggestion to other students seeking such a job was, "Don't." This negativism, in the face of a decent wage, perplexed us until he was asked whether his summer job had any advantages (social, career, academic, humani-tarian, other). His reply? "Academic. How many bones can be broken if a 180-pound man falls on his left shoulder from the thirteenth rung of a 17-foot ladder after launching his body with a twisting motion?" We hope his earnings covered the hospital bill.

A senior who was lucky enough to have a hack and chauffeur's license decided to put them to work as a taxi-driver in a large eastern city. He answered an ad in the local paper, convinced his employer of his general knowledge of city streets and public buildings, and took off—at $2.25 an hour, plus around $50 in tips for a part-time schedule. Aside from his anxiety about the frequent muggings and robberies of taxi-drivers in his town, this student found his clientele and the shiftless quality of his employment depressing, and he quit to work in a manufacturing company.

A student who earned $1.65 an hour delivering soft drinks states that he got the idea to apply for the job because he passed the soft-drink plant every time he went to town. He cut his hair short and convinced the personnel manager of the bottling company that he needed the money to pay his debts. Although the job turned out to be more or less what he had expected—hard physical labor, plenty of free soft drinks— the hours were incredible: twelve to sixteen hours a day. This sounded like a nightmare until a penciled description of the student's background, at the bottom of his interview sheet, changed our perspective. It said "no scholarship—heir to $2,000,000 pharmaceuticals fortune."

Whatever his reasons, this student chose not to turn to his captain-of-industry father for a $9 an hour position packaging pills or working out color schemes for capsules. You, too, can tackle the sickly summer job market on your own, but our best advice to you is to exploit your contacts for all they are worth. Your uncle John, your cousin Frank, your dentist, roommate, roommate's fiancée's brother, and high school phys-ed teacher are all important sources of job information, but when it comes to the reality of summer employment, the best jobs belong to Daddy.

The Pop Job

Freshman makes $5.75 an hour as steelworker's apprentice! Junior clears $7.50 an hour on heavy construction job! Southwestern student earns $5 an hour building municipal offices! Sophomore steelworker lands wage of $185 a week and senior earns $230 a week as a summer steelworker!

These joyful exclamations all reflect real student experiences in summer employment, and we only wish that we could have begun this chapter with an enthusiastic introduction, describing how initiative, skill, and perseverance had obtained these superb salaries for deserving students. Worthy young men they may well be, but their aptitude and attitude are beside the point when it comes to discussing their success in landing summer jobs. In every one of these cases, the student was hired by his own father. Steel and construction magnates appear to send a great many sons to college and they don't forget them when the summertime building boom rolls around. What is more, not a single student—of the hundreds we interviewed—had landed a high-paying job in the industrial or building trades without a close personal contact, and eight times out of nine, this contact was Pop.

Your position on this fact will vary primarily with the pull-potential of your own Pop. If he runs a tree nursery, and you're allergic to pine pollen, you lose. If he's an ornithologist, and you can't stand birds or if he runs a clothing store, and you can't abide the idea of selling sport coats for the sixth consecutive summer, you're out of luck. If he works for Paramount as a movie director, and you want to work in films, you win in a big way.

Unfortunately, there is not much that we can tell you about getting the most summer employment mileage out of the fact that your father owns a construction firm, your uncle John manages a Broadway theater, your cousin Frank is ambassador to Sweden, and your roommate's fiancée's brother is looking for extras to jet to the site of his newest film, set on location on the French Riviera. If you can't figure it out, none of this chapter has probably helped you much. We do urge you, however, to consider your contacts carefully and not to hesitate to utilize whatever pull you may be blessed with.

Think about the job you want, and perhaps a helpful contact will come to mind. You'd love to work outdoors, with animals—isn't your aunt Millie's next-door-neighbor married to a veterinarian? What about your father's cribbage partner—doesn't he live across the road from a horse farm? Wasn't your biology teacher just mentioning last week that the University Agricultural Extension was looking for summer help? Better still, talk about your job aspirations with anyone who will listen—friends, relatives, professors, classmates. If you're looking for summer research work, a teaching fellow may know which professor is seeking an assistant or a sophomore down the hall may remind you that his uncle's chemical plant hires student trainees. A contact through your roommate's father is almost as valuable as your own father's pull—and perhaps you can pay him back someday.

Many students, especially those who don't get along spectacularly at home, or who are especially conscious of independence, draw back from exploiting nepotism to gain summer employment. They are reluctant to sell themselves or to take unfair competitive advantage, or to sidestep the test of their own *individual* ability to land a job. These are perfectly acceptable and respectable attitudes, and we certainly do not urge any student to adopt any idea or behavior, simply for the sake of gaining employment, which goes against his or her conscience. However, we must offer the realistic advice that you should exploit your connections to as great an extent as it is comfortable for you to do so. Most people—not just students on summer vacation, or students looking for construction work—do land their jobs through contacts, to one degree or another. If you ignore your own contacts, you will be putting yourself at a *dis*advantage, compared to the rest of the unemployed.

Some students don't seem to have much luck, even if they *do* use pull. A young man who attended college in Connecticut worked during the summer as a laborer for the buildings and grounds department of a southern university. He worked operating forklifts, tractors, sod-cutters, dump trucks and other light machinery and vehicles thirteen hours a day in an all-out effort to resod the practice football field before the team returned in the fall. For this he received $1.65 an hour—but he doesn't seem to be conscious of any discrepancy between the work and his wages. "I so impressed my employer," he reports, "that I will be rehired next summer!" And how did he pick up this windfall in the first place? "My father is chairman of the science faculty there."

Another student lovingly described his two years as a municipal employee in a Midwestern town—$1.65 the first year, with a dime raise the succeeding summer. His first vacation was spent at the city dump; the next year, he graduated to painting curbs and street lines, cleaning alleyways and picking up trash. The source of this ideal job? "Pull. My mother and father were leading Democrats, and we had a Democratic mayor."

If Pop *can* get you a position, and you're willing to let him help you, try to make the most of this stroke of luck. Humility may dictate that a summer as a hod carrier at $4.90 an hour is a dream to be seized—but if you have a chance at being a bricklayer's assistant, at $3.80 an hour, consider it. Such training is hard to find and especially hard to arrange to be *paid* to acquire, and it could lead to future employment independent of Pop's contacts. If your father is the director of an art museum in upstate New York, you may get a fascinating position leading children's tours or coordinating nonprofit money-raising efforts for the acquisitions fund, or mounting an exhibition of contemporary graphics. Or, you could ask him to use his influence to help you work in a more modest position—perhaps taking entrance tickets or selling art postcards—in the museum run by a colleague of his in western Canada, an area that you've always wanted to visit. You could also do clerical work in a busy and successful gallery on Madison Avenue, which your father often deals with while representing the museum.

Mom Jobs?

If we can devote pages to the Pop jobs, where are the female equivalents? This is such a good question that it is bitter to have to record the extremely poor answers that the American economy offers us.

It is a fact that, although you are remarkably lucky if your father is a construction tycoon, you are both lucky and remarkable if your mother is one. Most positions of responsibility and high salary in American business and industry have simply never fallen to women, for a variety of reasons. You may, on the other hand, find your mother's pull helpful if she is a professional. Female nurses and surgeons may influence a hospital department to find a niche for you: one sophomore got a position at the admitting desk in a large clinic, at $3.10 an hour, partially on the strength of his mother's status as staff dermatologist. If your mother is a teacher, a social worker, a psychologist, or a scientist, she may help you to find a summer position in her program or project. *All* contacts should be explored, but it is simply true that you are more likely to get summer leads from your roommate's fiancée's brother than from your roommate's fiancée's sister or aunt or mother.

It is likewise true that female students invariably earn less, overall, than their male counterparts in the summer job market. Rare is the tycoon father who signs his daughter on for the summer construction crew at $7.50 an hour—and no such lucrative alternatives as physical labor and skilled building trades are offered to women undergraduates. There is virtually *no* legal employment open to a female college student that will bring her anything close to $7.50 an hour, if she wants to keep her integrity intact.

Individual women will undoubtedly earn outstanding salaries, but as we pointed out in the subsection on resort employment, equal pay is often denied for equal work; waiters are tipped more heavily than waitresses, and this general trend is present throughout the American economy. Parents may compensate for—or feed into—this trend, by expecting their sons to contribute substantially to their own college expenses, whereas a daughter's education is more completely subsidized. As long as tuition costs and living expenses remain the same for male and female undergraduates, the latter must make their financial plans with a realistic sense of the limitations that the economy is likely to impose on their prime income source: summer earnings.

* * *

Jobs are scarce and wages are down, compared to the lush summer pastures of the employment market in the late 1960's. The undergraduate seeking vacation employment in the 1970's will, at least until the economy perks up, have to bring to bear on this task all of his intelligence, skills, determination, personal contacts, and capacity to resist frustration. But repeated, thoughtful effort should pay off, even if your father is not a corporate giant. We will close on a hopeful note:

A New Hampshire sophomore was out of work. It was late in May, and he had postponed his job search until the eleventh hour. His father was an insurance agent, with no contacts that his son wanted to pursue. The student's grades were fair, his clerical skills nonexistent. No one was hiring. He had to make money to keep up his scholarship. What was he to do?

After several weeks of disconsolate pavement-pounding, he wandered out to the local racetrack, which had just opened its late summer season for trotting horses. The place seethed with customers. Perhaps? *Yes.* The track management offered him a job as a window attendant, passing out tickets and collecting bets. It paid only $1.80 an hour, but it was better than nothing.

The next summer he stopped by again—earlier, this time, expecting to be rehired for the window position. But his summer of previous employment stood him in good stead. Having observed his honesty and calm the previous year, the management absolved him from any more steamy hours of wrangling with unhappy bettors. He was given a new position, at $6 an hour, to conform with its significant responsibility. For the next two summers, he spent his vacations in the inner, air-conditioned corridors of the track office—lugging endless armloads of money from the betting windows to the vaults. It may not have been *his* fortune, but that initial excursion to the track really paid off.

* * *

Doubtlessly you will, at some point during your college career, feel a yen for faraway places. There was a time when summer jaunts to Europe were reserved for society honeymooners, aging industrialists, and wealthy adolescents indulged by their grandmothers with an "enriching" Grand Tour. Now millions of Americans visit Europe every summer and airline price wars have made it financially easier to get there. Perhaps you can afford it, too—by working for a while when you get there. You won't save up a fortune, but with luck, ingenuity, and planning, you should be able to make enough to cover your living and travel expenses. The following section will help you with the planning aspects of your European work experience.

Summer Employment Abroad

When American students picture themselves working abroad for the summer, they often imagine themselves in an exotic setting, learning another language, earning a steep salary, and touring the Continent on weekends and lunch hours. If your father is the president of an airline, or happens to be Conrad Hilton—why not? The rest of us must face certain realities concerning summer employment abroad.

The first limitation on a student's summer employment plans is geographic. You must concentrate your job search on areas with low unemployment rates—which rules out most of the world. Even the United States is not in a strong employment position, and unless you have extraordinary personal contacts, it is impossible to find summer work in Asia, Africa, or South America. Volunteer projects abound in these countries, but you will have to subsidize your own excursion. Australia and New Zealand offer what is probably the world's best concentration of summer job opportunities for students, but their distance from the United States means that few needy American students will be able to make the trip, to take advantage of the job bonanza. Capitalist undergraduates are not welcome workers in Eastern European countries. Already the field has narrowed to the point where "summer employment abroad" really only applies to opportunities in Western Europe.

Even within this limited sphere, the job situation varies from country to country. It is just about impossible for Americans to locate summer jobs in Southern Europe. Spain, Greece, Italy, and Turkey cannot offer you much more than volunteer projects and work camps. There are too few jobs in these countries for the native workers, and thousands of Southern Europeans go north every year, in an effort to find work. To compete with these workers is fruitless for you and unfair to them. In addition, most nations protect their own work force. In Italy, for example, an employer cannot hire *you* until he proves to the Ministry of

Labor that it is impossible for him to hire an equally qualified Italian to do the job—which is unlikely. Other countries with similar policies may relax their requirements for students who intend to work only temporarily within the foreign country.

Northern Europe presents a somewhat brighter picture. Norway offers some farm work, which students can combine with home-stays with agricultural families. Austria, Denmark, Finland, France, Germany, Great Britain, Ireland, Switzerland, and the Netherlands all offer some variety of jobs to American students. Among those to whom we talked who had held stable employment in European businesses (as opposed to tour leaders, volunteers, and *au pair* help), the vast majority had found their work in France—perhaps because French is the language in which most American undergraduates have fluency.

Israel, the exception to the no-job rule outside of Europe, is especially hospitable to American students. Agricultural work on kibbutzim is your best bet, if you are an unskilled American student seeking work.

Basically, the summer jobs available in Western Europe break down into five main categories: short-term skilled jobs, short-term unskilled jobs, trainee programs, positions as tour and group leaders, and volunteer projects.

Unless you speak the language of the country, have relevant work and academic experience, and a great deal of pull, you will find it nearly impossible to find an "interesting" job in such a field as social work, administration, public relations, teaching, architecture, or law. The American economic habit of accommodating vacationing students with summer employment is not widespread in Europe, which does not even, generally, employ its own students, much less Americans. If you do not know how to use foreign language typewriters and have no command of the local language, you will not be of much use in a European office, except in an English-speaking country. Even typing, the passport to perpetual employment in the United States, will not necessarily secure you a job in Europe.

Those short-term skilled jobs that *are* available, on the other hand, tend to be secretarial in nature. Most of this work is in Great Britain, where language is no barrier and where wages are far lower than in the United States. You will experience a corresponding decline in living costs within the British Isles, however, and your salary ($50 a week or so) will seem relatively adequate while you remain there. British salaries will probably not finance extensive travel outside of England, Ireland, and Scotland, unless you stay in countries such as Spain, which are inexpensive and not too far away. Paris is as costly a city to visit as New York, and your London salary will rapidly melt in the City of Light.

If you are highly skilled and interested in summer work in Britain or on the Continent, your secretarial prowess may pay your way. Foreign placement services are offered by Manpower, Inc. and by Miss Liberty, Inc. If you have any contacts in big business here in America, you should explore the possibility of summer employment in an international office of a large corporation, where the scenery may be foreign but the salary will be American and substantial.

You will have a clear advantage in obtaining European employment if you are bilingual. This is true of all types of office work, and some types of businesses, with many foreign orders, may offer jobs to translators and interpreters. The more common languages—French, Spanish, German, and Italian—are most in demand, but demonstrated fluency will be required. If you know Czech, Dutch, Danish, or another less frequently mastered European language, you should make your skill known to an employment or placement agency, or through a foreign newspaper advertisement of your availability for summer employment. Bilingual persons may also be hired to teach English in Europe as a foreign language. This requires more than just the ability to speak English, but a school or program may give you training and a try. Advertisements in such nationwide newspapers as the Sunday edition of the *New York Times* may alert you that such an organization is seeking potential teachers.

Short-term unskilled jobs are the positions that you, as an American student, are most likely to find. Many of these jobs are connected with the tourist industry, since hundreds of thousands of vacationers from North America, Great Britain, and the Continent itself swarm to distant holiday spots during June, July, and August. Hotels and restaurants require extra help, and may take you on. Some farm work may be available, particularly in the late summer, but it will undoubtedly be poorly paid. So are European construction jobs for students—not to be confused with the American equivalent, which is a lucrative Pop job. Factory positions are also available. One American student who flew to France the day his exams were over, without waiting for the term to end officially, landed a factory job at Rennes, France. He started the same day, earning $1.90 an hour for *eleven* hours a day of tedious machine work. This student found his job worthwhile, because it allowed him to break even on his European summer. His experience, however, points up several facts about European summer employment of which American students should be aware.

Unless you are employed by the foreign office of a United States corporation, you must expect a work experience that is quite different from your summer jobs here. Hours are long and salaries low, by American standards. Room and board are sometimes included in a job offer, particularly on farms and at tourist facilities such as hotels and restaurants. This will stretch your wage, but living conditions will differ from what you are used to at home. Some students have worked for a whole summer in Europe without ever having a day off, and if you get one, you may be too tired to do much exploring. The most common and best solution to this dilemma is simply to work for a part of the summer, and tour during the remainder. Although some students are content merely to stay in one city and share the life of their fellow workers, most—especially first-time visitors—prefer to put in a month or two of hard labor and then travel on the profits, rather than attempt a full-time compromise.

Two types of short-term unskilled jobs bypass many of these considerations because the expectations of both your employers and yourself will be closer to what you are familiar with. These are camp counseling jobs and *au pair* (mother's helper) or companion-tutor positions.

The European camp counselor's job is exactly the same as his American counterpart's. If you work at a camp in Europe, however, you will have to be fluent in the language of the country in which the camp is located. Some camps cater to American children abroad for the summer or to the vacationing children of American businessmen and diplomats who reside permanently in Europe. Others are international in emphasis and accept campers of various languages and national origins. Still others are simply local European versions of summer camp, not unlike those in the U.S.A., which may find it a novelty to have a foreign counselor or deliberately hire English speakers to provoke an opportunity for practice in the English language. In any case, you may polish your European language as a camp counselor, but such a job is no time to begin learning. Write to the embassy of the country in which you hope to work, requesting a list of its summer camps, with special reference to those that may hire American college students in the summers. Once you have such a list, contact the camps directly. You may also make your arrangements through the Camp Counselor International Exchange Program, the address of which is noted at the end of the chapter. This organization places counselors in foreign summer camps.

Au pair positions, limited mainly to women, involve live-in babysitting. A young woman lives with a family and receives a small spending allowance in addition to her room and board. Her function is not as impersonal as that of a hired babysitter or maid; rather, she serves the function of a helpful eldest daughter, assisting the mother with meals and light housekeeping, shopping, watching the children, and so forth. As a "member of the family," she usually has a chance to meet pleasant people, since employers of *au pair* girls are often middle-class professional families. In addition, she has an ideal opportunity to perfect her conversation in the relevant foreign language. Factory and farm jobs often put the American student, with his classroom fluency, in contact only with natives who speak in lightning slang—and in a resort, you may only speak English to the American tourists.

American girls frequently enjoy the knowledge of the visited country that they gain by living with a foreign family, but women of college age may find *au pair* jobs infantilizing. All agree that you are much better off if you work for a family who is vacationing and traveling, rather than established in its daily routine. If the family is stationary, you are all too likely to slip into the position of part-time, all-purpose housekeeper; if they travel, you are principally the children's companion—plus, of course, the recipient of a free trip. And no two-cent tour—a family who can afford an *au pair* girl can afford to travel in style. American families, as well as European ones, often hire someone to take the child-care worry off of Mama's shoulders during the holiday jaunt.

European families may also hire tutor-companions, the modern guise of yesteryear's governesses, to teach English to their children. These jobs are not as Victorian as they sound, and are open to men as well as women. Elderly people occasionally need similar traveling companions and secretaries.

A number of European placement agencies handle *au pair* and tutoring positions, and you may find listings of some of these agencies at your student employment office, or in the "Help Wanted" section of the college, local, and foreign newspapers. Your chances are better, however, if *you* take the initiative. If you seek a job with a traveling American family, place a provocative ad in your college, and/or in your city, newspaper, telling enough about yourself to show that you are responsible and to make potential employers curious. One enterprising freshman did just that. Two months later, she was in Rome—all her expenses paid.

To work for a foreign family, you should run your ad in a European newspaper. The London Sunday *Observer* and the Paris edition of the *International* [formerly, New York] *Herald Tribune* are two newspapers you could try. A junior at a Midwestern men's college who advertised his services in the Paris *Tribune,* found himself at a villa in Nice for the summer, soaking up sun and tutoring English.

If you run out of money while you are actually *in* Europe, try checking out newspaper classifieds and the bulletin boards at universities and student organizations (for example, the *Cité Universitaire,* in Paris), for notices of these jobs. You won't earn much, but at least you will be employed, on short notice, and your room and board will be secured.

Some of the most interesting summer jobs in Europe are offered by international organizations that sponsor trainee programs and skilled-student exchanges. Such programs tend to operate primarily for graduate students, but juniors and seniors (no underclassmen) are also accepted. The two major associations active in this work are mentioned here; their United States office addresses are listed at the end of the chapter.

The International Association for the Exchange of Students for Technical Experience (IAESTE/US) places American students with backgrounds in architecture, agriculture, engineering, or the sciences in appropriate offices, firms, and laboratories throughout forty-one countries, although most placements are made in Western Europe. This program has a December 15 application deadline and, like the following program, demands of an applicant a sound command of the technical language of the country in which he will be working.

Economics and business students are the focus of the *Association Internationale des Étudiants en Sciences Economiques et Commerciales* (*AIESEC/US*). This organization operates management trainee and technical exchange programs on five continents, including students from forty-nine countries. Some of the jobs available though this organization are sophisticated, others are merely a paid excuse for a European vacation, but most run on the "exchange" principle. An economics major who managed to find a Boston summer job for a French student was reciprocally presented with a "business internship" in Paris. This turned out to be a euphemism for "office boy," but the American student scarcely noticed the boring work: he was too busy exulting in his Parisian summer and touring on the weekends. When his job was over, he had plenty of time to travel more extensively in Europe and enough summer earnings to precisely break even on his working vacation abroad.

If you've been to Europe before, and want to go back next time for free, try to arrange a job as a tour or group leader. American travel camps for teen-agers often need bilingual students to serve as tour guides and group supervisors: consult *Sargent's Guide* to camps, or the Sunday camping section of city newspapers such as the *New York Times*. American Youth Hostels, Inc., hires undergraduates as tour leaders, provided that they are over twenty-one and have suitable previous travel experience. You might also look into the programs of the United States National Student Travel Association, Inc. The highly successful tours run for high school students by the Experiment in International Living may also hire you as a group leader, if you have travel experience and if your command of the language of your target country is superior. This program's minimum age requirement (twenty-four) will, however, rule out many undergraduates. The Experiment makes its summer staff appointments between October and April, so it is vital to apply early.

Certain travel agencies may hire guides for their organized tours or may offer a free trip to a student who arranges a group excursion flight to Europe. You should investigate these possibilities in your town. American Student Tours, Inc., is a company that specializes in tours within the Continent and flights to and from the U.S.A. If you sell the requisite number of flight tickets and tour commitments to other students, you may earn yourself free Atlantic flights and/or free travel on the Continent.

A most romantic vision, left to us from the days of three-masted schooners, sleek clipper ships, and New England whaling expeditions is the shipboard excursion. Freighter passage to India (or Western Europe) is not the penniless traveler's dream it once was, but it is not impossible to work your way to Europe by sea. The only problem is that you probably won't be able to stay there. Summer employment on shipboard is possible as a full-time proposition, but almost never for a one-way voyage. Ships cannot hire and train new personnel at every port; you must expect to spend most of your vacation on board, and if you cross the Atlantic, you should expect to recross it when your freighter turns around for the return passage.

You will need to prove your United States citizenship and qualify with certain U.S. Coast Guard regulations before you sail. Most shipboard jobs are held by union members, so you must begin by frequenting the employment offices on the docks until there is a job posted that no union member snaps up. Next you must secure the job, on your own, and obtain the employer's agreement, in writing, that you have been hired for a specific job. Take this letter to the U.S. Coast Guard Office, where you will be issued Seamen's Papers. Your last step is registration with the Seafarer's International Union and—seafarer, you're on your way. Detailed information on hiring procedures and labor regulations can be obtained from the National Maritime Union.

If you are in a position to put human rewards above financial ones, we urge you to look into some of the hundreds of fine volunteer projects and work camps in which American students may participate, outside the United States. These opportunities—unlike paid employment, with its strict governmental regulations and dependence on the vagaries of the economy—can bring you into direct contact with the peoples of Africa, Asia, South and Central America, as well as Western Europe. You may help out in a flood disaster area or in an innoculation project. You might work to build a school house, or an irrigation system. You might teach pre- and postnatal care, or conduct research on political organization in a Third World nation. You might do agricultural labor—plough and sow and cultivate and harvest with other young people from all over the world. This is the most direct way of making friends abroad and usually surpasses the parochial experience of a paying job in a limited sphere of European business, by its collective and exuberant nature.

You will invariably have to pay your own travel expenses, however, although room and board may be provided free. An American college sophomore worked as a farmhand in Les Fontenelles, near Besançon, France, under this type of arrangement. He and the other students in his project lived with individual farm families and shared their chores. After three months of milking the cow, cleaning the barn, feeding the pigs, and generally accommodating to a rural life style, the student had to jet back to his urban university, nostalgic but satisfied. He reports, incidentally, that this experience was invaluable to his fluency in French.

Volunteer projects with international aims are sponsored by a wide range of groups, with an equal variety of goals and styles. To begin your selection, we suggest that you consult the American Friends Service Committee and the book *Invest Yourself: A Catalogue of Summer Opportunities*. A third, excellent source of information on foreign volunteer service and work camps is the Coordinating Committee for International Volunteer Service, in Paris.

Once you have determined to arrange a working summer for yourself in Europe, you are faced with the necessity of finding a job. There are two ways to go about this. You can do it yourself or you can do it through an agency.

The former is the path of the independent, the impetuous, and those who have powerful contacts. If you have none, pause and weigh the independence of your choice against its impetuousness. Be forewarned that most European countries have strict rules concerning work permits.

In order to get a work permit, you must obtain a firm job offer *before* you leave the United States, and your employer must then obtain and send to you *in advance* the work permit, with which you will be able to enter his country legally as a worker. It is difficult to convince an employer 3,000 miles away that he should hire you sight unseen. If you do manage to arrange your summer employment independently, you must be sure that you allow plenty of time to make the legal arrangements: work permits may take up to two months to clear. Inquire at the embassy or consulate of the country you intend to work in, to check on the required papers. These offices can give you information, not only on the red tape you will face but on the up-to-date job picture in their countries as well.

An alternative to this correct and circumspect approach is to ignore all the rules and regulations—and just go. This plan requires capital—you must take along enough money so that you can afford to eat during the time it takes you to line up a job. The fastest and easiest way to do this is to turn up in a tourist resort and inquire at all the hotels, restaurants, and souvenir shops. Ask as early in the tourist season as possible, to avoid the hordes. Some tenacious undergraduates have done this successfully even in the Mediterranean countries. There are always those apocryphal students with initiative and blind luck, who, on the spur of the moment, land jobs languorously playing the guitar in a Parisian cave, or chauffeuring an Italian businessman, at an exorbitant salary.

If you decide to let an agency assist you in your job search, you may also simplify your travel arrangements and struggle with work permits. Before committing yourself to any summer employment agency, however, you should keep the following questions, suggested by the State Department, in mind.

What do you know of the organization? Do you have any friends who have used its services, and if so, what is their appraisal of them? Is there a campus representative with firsthand knowledge of the organization? Can the agency tell you of someone from your school who has used it before? Be sure to consult your college employment office and your professors.

What does this summer employment agency charge for its help, in comparison with other agencies? Service fees are almost always contained in the organization's promotional literature. Are the actual and total cost to the participant clearly outlined? Does the literature specify what is covered and, more importantly, what is not covered? What percentage of the total cost goes for administration?

Under what circumstances will the fee be refunded in the event of any sort of cancellation? Some agencies will return all but a modest service charge; others make no refund at all. Read the fine print!

Does the organization have an official base in the United States that would be legally responsible in the event of any complications that might require legal action on your part? In all business arrangements there is the risk of misunderstanding or even breach of contractual obligations. As an American you might find it difficult to protect your legal interests in a dispute with a foreign organization unless it maintains some form of representation in the United States that would be responsible to you under United States laws.

Does the organization appear to be a bona-fide work-or-study aboard organization, or is it possible that its major interest lies in the area of travel sales, for which it probably receives a commission? There are a number of thoroughly reputable commercial enterprises in the cultural exchange field whose primary concern is travel, but some are not sufficiently skilled in making the overseas arrangements that are necessary to arrange a rewarding and satisfactory student work-travel experience.

Does the organization offer any advantages in securing low-cost passage and maintenance for students? Among the potential advantages sometimes offered are student identification and discount cards. Such cards are sometimes internationally recognized and carry such benefits as lowered museum entrance fees. But unless the agency specifies exactly how, where, and to what extent these cards provide advantages, they may not possess any real value.

How does the organization advertise its programs? Does it present them in a straightforward, detailed manner or is the promotional literature vague about program specifics, but crowded with claims to and implications of official support? In regard to work-abroad programs, is the agency specific about the exact types of jobs available to American students: the hours, the pay, and what the jobs include in the way of meals and lodging? Read the fine print in the promotional literature and choose an organization that clearly spells out the disadvantages as well as the advantages of summer employment abroad.

A good international student employment agency can offer you many advantages by which to make your summer plans smooth and secure. Fees can range from $50 to $450, and different agencies take different degrees of responsibility for arranging your job, lodging, board, travel and working papers. Take the State Department's advice seriously, and carefully evaluate the agency or program that you select. Some organizations offer travel plans to and from Europe. Be sure to compare these with current commercial fares, since price wars and youth fares have brought many commercial rates within competing distance of group fares, and a commercial flight gives you greater physical comfort and far more latitude in your arrival and departure plans.

An exemplary agency for overseas employment is the International Student Employment (ISE), the student employment arm of the Council on International Educational Exchange (CIEE). For a fee of $25— which covers administration, prejob orientation, and your first night's bed and breakfast abroad, and which is refundable if you are not accepted by the program—this agency facilitates student employment in Great Britain, Ireland, New Zealand, and Australia. Students must locate their own jobs, but the agency helps with reliable leads on office, hotel, and factory work. Three-month temporary work permits are then provided, and low-cost travel can be arranged through the organization. Underclassmen are given preference, and the program's application deadline is May 1. Other organizations with similar aims are listed in the group of addresses at the end of this chapter.

However you land your job in Europe, you are bound to find that business, babysitting, or physical engineering has an entirely different aspect when you ply your trade in the shadow of the Alps or the Apennines. Concentrate on the Continent, not the profits—with luck you'll not only have a wonderful time but you'll break even. And *bon voyage.*

HELPFUL ADDRESSES

Student Employment Abroad—Agencies and Special Programs

International Student Employment
  (ISE)
Council on International Educational
  Exchange
777 United Nations Plaza
New York, New York 10017

Belgian Educational Travel Service
291 Broadway
New York, New York 10007

Eurojob
102 Greenwich Avenue
Greenwich, Connecticut 06830

A.I.E.S.E.C./U.S.
52 Vanderbilt Avenue
New York, New York 10017

American Study Tours, Inc.
210 West 7th Street
Los Angeles, California

National Maritime Union, AFL–CIO
36 7th Avenue
New York, New York 10011

Miss Liberty, Inc.
614 Murdock Road
Baltimore, Maryland 21212

American Youth Hostels, Inc.
20 W. 17th Street
New York, New York 10011

International Association for the Exchange of Students for Technical Experience
I.A.E.S.T.E./U.S.
866 United Nations Plaza
New York, New York

Association Internationale des
Etudiants en Science Economiques
et Commerciales

Coordinator of Overseas Employment Manpower, Inc.
820 Plankinton Avenue
Milwaukee, Wisconsin 53202

Camp Counselor International Exchange Program
491 University Avenue
Bridgeport, Connecticut 06604

Experiment in International Living
Putney, Vermont 05346

Summer Employment Abroad—Publications

A Word of Caution
Director of Public Information and
Reports Staff
Bureau of Information and Cultural
Affairs
Department of State
Washington, D.C. 20520

A guide for evaluating student work, travel, and study-abroad programs and agencies, free.

Employment Aboard—Facts and Fallacies
International Department, Chamber of Commerce of the United States
1615 H Street N.W.
Washington, D.C. 20006

Advice and information sources, $.25.

A List of Sources for Employment Overseas
Committee of American Laymen and Churches Overseas
National Council of Churches of Christ in the USA
Room 656, 475 Riverside Drive
New York, New York 10027

Sources of work with organizations occupied with world affairs, including business, free.

Employment Abroad: Sources of Information

Lists job opportunities country-by-country, including *au pair* and exchange visit agencies. Visa, residence, and work regulations. An expanded section on employment in England, Scotland, and Wales, $4.95.

Students' Europe: ASA Employment and Touring Guide
American Students Abroad
P.O. Box 36087
Cincinnati, Ohio 45236

Invest Yourself: A Catalogue of Service Opportunities
published by the
Commission on Voluntary Service and Action
475 Riverside Drive, Room 830
New York, New York 10027

Lists American, Canadian, International, and United Nations volunteer projects, including community action, intercultural exchange, and work camp programs, and conscientious objector alternative service opportunities. Summer and winter projects, $1.

Earn Your Way in Europe
Student Overseas Services Handbook
Student Overseas Services
Luxembourg, Europe

CIEE
777 United Nations Plaza
New York, New York 10017

A guide, revised yearly. The same publisher prepares free Area Fact Sheets containing information on travel, work, and study for students in the following areas: Latin America; U.S.S.R. and Eastern Europe; Japan; and Africa.

The Directory of Overseas Summer Jobs
edited by Charles J. James
published by
Vacation–Work
9 Park End Street
Oxford, England

Mademoiselle magazine reprints:
"Au Pair Jobs Abroad"
"Leads on Jobs Abroad"
"European Job Chart—Working in Geneva, London, Paris, Rome"
$.35 each. Published by
Mademoiselle Magazine
Box 3389
Grand Central Station
New York, New York 10017

Students Abroad: Summer Study, Travel, and Work Programs
published by
CIEE
777 United Nations Plaza
New York, New York 10017

Student Employment Abroad and in the USA—Publications

The World-Wide Summer Placement Directory
published by
The Advancement and Placement Institute
169 N. 9th Street
Brooklyn, New York 11211

A Compendium of summer and permanent jobs, projects, and awards.

None of the possibilities listed are volunteer projects; all involve salaries or defrayed expenses. For the United States or state-by-state breakdown of opportunities. Foreign openings also listed. Revised annually (December), $6.

Student Summer Employment, USA—Publications

Summer Employment Directory of the United States
edited by Myena A. Leith
published by
National Directory Service
266 Ludlow Avenue
Cincinnati, Ohio 45220

Extensive lists of addresses and openings for summer jobs in resorts, hotels, restaurants, summer camps, dude ranches, summer theaters, business, and industry. Advice on applications. Revised yearly in November, $5.95.

Summer Employment Guide
published by
University Publications
P.O. Box 20133
Denver, Colorado 80220

Directory of Federal Job Information Centers
available from the
United States Civil Service Commission
1900 E Street N.W.
Washington, D.C. 20415

A directory of local offices, listed by states.

Summer Job Directory
published by
Student Employment Exchange
P.O. Box 571
Vermillion, South Dakota 57069

Revised annually, $2.

The United States Department of
 Labor
Bureau of Employment Security
Washington, D.C. 20210

Offers a free booklet on summer jobs
and how to find them.

Chapter Five

STUDENT-RUN SMALL
BUSINESS

It's cold, and it's drizzling. You've been up Main Street and down
College Avenue, clutching your damp copy of the local "Help Wanted"
columns. Your boots are soaked, and that's all you have to show for a
lengthy job hunt. Nobody's hiring—or you've found nothing that suits
you. Why not head home and, while those boots dry out, create your
own job? You can, if you start your own business.

Do the people in your dormitory eat, sleep, or study? Sell them
meatball subs, water beds, typing services. The fact that you are reading
this book demonstrates a certain reconciliation with capitalism on your
part—after all, you could be studying *Steal This Book*. Why not, then,
put capitalism to work for you? In America there are buyers for everything from quick-frozen omelettes to gold-filled toothpicks. If you can
provide a product or a service to your community, you can become a
student entrepreneur.

Does the small business market seem glutted? Not at all—give it a
little thought. There are the basic needs of your fellow students: they
may rent a refrigerator from you, buy your handmade sandals, or call on
your rock group to catalyze the mixer. Consider the community around
you. Could students bartend at private parties, form a babysitting pool,
pick the fall crop of Macintoshes, or paint local houses? Organize it.

Recycle. Someone has already covered the market on turning
crushed champagne glasses from Lincoln Center into modular wine
racks, but there's still grist for your mill. Thrust that dusty old knowl-

edge of Latin or calculus back into the community of scholars: struggling freshmen or high-school seniors will pay you for it. You may want
to sink that organic chemistry book forever in the college pond, but
remember that generations of suffering premed students yet to come
would be happy to buy used texts: organize a cooperative bookstore.
Resell fur coats, sport coats, formal dresses, lived-in jeans, and old
leather jackets for those whose identity crises keep propelling them to
quick shifts of image. Trade on the escalating incomes and expertise of
your classmates by dealing in used stereo components, bicycles, motorcycles, or sports and ski equipment.

Sell convenience. Great Grandma made pudding from cornstarch
and chocolate. Grandma heated milk and mix on the same stove. Ma
just needed cold milk and a bowl, and now you and I can eat the
finished product right in the supermarket from a flip-top can. Same
product (give or take a little diethyl tributyl monostearate), but the
convenience factor made the sales. Most students type, but many will
pay to have the burden of final drafts removed when they've got three
papers due in ten days. Get your own work out of the way in advance
and you can clean up. (One sophomore not only made $2.50 an hour
this way, working at his convenience, but by typing term papers for a
course that he was taking himself, he picked up many good ideas to use
on the exam.) Most people are also capable of cleaning their own
rooms, doing their own laundry, and ironing their own shirts—but if
they would prefer to have *their* time free for something else, let them
pay you handsomely for *yours*. There may be a diner across the street,
but during exam week your fellow students will pay extra for the roast
beef sandwich they can buy in the dormitory court at midnight. Combine existing services, or increase their convenience: peanut butter and
jelly always sold better as a team, but some manufacturer actually
makes his living by selling them premixed in the same jar.

Co-opt the opposition. A great deal has been published on the "Students versus the Establishment" question, but many a freshman freak will
want a class ring before he's a senior, and when his fiancée asks him to
her college's Spring Ball, he'll be in the market for a rented tux. Provide,
provide.

But you believe that the needs are all filled and there seems no way
around it. No self-respecting student entrepreneur was ever foiled by a
satisfied campus—not for long. *Create* a need: then fill it. This is a
mainspring of the American economy. We crave this year's sports car or
the latest midi-skirt, when twelve months ago these items were only
gleams in the cunning eyes of their designers. Did the country know in

advance that it lacked a weekly television series featuring a talking palomino? Fortunes have been built on deodorants for odors most people never dreamed they exuded. Two Harvard juniors and a Cornell dropout started the first computer-dating operation in the mid-1960's, pleasing thousands of customers who had been previously unaware of their deep longing for a machine-matched mate.

The student-run business, then, is limited in conception only by your imagination, as it plays over the factors of your time, your skills, your capital, your interests, and your potential customers and labor pool. Be sublime: hire out the services of your string quartet to provide Corelli and Haydn at wedding ceremonies. Be ridiculous: provide a valve for all that pre-exam tension by organizing a late-night festival of old Road Runner and Heckle and Jeckle cartoons. Be your own boss.

If starting your own business seems more risky than being on someone else's payroll, the advantages of being self-employed are often ample compensation. First of all, you will be able to arrange your own flexible work schedule. More important, you will have a chance to do what really interests you; your work should be much more exciting than the part-time jobs you'd find at the student employment office. Running your own business is challenging, and if you use your wits, you may be able to pay yourself much higher wages than you could earn working for someone else. Being independent is often lucrative as well as fun.

Your business need not be elaborate—many a dog walker has earned a good wage with zero investment in equipment and skills. And many simple businesses grow and grow. You can easily start your business and minimize your risks if you follow good business procedures and keep in mind the points of operational technique that are now discussed.

Know Your Product

Whatever you sell, whether it is a commodity or a service, you must know your product. This means that you must have conviction in your ability to give your customer something of value. Although many of our great corporations provide examples to the contrary, as a small businessman you must face the fact that rip-off sales will not keep you in business for long. Your community is too small, and unlike the telephone company, you are probably not a monopoly. Students are skeptical consumers, so providing a good for your customers ensures your business success as well as your own sense of satisfaction and integrity.

You may meet legitimate needs that are not your own: in your eyes, class rings may be superfluous trivia, but it is not unfair to sell one to the classmate who may focus a deep feeling through this tradition. It *is* unfair to con him into a purchase that will turn his finger green. If you provide a worthwhile service or produce a useful product, and if your price is fair, you should expect to make a profit from your work.

If you know your product well, you will be able to realize its full potential marketability. Don't limit yourself to the obvious market— familiarity with a product may bring new ideas and new uses. Imagine the delight that the manufacturers of cigarette papers have experienced in recent years. They don't put out Stars and Stripes papers for their faithful old tobacco-pouch customers. Knowledge of the product may help you to avoid problems, as well. Small fortunes may be made on campus by catering to the water bed fad, but know your product, and insist that every customer buy a waterproof liner. One leak could be worth a thousand sales—in bad publicity and a dismayed dean, if the two tons of water happens to have flooded a freshman dorm. Many salesmen never sell anything unless they use it themselves. "Water" coolers in the Coca-Cola offices hold only the company product. You can avoid extremes and still turn familiarity with your product to your profitable advantage.

Market Research

STOP. Before you rush off to the wholesaler's to stock up on water beds, stop in your tracks to consider the work that you must do first: your market research. Market research is the first step in starting *any* business. Don't be frightened from this indispensable task by its fancy name. Researching your market simply means identifying your customers and estimating the income that you can expect your business to produce. This allows you to evaluate your economic prospects, both in advance and as your business venture continues. Anticipation, based on data, can help you to plan ahead for maximum profits. And, finally, if your scheme is risky, market research can give you a look before you leap.

Once a business idea has crystallized, *expenses* are usually fairly easy to figure out, since you know in advance approximately what supplies you will have to buy and what labor must be hired. These prices and wages will be reasonably standard and predictable. Although needs for materials and labor will increase as your operation expands, it should be relatively simple to figure out what your expenses will be at any given level of business. If you run a bus service and your major expenses are $15 for posters and $35 for each forty-four-passenger bus, you know what your expenses will be for twelve passengers, forty-four passengers, or ninety-eight passengers.

What you won't know, unless you have sold your tickets in advance, is how many buses to hire. How many passengers can you count on, and at how much per head? If you are selling snacks instead of rides, how many hot dogs do you buy? Is it worth it to stay open until 2 A.M. and to hire an extra man to work those hours? If your product is a magazine, will a mailing to potential subscribers pay for itself? Should you try to sell ads? Should you print 5,000 copies or 50, or 5? Should you print at all?

Market research should be aimed at answering these questions of demand and income for your particular business. The larger the potential business, the more money, time, and effort should go into market research, in order to minimize your risks. The highly publicized television-rating services are simply a gigantic and competitive form of market research, serving an even larger and more competitive commercial realm. Several concrete examples may help you to apply research techniques to your own situation.

You go to an all-male college in the deep woods. Every weekend, it's the same gripe: there's no easy and economical way to get to the local girls' college, fifteen miles away. Is there a fortune to be made, you muse, by running a bus service between the campuses on weekends? A great idea, so—*stop,* and do your market research.

There are 1,000 students on your campus, 50 per cent of whom you expect might use your bus service. You compose, mimeograph, and distribute through the dormitories a short questionnaire, asking when people travel, whether they would utilize a bus, how often, at what ticket price, and so on. If your venture were smaller and your memory reliable, you might simply spend an evening or two asking around in the dining halls, keeping a mental record of how many potential customers you've discovered. If you're exceptionally thorough and ambitious, you'll go to the girls' school and do complementary market research *there.*

The data is in. You find that your original estimate of 50 per cent was way off. Only 25 per cent of the students are genuinely interested. Your fantasized fortune shrinks, but your market is still large enough to provide a profit. What's more, you have discovered that most of those who are interested are freshmen and sophomores—so you needn't bother with deluging the upperclass dorms with advertising. By knowing your market, you can concentrate your efforts for maximum profit.

The next step in market research is to figure out your expected income. Will your business efforts prove financially worthwhile? You should first estimate your expenses. You decide that you want to spend $10 on advertising and you know that the sixty-seat buses will cost you $85 each. At $2 per seat, the first full bus will bring you a $20 profit, and you'll make even more on each additional bus (the first bus will have absorbed your advertising costs). By selling tickets in advance, you can estimate how many buses to hire and how full they will be. If a flu epidemic grounds your clientele, as shown by your advance ticket sales, then you can cancel the trip if you can't anticipate at least breaking even.

Market research is a useful tool long after you've pocketed that first $20. Are your customers satisfied with the service? Can your business be expanded? Try giving another questionnaire to the passengers. It will give them something to do on their rural journey and may bring you profitable suggestions for a better schedule of arrival and departure times or different boarding or unloading locations. Would a rest stop at a roadside bar make the trip more attractive? Should you set up special runs during Homecoming weekend or arrange transportation to the local ski slope? If you come into frequent contact with your customers and seem receptive to suggestions, you can conduct this research in conversation. Written or oral, these inquiries will bring you new ideas and fresh profits.

Market research may help you to earn money, and it can also keep you from losing money. For example, let's say you want to establish a birthday cake service, contracting with the parents of students at your school to deliver a cake "from" the parents on the students' birthdays. It may work, but research should be done first. If there are 10,000 students at your school, it will be expensive and time-consuming to contact all of the parents. The results of a test mailing to 200 parents (selected at random) could be projected, however, fairly accurately over the entire student body. What if you receive only ten favorable replies— not much of a response, and far too risky to start a business on. This is disappointing, and your mailing has shown a loss of $.05 per letter, in third-class postage costs. But compare this $10 loss to the $500 that would have been spent on the complete (10,000 parent) mailing. And consider the time and money you might have invested in starting your business, only to find out that there was no market for it. Occasionally an idea is a natural, and you know that cautious tests are unnecessary. When it comes to a few dollars or cents of profit figured over a large number of customers, however, careful market research can really pay off. Only $.05 *profit,* on the average, from each of 10,000 parents would provide a decent remuneration for a hard month's work. Size up your market in advance, and you'll know what to count on, and how and when to go ahead.

One last word of caution. Market research can be tricky. Try to get help from a marketing or statistics professor in designing any tests. For example, one group of students planned to publish an alumni magazine. To send a mailing to the 88,000 alumni would have cost them $8,800, so the students decided to mail to 800 alumni, chosen at random, in order to gain a sampling of the market. In the questionnaires, the students asked the alumni whether they would subscribe to the magazine (at $15 for a one-year subscription) and what suggestions they had for its content. The results of the survey indicated that the full mailing would sell 40,000 copies, at a large profit. To be on the safe side, a brochure was printed and sent with a letter—again to only 800 alumni —when the first issue was ready. This second test produced disastrous results, indicating that if the full mailing had been done, the students would have lost $7,000.

What happened? Evidently it was one thing to ask the alumni for opinions on what they *thought* they would do if they were sent a brochure—and another thing entirely to send them the brochure and ask them to order and pay for a subscription to the magazine. The more the "test situation" differs from the "real situation" that is planned, the more likely it is that the test results will be misleading. The students who were preparing the alumni magazine could have saved themselves a great deal of trouble if in the *first* mailing they had asked the alumni for both their comments and a check for a one-year subscription.

Time

Always ask yourself "How much time will it take to run this business?" Will you have to stay at school during vacations or during the summer to keep it going? Can you delegate the work to others, or will you have to do it all yourself? Naturally, you can only guess, and even the cleverest people (Ford-Mustang) miscalculate sometimes (Ford-Edsel). But you should be able to make a budget of the time required to put your idea into action.

Some businesses will require only as much time as you wish to spend. If you are able to sell class rings on campus, you need make only as many calls as you have time for. Also, you can find good salesmen to work for you if you are willing to give them a healthy commission. Other businesses will commit you to working even when you would prefer not to. If you mail a letter to every student's parents offering to deliver a basket of sun-ripened Florida oranges to his snowbound door each week, you will be obligated to make your deliveries, exams or no exams. In almost every case, though, you should be able to control the size of your business (mail only to 200 parents as a test), or to hire enough help to handle your overload.

Risk

Almost every business involves financial risk. As a student entrepreneur, your aim is to keep your risk as small as possible. When you anticipate a business venture, you should always try to envision the worst financial loss your idea could result in, as well as its most lucrative possibilities. You plan to open a concession stand at your university's basketball games. If you spend $200 renting a Coke machine and a hot-dog cooker, buying the food, and paying for labor, then you stand to lose $200. How does this risk stack up against your potential profits? Can you afford the gamble?

Make up a budget with all the expenses you can think of, plus a little slack in the form of an estimate of miscellaneous or unexpected costs. Your concession stand budget might break down this way (the expenses of a real business would probably need to be itemized in greater detail):

Expense Budget

Machine Rental	$50
Food Costs	75
Advertising	10
Labor	35
Miscellaneous	30
Total	$200

Now estimate the amount of business you will have. The more revenues you take in the higher your expenses and profit will probably be. You should be able to identify a break-even point in sales, at which your initial investment has been recouped and you will begin to make money. The budget is vital to your decision as to whether or not to put an idea into action. Great corporations, in fact, usually make up *three* budgets for each product they consider: a best-possible success budget, a worst-possible failure budget, and a most likely sales budget, which reflects the probable real compromise between the two extremes. Consider your concession stand:

Worst-Possible Failure

Sales	$ 0
Cost	200
Profit	−$200 (Loss)

Best-Possible Success

Sales	$350
Cost	200
Profit	$150

Most-Likely Sales

Sales	$250
Cost	200
Profit	$ 50

The possibilities shape up as "terrible," "terrific," and "so-?" Which can you count on? The precision-minded entrepreneur answers this question by means of a simple and statistically justified tool: the "expected profit." Multiply each profit by the estimate of the probability of its occurrence that you derived from your market research. (If 10 per cent of your questionnaires indicated that you could expect $250 in sales, then the probability of that level of sales, and its corresponding profit level, is 10 per cent). Now add the three results to get your expected profit.

Market research shows, in the case of your concession stand, that you stand a 10 per cent chance of losing $200 (worst-possible failure), an 85 per cent chance of earning $50 (the most likely sales), and a 5 per cent chance of making $150 (the best-possible success). Your calculation of expected profit would look like this:

10% × −$200 (worst)	−$20.00
85% × + 50 (most-likely)	+ 42.50
5% × + 150 (best)	+ 7.50
Expected Profit	+$30.00

Your expected return, when risk (expressed in terms of probabilities) is taken into account, turns out to be only $30 on an investment of $200. In terms of percentages, this is only 15 per cent ($30/$200)—a narrow margin of profit. This preliminary paperwork indicates that your proposed business is a risky one—proceed with caution. Your figures may foreshadow a landslide profit or a staggering loss—you can act in accordance with your expected returns.

Remember, however, that although this is a valid procedure employed by many large companies, your calculation of expected profit is only as good as your estimates of the probabilities involved. Your market research will make or break these estimates. False guesses or insufficient data can throw your probabilities off and lead you into an unsuccessful business—or stop you from undertaking a potential money-maker. Even if your prediction of the size of your profits does not assure you of a direct hit, it will at least give you an idea of whether or not to pull the trigger. Intuition counts, but force yourself to take a realistic look at your prospects on paper. By clarifying your intuition, you minimize your financial risk and heighten your potential for profits.

Records

The first rule of sound business procedure is to keep good records. Good records protect both you and your customers, and will aid you in your market research. You needn't set up an elaborate bureaucracy, but you should keep your correspondence and bookkeeping complete and up-to-date. Those clear, simple records will prove to be an invaluable asset.

Set up a separate checking account as soon as you start your business so that your personal and business expenses are maintained separately from the beginning. Deposit all funds from the business (and *only* business) into this account and cover all your business expenses from it. This account will help you keep track of your costs and profits and to check on how your money was spent. The canceled checks will be needed at tax time.

Retain and file all receipts and correspondence. Never send a letter unless you have a copy for your files. It is also important to have dated notes of all your meetings, conversations, and oral agreements. It may seem trivial at the time, but such records can save you money, customers, and the pain of an unresolvable misunderstanding. If you take your roommate on as your sales manager, write him a letter repeating the terms of employment that the two of you have agreed on, and keep a carbon for yourself. It may save your friendship, when his commission comes into question six months later. And although you're positive, as you hang up the telephone, that you will remember what you've said, three weeks from now you won't be sure, and how will you persuade the other party that you have things straight? You will be amazed at how quickly you begin to confuse John A. Walters at the City Trust Company, who wanted a half-page ad, with Walter J. Johnson at the Citizens' Bank, who told you to see his ad agent at J. Walter Thompson.

Accurate records should tell you which advertising media are most effective, which periods of the year (or day) bring your sales peak, and who your best salesmen are. They will prompt you to pay your creditors on time and will let you know who still owes *you* money. What's more, you will be able to prove it.

As your business grows, you will need more records. But start out by being accurate, stay simple and your business records can become a resource rather than a curse.

Hiring

Your business is successful! Congratulations—but remember that you are a *student* entrepreneur. Unless you'll be satisfied with lower grades, you may have to hire assistants. Being an employer is a complicated situation, and the employer-employee relationship is one of the most important aspects of the business. You've already mastered the art of keeping the customer satisfied—remember that if your employee feels he is receiving an honest return for his effort, it will show in his loyalty and performance. If you set up a sweatshop, you may get away with it in the short run, but in the long run word will get around and you will find yourself left with no one to exploit.

If you hire your friends, you will have to deal with the fact that it is often difficult to criticize a friend's work or to make demands on his time. You may have to choose between losing the friendship or settling for sloppy work. On the other hand, it is obviously convenient to have an employee who is nearby. If your friends and roommates are part of your business, they have an incentive to answer the telephone and to take careful messages; furthermore, they'll be easier to find than classmates living at the other end of the campus. A compromise solution is to hire a conveniently located stranger. Once you are his employer, his sense of duty to his work will depend largely upon how well you pay him. You have several alternatives.

1. *By the hour*. This is the easiest method to calculate and the most secure for the employee. However, you have no way to inspire him to perform faster or to do better work. It's really remarkable how variable typing, delivery, folding, or mimeograph-cleaning speeds can be.

2. *By the piece.* This is ideal if you can work it out. The employee gets paid for exactly what is accomplished. If the work if done quickly and well, the employee's hourly wage will be high.

3. *A combination of No. 1 and No. 2.* This is often an effective compromise. If you would like to see your employee earning about $3 an hour, but you want to make sure that he does fast work, offer him $2 an hour plus a piece rate, which, by your calculation of what a "fast job" is, will add another $1 per hour.

4. *Commission.* This is really the same as "piece rate," but it involves sales, not mechanical operations. You pay a fixed percentage of total sales to your salesmen; you can set the pay to increase after a certain amount of sales as an added incentive. You can guarantee a minimum wage per hour or offer bonuses at certain levels of sales. Bear in mind the requirements of your particular business when you institute a bonus or commission system.

5. *Fixed amount.* This is the safest method for you. Simply define explicitly what you want done and how much you will pay for it. Be sure to make your terms clear; otherwise your indignant and penniless employees may insist that they have done their job while you insist that they have not. Do not pay them unless the job is done as you instructed. If there is quality involved that is hard to quantify, you may offer a fixed amount plus some extra percentage (at *your* discretion) if the job is really outstanding. Frequently the amount you offer divided by the time the employee spends does not result in an hourly wage that you think is fair. Someone often feels underpaid or at least disappointed.

6. *Profit share.* This is also a safety measure for you, as well as an excellent incentive for your employee. Offer to pay them a percentage of your business' profits. You may wish to set a limit on the amount he can earn (25 per cent up to $400), but be prepared to give the employee the chance to make an attractive amount. Otherwise, he will have no reason to agree to both the risk and the wait (until the profits are reckoned) for his cash. You may have to guarantee him a certain minimum; you cannot expect him to risk walking away penniless if your business fails. For this reason, profit sharing often works best in combination with other methods of payment, for example, an hourly wage of $2 plus a small profit share. Profit sharing can give your employee a feeling of partnership in your business and a correspondingly greater interest in its success. If the business does well, he should be paid more, and because profits are high, you will be able to afford it.

There may be other ways of paying your employees that are particularly well suited to your situation. An important general rule, however, is to pay your employees fairly. Make sure that your employees know exactly what to expect so that if they agree to your terms they won't be disappointed.

You have no legal commitment from these people, and if they become dissatisfied with poor wages, you have no guarantee they won't quit when you need them or that their work will be of high quality. If you cannot make a good profit after paying good wages, then the business is not worth your efforts anyway.

What is fair? Fair wages vary greatly from college to college and with age and talent. Less than $1.50 per hour sounds like slave labor; $1.50–$2.00 is probably decent in many areas; but the going rate might be as high as $3.00. Naturally, you have to pay more for special skills. A good student artist, for example, may earn $10 to $50 per hour for actual brush time. In wages, as in values, you must watch your competition.

Tied in with this question of what is fair for your employees comes the equally important question, what is fair for the entrepreneur? The answer to this is arrived at by a process of elimination. If the entrepreneur is paying fair wages and the employees are happy; if the product or service is worth the money charged and the customers come away and remain satisfied; if the business is operating legally and is competing ethically; and if any other people (except competitors) with whom the business comes into contact—suppliers, university officials, and so on are satisfied with its performance, then the entrepreneur is entitled to any money that's left over. The amount of $20 an hour should not embarrass anyone who has met these conditions. A $2,500 profit on birthday cake mail orders, when the deliverer of the cakes earns $2.50 per hour, is "fair" and something to be proud of (as is donating 10 per cent of that profit to the scholarship fund—but that's *your* business).

Going It Alone versus Partnership

Either before you start your business or after you're well under way, the opportunity will present itself to enter into a partnership. Three immediate benefits can be derived from entering into a partnership: (1) You and your partner(s) pool both your resources and ideas, (2) a partnership provides reliable backup personnel, each person having a stake in the business' success, and (3) you share the financial risk.

Choosing a partner depends a great deal upon individual circumstances, but you should keep in mind that a good partner will have strengths in the areas in which you have weaknesses. For example, you may be a great schemer with lots of phenomenal advertising and promotional ideas but with little aptitude for bookkeeping. Try looking for a partner who has plenty of business experience and who likes to pay attention to details. Fighters and rock groups have their managers; playwrights and producers have their backers. Gilbert had Sullivan, Masters has Johnson, and even John Lennon worked with a group for a while. You may find a pattern of partnership that suits you and *your* business.

Another thing you should consider if a student business organization exists on campus is going into partnership with it. The benefits of such an alliance are numerous. The already established student business organization can provide you with help in setting up your records, advertising, and fund raising. And you will find yourself the instant heir to the business contacts and experience of dozens of your fellow student entrepreneurs.

The main disadvantage to any partnership is that you lose some autonomy. Each decision you make will require the approval of at least one other person. This should be a prime consideration when you're considering entering into a business partnership.

Obtaining Capital: Selling the Business

Some businesses require no capital. Most of the ones suggested in this book require a greater risk of time and effort than of money. Many, therefore, can be started out of personal savings. If not, you will have to seek funds elsewhere.

An obvious source of capital is your parents. They may go along with you where a banker would not.

Another source of money is your prospective supplier. For example, if you need a motorboke to deliver birthday cakes, your bakery may decide that the business you could bring in is worth the risk of loaning you money for the bike. At least they may give you easy credit for a while.

Student organizations on campus may be willing to take the risk that you face if you offer them a small share of your profits. On many campuses the newspaper or yearbook has a healthy surplus of funds. Interested businesses in the community who wish to encourage entrepreneurs might also back you.

One intriguing idea is to sell shares to your classmates. If you need

$500 to furnish your grill and you can find 100 people to buy $5 shares, you would get the financing you need and retain 50 per cent of the stock for yourself. More probably, you might find four or five students who could afford a substantial investment in the hope that they might double their money in a year or two. Still more practical in the case of the grill is to persuade the dorm committee or student government to come up with a loan. By all means, try the loan department of your local bank; a cat can look at a king. Your image will be crucial. Achieve the proper alchemical proportions of dynamism and financial responsibility, and the most conservative banker will come through for you. No doubt you will need a cosigner, however, and possibly some collateral, from parents or elsewhere.

The American economy is not termed *capitalist* for nothing—free enterprise is rarely free. But the nature of the system is such that, despite your age and probable inexperience, you will probably be able to raise the necessary capital to start your business and nurse it past its infancy—if your idea and your ability make the grade.

The search for capital may be part of the birth pangs of your enterprise, but it is not too soon to consider its potential demise. Since you are a student, your business may reach old age soon after it is born. If you escape from a dull dining hall job in the spring of your sophomore year and begin to set up business for your junior year, then after a year and a half of operation you will be faced with the problem of what to do with the business after you graduate. If it has been marginal, surviving mainly because of your particular talents and hard work, you may decide to let it die. But if it falls somewhere in between, you may be able to sell the business.

If you own fifty refrigerators that you have been renting, you may either decide to sell the machines to individual students, to a used refrigerator dealer, or to a freshman or sophomore who would like to continue to rent them. Along with the refrigerators go your experience in sales and management, your records, your market research and organizational set-up—which are certainly worth something.

Hopefully, a fair and amicable arrangement can be worked out so that you do not wreck the college career or family finances of the student whom you talk into buying the business. A good protection for you and your buyer is some profit-sharing arrangement, whereby you instruct the new owner carefully and provide him with an attractive deal, and receive in return a dividend for two or three years. Another idea is to sell the business to one of your employees, who already has enough experience to know the true value of the business and to run it well after you leave. In transferring ownership of your business, you should make sure that your buyer knows of any credits or debts that the business has accumulated.

Another kind of "selling the business" involves nothing at all tangible (no inventory or capital equipment), only your experience and your company name. Anyone may be allowed to set up a bartending business, but not everyone will know the tricks you have learned about running the business well; they will not have your mailing list of steady customers; they will lack your (now fairly well-known) company name. Again, it may be fairest to set a student up with your business in return for a 10 per cent (25 per cent? 50 per cent?) share in the profits for the first or first few years of its operation.

Help from the Community

You can get a lot of help from people in your college and local community. The idea of a student running his own business arouses interest and paternalism.

One excellent source of help may come to you from the local news media. If you open a store, you can expect free stories and possibly some local radio or television coverage. A middle-aged gentleman opening a store may not be news, but you—nineteen-year-old sophomore, supersalesman—are a novelty. "Local Boy Makes Good." "Collegiate Captain of Industry." Your bid at fortune rates at least one celebration in the local newspaper. If you start your business in a large city, there are several people to see at the paper. The first is the business editor—your business has a lot to do with students, campus life and the important field of financial aid. Second is the editor in charge of the field under which your business falls—the society editor for a bartending or entertainment agency, the book review editor for a guide to the city, and so forth. University seniors who started a restaurant in Somerville, Massachusetts, recently were featured in a *New York Times* article, under the by-line of a food editor; not only was the establishment praised, but one student cook was photographed in the pantry and several recipes of his were published, to tantalize the restaurant-going reader. Don't be shy—by convincing a newspaperman of your newsworthiness, you get him a story and yourself priceless publicity.

The public fascination with youth and student enterprise is enormous: don't underestimate it.

This interest may help you get other help from the community besides free publicity. A local lawyer or professor of law might consent to sit on your "Board of Directors" and offer his $50-an-hour counsel for free. A local accountant or professor of economics might help you to set up your books or answer your questions about taxes and accounting. Local businesses may allow you to place posters in their windows, permit you to use their machines, or give you general business advice. You may be surprised to see how willingly important people will sit down to lunch with you and pour forth really valuable information, suggestions, and criticism. These people know how to get things done, where to buy materials (where to find out where), what billing and purchasing procedures are standard, and so on. Of course, if you plan to go into direct competition with a business, its owner will not be of much help to you. But the owner of a similar enterprise in your hometown a few hundred miles away might be delighted to tip his hand if it is clear to him that he is safe from competition.

It is up to you how much you capitalize on your "needy student" status. Certainly you will get the breaks because of your special position; but these favors should not be sought out or requested on the basis of sympathy alone. A master craftsman usually enjoys passing on his skills; so does the successful businessman. The local printer may well be flattered if you ask his guidance in setting up your broadside handpress, and a furniture leasing agent may get some gratification from helping a young entrepreneur organize his refrigerator rentals. The Horatio Alger aspects of your upward struggle may reawaken an aging capitalist's romance with free enterprise.

Although you may well feel uncomfortable asking for favors that amount to fists of money, you should *not* feel uncomfortable asking knowledgeable people for their advice and experience. Nor should you underestimate the importance of what can be learned from a big-business executive about a tiny student business. Will his recommendations prove valid for your enterprise? Test them out. If the people you consult are good businessmen, chances are that you'll eventually be handing down their advice approvingly to your successors.

Advertising

Few businesses have ever succeeded without effective advertising. You not only have to be in business but you have to let the people *know* you're in business. As a student business your advertising budget is necessarily limited—but that needn't stop it from being effective.

First, think about what advertising is—it's communication. The job of advertising your job is to communicate effectively with people. Well designed ads are important, but so is the use of all of the channels that are available to you in reaching your target audience of potential customers. If your school has a radio station, perhaps you can arrange to buy advertising time cheaply. Better yet, you might be able to arrange it so that you're interviewed on a news program, or maybe you can get a friendly disc jockey to give you a plug every now and then. Next there's the college paper. Your new business surely rates a news story and the paper might even be willing to run a free advertisement for you.

Have you ever received "10 per cent off with this coupon" or drunk a free Coke "with every Big Burger purchased" because you mentioned the name of a radio station, as suggested by the disc jockey in the restaurant's ads? These offers serve the advertiser in two ways. They bring you new customers, who are drawn by your something-for-nothing deal. What you count on is that many will discover that they like your product and stay with you long after the discount lapses. In addition to expanding your market by discount "introductions," you will find this pattern of advertising to be a good method of judging how effective your newspaper and radio advertising are. By keeping a careful tally of the advertising sources "mentioned" to secure a discount by keeping a careful tally, you'll know which media are bringing you the most business, and can then judge exactly where to put the bulk of your advertising budget.

But don't stop at radio and newspaper advertising. Dress up in a sandwich board and patrol the campus. Hire a one-man band, a hurdy-gurdy, or a dancing bear. Get a skywriting friend to paint your slogan in the air over the Homecoming Game. Try mimeographed handouts, posters, word-of-mouth—anything that will let people know that you're selling something *they want*.

Technical Information

There are, of course, technical problems you will have to deal with when setting up your business. You will want to consider procedures for using the mails, writing letters, sending bills, and answering legal and tax questions.

Mailings

First-class mail is usually more effective than third-class or bulk-rate mail, although it is more expensive. If you are trying to sell something, it is probably worth the extra pennies to be a first-class salesman instead of a "junk-mail" man. In fact, where practical, you should use commemorative stamps instead of an impersonal postage meter or (worse still) a printed permit.

All mailings represent a compromise between personal attention and efficiency. You have probably tossed out—unopened—letters that were clearly part of a machine-processed mass mailing. Your own priorities, as you prepare solicitations, will depend upon the demands of your particular business. Preparing sheets of address labels and then sticking them on envelopes is faster than addressing each envelope individually. On the other hand, it is more effective to type, or even to write out, each address. The more personal the letter looks, the more likely that it will be read. Adhesive-backed, unperforated labels balance speed and appearance.

You should present your prospective customer with an attractive letter. It is almost always worth the money to print sample stationery; if your letterhead is blank, you can have your form letter printed beneath at the same time. Be sure to leave the salutation and first paragraph blank, so that you can personalize each form letter by typing in the addressee's name and a special greeting. If you prefer to save money and have the letter mimeographed, be sure that the stencil is perfect and that the letter looks attractive.

Distinctive stationery and a strikingly designed letterhead can make a positive impression for your business before a word of your message is read. You can create this lure toward your sales pitch for little or nothing more than you would pay for a pedestrian layout. An investment of time and thought can also make your name memorable. All business correspondence at the Hershey Chocolate Company is printed in luscious brown ink. Your letters need not go out in your school colors (purple and green), but remember that even printing details can be resources for you to exploit.

The letter itself should be simple, sincere, and *interesting*. You may think it sufficient to state your case clearly, but you're wrong. If the letter is hard to read (one huge paragraph) or dull, your response rate will fall dramatically. The first sentence is crucial. Compare these: "In order to raise money for my college expenses, I have started a . . ." and, "Your son's birthday is this month—we can deliver a birthday cake for you." Many more customers will read the second letter than the first.

It may prove useful and interesting to send out several different kinds of letters, noting which one brings in the best response. Whenever possible, pay the return postage for your customer by enclosing a business reply card or envelope; it may increase your response rate significantly. (Consult your post office about a permit and about all of their different rates and regulations.) At the same time, you can code the different letters by using a mark on the back of some reply envelopes and not others. Then, next time, use only the approach that brings the highest response. This is the sort of thing that will make your work interesting, while your profits grow.

If you plan to do much mailing, it is worth your time to figure out time and money-saving ideas. There are machines that stuff envelopes, seal envelopes, stamp envelopes; there are also machines that "hand-sign" letters, type "individual" letters, and fold inserts. There are permits for reply mail, for bulk mail, for nonprofit organization mail (in case you are reading this chapter with an eye toward improving the financial position of your yearbook or debate society), and for omitting the postage stamp or meter. There are special "postage saver" envelopes that go third class but look almost first class, and there are electric collating and stapling machines.

It is certainly unlikely that you would need to buy any of these machines—but very likely that you can find someone in the mailing business who wants you to use his machines to do your mailing. Better, you may be able to find a business that is friendly to you and will allow you to use its machines free. The best place to look is your college administration—no doubt they have many of these machines, as well as computerized mailing lists that you might persuade them to run onto your envelopes.

Writing Letters; Sending Bills

The ability to write a good letter is important, particularly in business. It is not difficult to write a satisfactory letter ordering some product—just make sure you are clear and precise. The recipient will ignore your poor spelling, poor typing, or poor phrasing, because you are bringing business his way. These flaws are not so easily forgiven, however, in a letter that "sells" instead of buys. It is much harder to write a letter to get a dean to go along with your water bed scheme, a grocery store to advertise in your magazine, or a parent to buy a birthday cake for his son through you—in these letters you've got to be *convincing*.

You may already be used to proper business form. If not, we have prepared some fictitious examples of business letters in the pages that follow. The first is a request to the college administration for permission to do something. The second is a simple sales letter. The third is a publicity-seeking letter, and the fourth is a collection letter.

No doubt you have written many letters before, but it is likely that you have never sent a bill. In most businesses it is customary to send the bill soon after you have performed your service or delivered your product, and to allow the customer thirty days in which to pay you. If he does not pay within the time agreed on, you send him a "statement" (not another bill), which reminds the customer of your first bill.

Money that you are owed by a customer is called an account receivable. In most cases, accounts receivable are almost as good as having cash, since you should only be dealing with people whom you expect will pay you. Someone who takes a couple of months to pay a small bill is not dishonest—he just needs some friendly reminders. There are people, though, who make a practice of not paying their bills unless they are forced to. There are also people who are really tight for cash, and delay paying their bills until they can pull themselves out of their financial difficulties. Finally, there are people who would like to pay you but who go out of business. An account receivable that is not collected is called a bad debt. Some businesses know statistically that a certain percentage of their accounts receivable will turn into bad debts. This percentage is particularly high, for example, in the magazine subscription field, since a customer knows that a big magazine's threat that it will go to court over a $2.97 bill is probably an empty one.

If you cannot collect all of your accounts receivable by the friendly (or not so friendly) reminder system, you may decide to take stronger action. You can write to Dun and Bradstreet, Inc., for a brochure on their collection agency and related services (check the telephone book of any major city for an address or number). A more interesting way to try to collect a bad debt is to file suit in a small claims court. If you win, you won't have to split the money with a collection agency. The small claims procedure is relatively easy—you don't need a lawyer and the costs are very small—but regulations vary from state to state. Call your local courthouse and ask to speak to the small claims clerk (if there is one). Explain your problem and he will be glad to tell you how to proceed.

Legal and Tax Problems

Your thriving new enterprise may be a *student* business, but it is nevertheless a *business* and is subject to certain regulations. One thing that new student entrepreneurs ask is "Well, if it is a business, should I incorporate it?" The answer, in almost all cases, is "no." The expense of incorporating (in some states it is almost $300!) simply isn't worth it. To be sure, you have a business, but most likely it is run by you, and maintained by you, and there is simply no need to enlarge the "executive staff."

Although you don't have to incorporate, you *do* have to pay taxes—which is one of the main reasons for maintaining a separate checking account and good records. The Internal Revenue Service publishes an excellent booklet entitled *Tax Guide for Small Businesses,* which is available from any I.R.S. office. Be sure to consult it from the beginning of your business efforts, so that you will be well prepared at tax time. Another item to watch is the sales tax. Regulations vary greatly from state to state—some states tax food, others don't; some tax almost everything, some tax almost nothing. As a businessman, however, you will be expected to submit to and to collect the state taxes on all taxable items that you sell. "I didn't know—" won't have much effect on the authorities. You are legally obliged to find out your tax responsibilities—but learning isn't as complicated as it sounds. Check with your local tax authorities on their exact regulations and methods.

In taking care of your business identity, you should not lose sight of the *student* part of "student businessman." With all of this tax money changing hands on college grounds—which are by law tax-exempt—it is *absolutely imperative* that you get permission from the appropriate dean before starting any business. This cannot be stressed enough. Also, the college is more likely to be a help than a hindrance: perhaps the dean will consent to sit on your advisory board!

If you follow good bookkeeping procedures and maintain fairly friendly relationships with your creditors and debtors, you probably won't need a lawyer. If your university has a law school you may be able to get a law student or even a law professor to give you some free advice. In most cases, your legal problems aren't worth worrying about in advance.

By now, you may already have an idea for your own business. If not, the student businesses described in the next section should give an idea of the possibilities and procedures for earning your first million. We suggest that you read through all of the business suggestions, even the ones that seem inappropriate to your situation, because there is general advice in many that may be helpful to your success with the business that you are most excited about.

Agencies and Solicitations

The most traditional (and often the most lucrative) student businesses have been those in which a student represents a company on campus. Many students have worked their way through college representing everything from insurance firms to magazine companies. If your college is large, or has been around for a long time, it is likely that most of the ideas that follow are already being realized. Whoever controls the agency you covet, however, is bound to graduate—try working with him in the hope of becoming his successor. There are, of course, hundreds of possibilities. The following are just a few to give you an idea of the scope of the market. Names and places to contact are listed at the end of this section.

Most of the major airlines in your area probably like to have a student representative on campus, to distribute their promotional material, place their campus advertisements, and talk up the airline generally. These jobs often pay well, particularly because the airline may hope to recruit you for full-time employment after graduation. With the youthfare price war, airline campus representatives are kept busy publicizing the latest rates and selling students on the comparative advantages of their particular airline. You may get special rates when you fly, as well as a salary or commission.

Look into other aspects of the transportation industry. The Greyhound Bus Company, for example, offers a 10 per cent commission on group sales and charters. Contact the marketing representative at your local Greyhound station for details.

If you're a female, *Mademoiselle* magazine runs a campus marketing program in which you might be interested. Company X wants to know what percentage of college women buy striped jeans. Your assignment is to distribute and collect 100 questionnaires concerning this question from women on your campus. This type of standard research pays $2 per hour.

One of the most lucrative campus representative programs is insurance sales. Students earn, typically, between $1,000 and $3,000 per year selling insurance to their classmates and to graduate students. Healthy young persons usually obtain insurance at bargain rates, and insurance companies want to make student populations aware of this. The work involved is not difficult and is often challenging.

Another old standby is selling magazine subscriptions. Don't pass it up because it's "old"—it is also profitable. You will receive commissions for the subscriptions you sell. At the same time, you will be saving your customers the trouble of having to figure out where to go to subscribe at the special rates that are available to students.

Time, Inc., has pioneered this area of student employment and hires a large number of representatives each year, as do other magazines and major newspapers.

If you are interested in writing for these publications, you could also investigate the possibility of becoming a campus news representative. Campus unrest and the popularization of the "youth culture" have led many publications to seek out students on major campuses, to be their on-the-spot reporter—or "stringer." If the chairman of your Biology Department wins the Nobel Prize, or if a new approach to Afro-American studies is pioneered at your school, you may end up writing a story with nationwide coverage. Or you may simply be asked to glean student opinions on a presidential hopeful. In any case, you may be paid for keeping your eyes open to campus affairs.

In addition to magazine subscriptions, bus tickets, and insurance, students buy class rings, personalized stationery, beer mugs, class banners, special college T-shirts or ties, and so on. Commissions on these items are usually *very* generous, and students who have sold them have earned quite a bit of money.

You should note, however, that there is a general trend away from "college identity" items and the rah-rah spirit that once made these items so popular. The older and more tradition-conscious your school is, the higher will be your percentage of sales among the student body. For most of these items, freshmen are the best market. They are the most enthusiastic and present a new market year after year. If there are 2,000 freshmen in your college, you might aim to sell to 200 of them.

Your sales pitch might run something like this: "You are bound to buy a school ring sooner or later, and prices go up each year. Why pay more next year for the same ring—and have one less year to enjoy it?" The new customer will fill out one of the order forms your ring manufacturer has supplied, and you will determine the customer's ring size with one of the manufacturer's sets of sized rings. The ring is likely to cost your customer about $40, depending upon the ring selected, and makes a good Christmas gift from his parents. (This suggestion might warrant a test mailing to parents.) Of the $40, about $25 goes to the manufacturer, who makes the ring to order in about six weeks and $15 goes to you. Part of the $15 may be used for general business expenses, or may go for advertising costs (such as a mailing to alumni wives suggesting that they buy a ring as a gift for their husbands). Even so, you should be left with well over $1,000 for your efforts. The same principles apply equally for selling other college identity items.

The main student store probably sells many of these items and you should try not to anger them when you try to compete. If you are imaginative enough to think of an item *not* already being sold at the store, then you will have a much easier time and you will alienate no one.

In all of these cases, as with most business/agency ideas, you act as an agency for a much larger company. Be sure to check with college officials before you begin posting notices, canvassing door-to-door, or operating an agency from your room; deans become irritated at many things if they are not identified in advance.

Instead of representing another company you might try starting your own company and, eventually, hiring your own agents. Students may wish to rent television sets or refrigerators from you, if you will take care of all the headaches of moving them in and out and guaranteeing reliable (free) repair service, should anything go wrong. You may be able to purchase a small inventory of these machines and then watch them pay back your investment plus a profit.

Small refrigerators are usually best to use. They are adequate for most students without taking up too much space in their rooms. They cost you less, they are easier for you to move and store, they use less electricity, and they are therefore less likely to cause problems with the college electrical system. If electricity has been a problem in the past, try Norcold (Sidney, Ohio), which only uses as much electricity as a 50-watt light bulb. Other manufacturers of small refrigerators are Tapp (Miami, Florida), Fridgette (Ero Industries, Chicago, Illinois), and Delmonico (Maspeth, Long Island). General Electric and Frigidaire also make small refrigerators but are less likely to deal with you directly and at their lowest price. This industry is highly competitive, and it would be to your advantage to shop around by telephone to find the best price and terms.

With any new refrigerator, the first ninety days are the critical ones and are covered by warranty. If no problems have occurred in ninety days, the refrigerator is likely to last at least five years and possibly ten or twenty. You should be careful when moving the refrigerators around, though, as the cooling and electrical systems can be easily damaged.

If you can't afford or don't wish to invest money in new refrigerators, you should be able to buy decent reconditioned refrigerators for

$25–$65 apiece, depending upon their size and age, and your luck. Perhaps you can buy refrigerators from graduating students for even less. A fair price for the rental of a refrigerator that is delivered, cleaned (at the beginning of the year), and repaired free, if necessary, is anywhere from $25 to $50 for the school year. Do a market survey to see if the students in your school are willing to pay that amount. With four or five students in a room, or with fifteen on a floor, $40 doesn't amount to much from each pocket. If you cannot afford to buy television sets or refrigerators, you might approach a large appliance store to set up a rental business with you as the manager and head salesman. (IMPORTANT NOTE: Before renting *any* electrical equipment make sure that the electrical wiring is adequate in the building in which the appliance is going to be used. There may be college rules on appliance use that you must also consult and abide by.)

Any agency you set up will eventually require salesmen. The following story will give you some idea of what to expect. Sixteen salesmen were hired in one student ring business. Each was given the same amount of territory, the same instructions, and the same sample case. Two of the sixteen salesmen sold less than five rings. One sold more than 100 rings. The point is that you should be very careful when you choose your salesmen, giving them small enough territories so that the ones who are not ambitious or effective can be replaced without losing too many customers. Try to train them to sell well but not to be obnoxious or overly aggressive. Make sure they know a lot about their products and are satisfied that they are selling a good value. Pay by commission, possibly outlining some sort of incentive plan for high sales (10 per cent commission for the first fifty rings, 12 per cent for the next fifty, 15 per cent thereafter, for example). Make sure that they keep careful records, and that they bring in their cash and reports daily. In order to keep anyone from skimming the best customers and easiest sales from a territory, try to compile lists of the people in each territory and have the salesman write down what happened in each case. If he gives up after the easiest sales, at least you will know what prospects have not been contacted.

Useful Addresses

MARKETING SURVEYS

Campus Marketing Editor
Mademoiselle
420 Lexington Ave.
New York, New York 10017

INSURANCE COMPANIES

Provident Mutual Life Insurance
  Company
4601 Market Street
Philadelphia, Pennsylvania 19101

The Northwestern Mutual Life Insurance Company
720 East Wisconsin Avenue
Milwaukee, Wisconsin 53202

MAGAZINE SUBSCRIPTIONS

Burce A. Basnet, Manager
College Circulation
Time, Inc.
Time & Life Building

Rockefeller Center
New York, New York 10020

STATIONERY

Golbestat Corporation
128–168 Thirty-Second Street
Brooklyn, New York 11232

BANNERS, FLAGS, ETC.

The Nixon Company, Inc.
Nixon Building
Indian Orchard, Massachusetts
  01051

RINGS

John Roberts Ring Company
Norman, Oklahoma

CUSTOM-MADE SHIRTS

J. Packard Ltd.
1316–1320 Plum Street
Terre Haute, Indiana 47808

Services: Bartending, Entertainment

If your college is located in a large community, there will probably be many parties given among the faculty and in the "outside world." Student bartenders are very popular at these parties because they are attractive, articulate, and relatively inexpensive.

Learning to mix the most common drinks is easy, but important; just as important are your appearance and attitude. You do not necessarily need to be twenty-one to bartend at a private party. However, state laws vary; check your local regulations.

It will take time to build a good reputation, which is something to think about before hiring your staff and opening a bartending agency. If you have ten eager bartenders working under you, you will need at least ten parties a week. Business on that scale will not appear overnight, especially if you yourself do not wish to take more than one job a week. There are several ways to build this reputation. One way is to talk to any friends you may have on the faculty or in town who may be giving parties. They will probably be happy to hire you if they need help. Once behind the bar, you will be able to show your worth to many prospective employers. The word will spread.

The only equipment you will need is a clean bartender's jacket. It might also be wise to have some match books made bearing your name and telephone number. This is good publicity and is not expensive, and your employers will probably be happy to use these matches instead of their own.

The amount you should charge per hour varies with the community and with how good you are. (Do you add life to the party? Can you play the piano on request? Are you an enthusiastic helper after the party is over?) Here again you should look at the competition. You should probably set your rates somewhere between $2.00 and $3.50 an hour, with some minimum number of hours, for instance three or four, regardless of how long the party actually lasts. Of course, if you do a good job, you will often get a good tip. A $5 tip divided over three hours' work gives a good boost to the wage.

If you are hiring other students, you should send bills to your customers, instead of having your employees collect cash at the party. Supply your employees with jackets and matches, teach them how to bartend, explain the standards they will have to maintain to protect the good reputation of your business, and let them keep any tips they earn. You should pay your people a standard hourly wage (for example $2–$3 per hour) plus transportation, if there is any. Then tips, when they come, will be a bonus. Make it a strict rule that your bartenders cannot contract for parties on their own—they have to go through you. This is not unfair; you are supplying them with instruction, a steady stream of employment, and a fair wage. In return, they should agree not to take jobs on their own and bypass you.

At the same time, *you* must play fair: if you are charging your customer $4 an hour, do not pay $1 an hour wages and expect good service in return.

It is important to list a telephone number that will be answered and to provide your roommates with an incentive to take good messages and to be good salesmen. Why not offer $.25 per message, or per actual order taken? NEVER FAIL TO SHOW UP ON TIME: reliability is vital to your customers. Also, as a rule, do not drink on the job. Often your tip will be topped off by that half-empty bottle of Cutty Sark. Celebrate when you get home.

Naturally, one drawback to the bartending business is that people are generally having parties when you, too, would like to be giving or attending a party (for example, New Year's Eve). Having a whole corps of employees increases the chance of finding one who is free on a Saturday night.

You will soon learn what a host or hostess looks for in a good bartender, and you will get ideas for doing a particularly good job. Setting up the bar and cleaning up after the party are usually expected. If you have a good place to buy it, you might offer to bring extra ice to the party, extra bottle openers, rented glassware, a martini shaker, and so on. Why not call the hostess a few hours before your arrival time to reassure her that you are coming and to ask whether you can pick up anything for her on the way over—napkins, toothpicks, cheese spread, pretzels, or Maraschino cherries? In addition to being reimbursed for your expenses, your thoughtfulness will no doubt result in a lot of business tips and good will.

Somewhat similar to the bartending business are entertainment agencies. In this case, you find talented bands, light shows, pianists, magicians, and other entertainers and offer to act as their agent. Advertise to the community that you can fill almost any entertainment needs—tailored to the budget requirements and audience of the individual organization. Talk to fraternity chairmen, high school prom committees, and so on. Have your groups announce your services (musically?) at dances for which you have arranged live music. You may also want to advertise on the radio or in the newspapers.

Bands will fit in well with your bartending service, especially if they can play popular music as well as rock. Don't overlook the possibilities presented by wedding receptions, Bar Mitzvahs, and other large gatherings that may require music as well as liquor. When you are discussing bartending arrangements for the party over the telephone, you can suggest the band as well.

In addition to your bartending, and/or entertainment agency, you might also try catering. Be careful though—the catering business is full of pitfalls and can require a fairly large outlay of capital, which the bartending business does not. If you or your friends have a flair for cooking, however, you might start with an hors d'oeuvre and canapé service to augment your cocktail-party business. You could provide standard tidbits, as well as accepting suggestions from your hostesses and offering a few specialties—academic communities are especially enthusiastic about foreign and exotic foods. If tea cakes and pastries are your forte or if you take special delight in French luncheon dishes or skilled Chinese cookery, you might sell your talents to the community. The point to remember is: start small. Helpers and equipment can be added if you are in constant demand; a number of students have ended up owning and managing restaurants from such humble freshman beginnings. Make certain, however, that in preparing and selling food, you are complying with the rules and standards of your local Board of Health. (Female employees may have to wear hair nets!)

A better arrangement might be to work out a deal with an already established catering agency, whereby if your hostess desired catering as well as bartending you would refer her to "your" catering agency. A fair price to charge the catering agency for your referral service is 10 per cent of its fee.

Children's Party Service

Yet another entertainment service you can provide (if you like children) is a children's party service. For many parents, children's birthday parties rank second only to taxes as THE horror of modern life—and they will gladly pay you to run the entire party. The key idea in running a children's party service is that *your parties must be good*. They don't have to be gimicky or elaborate, but if they are disastrous, you will feel badly, and so will everyone else. You should have really amusing and entertaining things for the children to do; children are much less gullible than adults and they will not tolerate particularly asinine games.

It is much better to have too many things for children to do than too few. You should end each activity when anyone tires of it. Eventually you will accumulate a wide repertoire of games and activities. Outdoor games are often exciting—even ordinary ones such as kick-the-can and spud. "Capture the Flag" should absorb anyone under thirty for an entire afternoon—if you've got the space. Most of the conspicuously "party" games do not have the staying power of old favorites such as treasure hunts, but if you can find a *good* new game, everyone (including the parents) will remember you for it.

Good parties often focus on a single activity, such as a movie (which you can rent), a treasure hunt, a trip to a fire station or farm, or to a real circus. Activity-centered parties are usually more successful than theme-centered parties (wild west or circus), which are often dreadfully artificial. A nearby holiday (Christmas, Halloween, the Fourth of July) may provide a better theme. If you perform any type of entertainment—magic tricks, for example, you can make the party something special. Needless to say, the children's safety should be your highest priority. Transportation and adequate supervision must be arranged with care, and although a beach party sounds like fun, make sure that a helper has had life-saving training.

You must be careful to plan the party with the age of the guests in mind—for the length of the party and for the activities. Children aged nine to twelve often prefer parties exclusively for their own sex. Young children will not play each game very long, and older ones need more challenging games.

Your service will be most successful if you charge a flat rate—based on the number of guests and the time span of the party—which should include everything: food, favors, your services for running the party, and a cleanup after the party. Children like simple food: potato chips, plain cookies, ice cream, milk, juice or soft drinks, and, of course, the cake. Bake it yourself or make arrangements with a bakery. Be sure to find out the birthday child's favorite flavor—and don't forget the right number of candles. If you plan an excursion as entertainment, make up box lunches (or get the kids to bring their own and supply a beverage and cake).

As in all businesses, try to get your supplies wholesale. You may also end up hiring helpers, particularly if you intend to take twenty-five eight-year-olds to a Walt Disney movie or to the zoo. For a typical party that lasts for three hours with twelve guests you might charge $25. If you do a party every other week for the entire school year you could expect to clear about $350.

Parents whose children enjoyed a party that you arranged will hire you when their own child's birthday comes around and will recommend you to their friends, so your advertising costs should be minimal. Tips may also come your way. A fringe benefit is free cake and ice cream—and if you plan your party well, you too will have a good time.

Parent Mail Orders

Even grown-up children have birthdays, and you may be able to provide a great service to the parents of your fellow students by delivering birthday cakes to their hungry sons or daughters. If this is not already being done, go to the proper college official with your idea and ask him to let you use college lists of the home addresses and birth dates of the students at your school. Send a letter to each student's parents about a month before the student's birthday offering to deliver, at an appropriate time, a cake chosen from among several flavors, sizes, and prices (probably in the $4–$12 range) and suitably inscribed with whatever message the parents desire. Find a good, conveniently located bakery that likes your idea and negotiate prices with the owner. The bakery should be pleased to cooperate, because you are bringing it business that would not otherwise come its way. If you bought twenty cakes a week, you might get the cakes at half of the going rate.

If 3,200 of your fellow students have birthdays during the eight months of the school year, you would be sending 400 letters a month, at a cost of $.15 each (postage, letter, reply card, envelope, addressing, stuffing, mailing), or $60. If you write a good letter and receive a 25 per cent response (that is, the ratio of orders to letters), then you would be delivering 100 cakes a month, or about three a day (which is no great strain). You could deliver the cakes yourself by car or bike, or you could hire an energetic helper. In any case, you should make sure your system is virtually foolproof (will your cake come on the wrong day?). Never let a customer down.

If the average order is for an $8 cake, and $4 of the order goes to the bakery, then you would have $400 a month to pay for your mailing ($60), the wages you might decide to pay a delivery helper, and yourself. You should be clearing over $2,000 for the school year.

You may be able to think of other things to sell. A group at Mount Holyoke mailed letters to parents offering to provide an exam period "survival kit" (oranges, cookies, chocolates, and aspirin) for their offspring. Another possibility is a "fruit basket" each week: see if the local florist can supply you with inexpensive baskets of good fruit. If not, check with your grocer about quantity rates—maybe you can design your own package. Then offer to deliver it to the students; parents are always worried about their childrens' vitamin intake, and students will enjoy a good pomegranate now and then. The important thing to remember if you want your business to last more than a single season is that you *must* deliver high-quality goods and at the time agreed upon.

Furniture Moving Agency

Springtime on the campus is a good time to have a bulk supply of cardboard boxes of various convenient sizes on hand. Along about Groundhog Day, you should put in your order to buy these boxes in quantity and in late May you can sell them—at a considerable profit. They can be advertised for storage and for carrying books, clothes, and records from one dorm to another.

At the same time you might become a liaison between a moving company in your area and students and faculty who will be moving at the end of the school year. You can provide a needed service to the students as well as earn a good-sized profit for yourself.

There is a large market for this type of business in a university community, particularly in the graduate schools. The most effective method of reaching your market is through direct mail. You can obtain a list of your potential customers from the university directory. Send information to all students who live off-campus, who are graduate students, or who are finishing their programs during the current year. Your mailing should be professionally done—hire a competent printer. Your information sheet should include the name of the company with whom you are dealing and a telephone number through which the potential customer can get an estimate. Always bear in mind that you are selling a service and, therefore, must try to make your customers feel that they are getting something special.

You may need a part-time secretary or an answering service to type the names for your mailing list and, once your calls start coming in, to handle them and to keep records and files for you. Other than that, the only initial investment will be for your telephone and the costs of the mailing. Write up a budget to work with. Try to figure how many moves you have to get to break even and also, as a goal, how many you need to make a satisfying profit.

As an agent you are in a good position to get the best service for your customers. Be sure that the firm with whom you are dealing is reputable, and make certain that they understand that if they do not give high quality service you will take your business elsewhere.

Most important for making this a worthwhile business are an imaginative marketing strategy and quality service. Don't waste your money advertising in the wrong places or at the wrong time. If your business proves successful, however, you might consider expanding by advertising in the late summer as well—spring is moving-out time, but the start of the school year sees many members of the university community moving *into* their nine-month residences. See how creative you can be in finding prospects to mail to—for example, go through the classified ads to see who is trying to sell or rent his house or apartment. He may need a lot of furniture moved in the near future.

CAUTION: When you see the rates that professional movers charge, you may be tempted to go out with your van and your roommates, and take on some of the local jobs yourself. (One mover charged $66 to a student who wanted his piano moved from a freshman dorm to his upperclass dorm, 200 yards away!) You should check very carefully into the insurance problems that are involved, however, partly with regard to your damaging someone's antique baby grand, and partly with regard to having it land on the big toe of one of your workmen. You can get into a great deal of trouble if you are unlucky and have not checked out your responsibilities beforehand.

Publications

There are many types of publications that you could put together (calendars, blotters, newsletters, movie guides, and the like), and all of them can be profitable.

You could prepare a desk blotter, for example, to be given free to all students at the beginning of the school year, and print on the blotter ads that you sold late in the spring or early in the fall before school starts. An estimate of how long it will take to print your blotter should help you to decide when to sell ads. Find out from the printer, as well, how high your costs will be, and figure from that how large and expensive the ads should be.

If you are at all artistic, you might offer to design ads for your customers: "Sir, this blotter will be staring your customers in their face all semester; whenever they want to order a pizza (find out what's playing, buy a new pair of jeans, and so on), they will have your name, number, and address right in front of them. I sketched out what I thought might be an effective ad for you. Do you like it?" People find it harder to turn down your service when they see their name in print. Your blotter can charge higher space rates than the school newspaper, because you may have a larger circulation (free to everyone in the college) and a much longer exposure time—the newspaper comes out daily and is read only once whereas the blotter will stay around for months. If the blotter you design has handy telephone numbers, or a calendar, or a schedule of sports events and vacations, it will be extremely useful to the students; businessmen will understand this.

Don't let the printing aspect of this business idea frighten you; it is surprisingly simple to lay out and produce a blotter, and the printer you choose will be happy to give you help and advice. Once you have sold the ads and printed the blotters, make sure that you or someone you hire delivers enough blotters to each door in the college, plus a few to each of your advertisers along with your bill and a "thank you." This may go a long way in securing you their repeat business the following year.

You have to print advertising on both sides of the desk blotter so that students cannot escape the ads. Prices vary widely, but it will probably cost about $800 to set in type and print 5,000 blotters—shop around for the lowest bid, but use a good quality of blotting paper. If your blotter is 20 inches by 24 inches, or 480 square inches, and you plan to use 80 square inches for a calendar or football schedule (or ads for your other businesses, if you're a true entrepreneur), then you have 400 square inches to sell (which includes the identical 400 square inches on the opposite side). If you charge $3 per square inch (use standard sizes and have a discount for the larger ads), a customer can buy a decent 2 inch by 4 inch block for only $24. After salesmen's commissions, printing, and delivery, you could show a $600 profit or more, which would be your wage. If the ads do not sell, you've lost your own time, but very little money, since you can cancel the project. If business is terrific, you should consider producing a new blotter each semester.

Mimeograph your ad contracts, send your bill with a few samples of the blotter and keep good records of who has paid and whom to see next year. Your bill can simply be a piece of stationery with the customer's name and address, the product or service you have supplied or rendered, and the amount he owes.

You can print up and sell ads for other useful publications, or you can actually try to sell the publication itself. When you put a price on your publication, however, your circulation becomes uncertain (but *certainly* smaller), which cuts down your ad rates; furthermore, you may then have to start dealing through campus stores, who will require a 40 per cent share of the retail price to sell your magazine or book. Although a price cuts down your circulation, most advertisers know that a *paid* circulation is better than an unpaid circulation. (Would you just throw away a magazine you paid $.50 for?) For example, the longer you keep a publication, the more likely you are to respond to the advertisements it carries. It is also true that a paid publication often has a specific audience. If you publish a *Winter Guide,* with information on winter sports (skiing, cross-country skiing, snowshoeing, snowmobiles, skating, and hockey), in the area of your school, and if you include information about travel, equipment, and accommodations that are within students' means, you are in an excellent position to sell ads to ski shops, lodges, bus lines, sports stores, and so forth. You could write and publish, as a pamphlet or booklet, a student guide to the college town, listing hotels, restaurants, movies, sights, night clubs, and so on. A humorous style does wonders for sales, and remember, too, that there is a good advertising market in any large town for such publications.

A more ambitious handout project is a weekly Calendar of Events at the college—what is playing at the movies; what special lectures are being given; sports events; performances; radio, TV, and train schedules; and so on. Here you are faced with deadlines to meet each week, quality to maintain, and a staff to supervise. On the other hand, instead of selling ads one by one you'll be able to sell a whole season contract (a half-page every third week, for example, for one firm; an eighth of a page in every issue for another), plus seasonal ads and advertising for special events (rock concerts or Winter Carnival).

You could also set up a magazine (literary, humorous, or other type) that comes out a few times a year; undergraduate magazines, however, usually tend at best to be tenuous financial successes.

Perhaps a better bet is a college telephone book, with Yellow Pages and ads. You might be able to sell this instead of giving it away—with a sales force, you could spend a day or two at college focal points (dining halls, library entrances, the TV room) selling the books at $1 each. In addition to that revenue, you should be able to obtain small ads or listings from most of the businesses in town. The telephone company might buy a back cover ad, for example, since you're doing them a service. The college may be willing and able to supply you with all of the student telephone numbers from registration cards, or you may have to distribute and collect forms.

The one-time efforts of several Eastern schools in the late 1960's are examples of student publications that made runaway profits and had circulations far beyond the campus gates. Princeton called its highly successful dating guide to women's colleges *Where the Girls Are* and Amherst responded with *Where the Boys Are*. Another venture into humor and sexism—Yale's magazine *The Rites of Spring,* about spring vacation spots—gained 50,000 readers. These ideas might work again, for particular regions. The granddaddy of the money-makers was the parody of *Playboy* put out by an undergraduate humor magazine, the Harvard *Lampoon,* which sold ads on Madison Avenue, persuaded Hugh Hefner to loan his publisher and distributor, and produced a spoof—complete with a living-color fold-out—that sold more than half a million copies, all over the world. This little venture yielded its creators a profit in the neighborhood of $150,000. Such an enterprise requires some capital investment, of course, but the writers not only made a killing but went on, after their graduation, to found a national humor monthly.

Many other possibilities also exist. The Yale newspaper is highly successful with "career supplements," in which it gives advice about working in some industry. This paper sells thousands of dollars worth of advertising to companies in that industry. You can try a special skiing or surfing magazine, a special on cars and motorcycles, a special on records and stereo equipment, or a special on computers—depending upon your own interests and your estimation of the advertising potential.

Food: Food Vendors, Grill, Vending Machines

College students have often earned spending money by capitalizing on the inadequacy of institutional food. After a cafeteria breakfast (which half the students sleep through), a cafeteria lunch (cold cuts?) and a cafeteria dinner (no seconds on "mystery meat"), you may have an enthusiastic market for evening snacks.

One way to service this market is to fill a cart or basket with doughnuts, drinks, and sandwiches and to wend your way from dorm to dorm at prime hunger time (10 P.M. to midnight). The obvious drawback to this approach is that prime hunger time may also be your prime study time. However, if the idea works, you may be able to hire several "food vendors" to do the selling for you while you read Plato or physical chemistry.

It is essential for your food service to be well advertised. You might try posters, handouts and/or word of mouth. You should also try to make your service available at the same time very night. Alert each dorm to your arrival. A simple but effective method is to blow a piercing whistle (or ring a cow bell), and then scream "foooood maaaan!" Then wait in the corridor and listen to the music of slamming textbooks and tinkling change.

You should be careful to provide good food at low prices (you have no rent to pay, no equipment, no janitors to hire, and so on—your prices should be reasonable) and to provide your service with a good sense of humor. (Some students may be poor sports when their concentration on physical chemistry—or Plato—is shattered by the clang of a cow bell.)

In buying supplies, work out wholesale prices with local suppliers and be sure not to stock up with more than you can sell; either it will go to waste or turn stale, before it can be sold. You'll do best if you limit your menu—concentrate on a few types of subs or deli sandwiches. Market research will tell you what items will be most welcome so that you can plan your stock of food and drink. Bear in mind that you cannot sell alcoholic beverages without a liquor license. Also, be sure to check for permission to go around the dorms making sales in this way.

If you average two hours a night selling and one hour a day getting supplies ready, and if you want to earn at least $2.50 an hour, you will have to clear at least $7.50 on an average night. If the average purchase is $.60 (sandwich and soft drink), and you have a 100 per cent mark-up, you will have to make at least twenty-five sales in two hours ($15, of which $7.50 is profit). With any luck, you ought to do better than $15 worth of business a night.

It may be a good idea to start a grill in your dorm, fraternity house—or even off-college property. Check your competition carefully and keep these things in mind about your classmates: they will tend to patronize the *closest* store, especially in bad weather or when exams put time at a premium, and they will tend to patronize the place with the lowest prices.

You have several advantages here. You may be able to get rent-free space in the dormitory basement because you will really be doing your classmates a service: speak to the dean. You will be able to hire fellow classmates as counter help. The combination of little or no rent, reasonable labor costs, and minimal advertising and overhead should insure low prices.

One of your wholesale suppliers will probably give you a nice menu sign and you should be able to make money from vending machines, a juke box, and pinball machines: the ultimate attraction. Put up a dartboard, and have a tournament. Paint the walls black, with gold stars on the ceiling or invite the whole dorm to paint murals on the walls the first weekend. Invent your own specialities and gear your small menu to the taste of your classmates. Have special sale nights—give away a triple decker to every hundredth customer. Stay open according to the habits of your clientele—9:30 A.M.–12:30 A.M. for example. This is another advantage you have over a professional operation—you only operate and pay wages at the peak period.

You will have to make an investment to get started unless you can convince your fraternity brothers or dorm committee to pay for a counter, a few tables and chair, a grill, and a refrigerator. From there you should play it by ear. If you can find a second-hand cotton-candy machine inexpensively, you might attract a lot of attention. Experiment with shakes and floats. Try sandwiches, instead of the perennial grilled hot dogs and burgers. One school grill does a brisk winter business in hot spiced cider and bagels with cream cheese. Supply what students want to eat, but your college doesn't provide: yogurt, large salads, cottage cheese, late breakfasts, brownies, home-baked cookies. If your campus is becoming aware of natural foods, try supplying fresh fruit, brown rice, or soy sauce. Invest in a juicer, and make healthy drinks out of carrots and cabbages. Your classmates will enjoy the variety of your offerings and appreciate your efforts, and will tell their friends in nearby dorms. Bear in mind that you will need $30–$50 of business a night to break even.

You might try to cash in on the Sunday morning doldrums, taking orders during the week for eggs ("any style") and bacon, toast, and juice, delivered to bedside at a specified time. This is obviously not a big money-maker; on the other hand, the work involved is small. You should post convenient sign-up sheets for the breakfasts and try to get people to sign up for a "season ticket" instead of one Sunday at a time. You can buy the supplies you need on Saturday afternoon and cook and deliver for two to three hours on Sunday. If the standard breakfast is $1.25 (two eggs and two strips of bacon, a piece of toast with butter and jelly, a glass of orange juice and milk or coffee), you will probably make $.50 on each. (This is taking into account costs such as paper plates, cups, and so forth.) If you sell twenty-five breakfasts a week, you should clear between $400 and $450 for the year. Tie up with a dis-tributor—student or commercial—of Sunday newspapers, and add yet another dimension to your operation.

Another idea is to rent a vending machine or two—major companies will make this especially easy for you. Your only chores are to be around when the deliveryman comes and to avoid losing too many empties. There are lots of other food machines, though, that can make you a good profit, if there is sufficient demand. Check the Yellow Pages under "Vending machines." You may have trouble getting permission to install the machine on college property and you may have to spend a little money insuring the machine against the possibility of its being broken into or falling over on someone.

In all food businesses, you must be careful to be honest and profes-sional. You are *not* exploiting your hungry friends ("Hey, roomie, have a coke—$.45?") but are providing a reasonably priced service to strangers.

Dresses and Jewelry

Bright, simple dresses and earrings are fashionable now. If you sew your own clothes and enjoy designing, you might build a business on your talents.

Your first problem will be to decide exactly what to sell. No matter how diverse your talents may be, limit your production—at least in the beginning—to a relatively small number of things that you can make well and quickly.

Once you have decided what to sell and you are sure that you can make it quite well, you must decide how to sell it. You have several options.

Through a Store—

Many stores, particularly in college towns where people like folk-style clothes, are glad to buy handmade items. If you are very lucky, or if you are already well-known, you might be able to persuade a store to buy a stock of your product outright. However, most stores are not willing to risk so much—they dread having sixty dusty, homemade bikinis on their shelves in December. Many stores will agree to take your goods on consignment, which means that they will display your wares and keep a substantial commission—often 40–50 per cent of the sales price—on whatever goods they sell. If your goods don't sell, then the store will simply return them to you—having lost nothing on you but display space. If this sounds unfair to you, remember that the store will do your selling (if your goods sell), which will save you time and give you a certain amount of publicity. Handmade clothes and jewelry sell for very high prices, and even if the store keeps 50 per cent of what they sell your clothes and jewelry for, you should end up with a high hourly wage, since you don't have to spend time selling your goods or invest in advertising. If you ever want to cite your designing experience, your credentials will be much more impressive if you can say that you made clothes for a store, rather than just for "people who wanted them."

Both consignment and out-and-out selling to stores demand that you have a fairly large stock of goods *already made* when you begin business. If you sell dresses, you may have to make the same dress in six different sizes—and sell only two of them. If you cannot afford to take such a large risk, you can make one-size-fits-all items such as scarves, earrings, or caftans. Another alternative is to persuade a store to open a custom-made corner featuring your product. Here you would only have to make a few samples; interested customers could order the sizes and colors that they chose through the store. If you enter this kind of business, you will have to decide whether to deal only in standard sizes (5–15) and a preselected range of fabrics and colors, or to cope with the eccentricities of your customers' shapes and tastes. If you do the latter—and make real "made-to-order" clothes—you should charge more, and you must be quite sure that you really *can* fit clothes to people of all shapes and sizes. Sandal makers are often very successful with this custom approach.

Direct Sales—

If you want to bypass the complexities of dealing with a store or if you cannot find a store to sell your wares, you could try to sell your goods directly. If you want to make much money this way, you will have to begin an energetic sales campaign, but if you succeed, you can keep for yourself the 50 per cent that a store would have kept in commissions. After you have checked with college officials to see whether you can run a busines from your room, you could put up posters advertising your designs and put an ad in your school newspaper. (A commercial ad will give a much more professional impression than an ad in the classified section.) Remember, too, that you are your own best advertisement: dress in your most attractive and eye-catching designs. Satisfied customers wearing your clothes will bring you attention and more orders. See if you can sell clothes to some publicity oriented enterprise: a teen-age beauty contest or a rock group. Just as in working with a store, you will have to decide whether to sell "semiready-made" or "made-to-order" clothes. If you are on your own, made-to-order clothes are probably your best bet—people can't buy them off the racks anyway. But impulse buying is rare in the made-to-order markets.

No matter where you are selling your clothes, you should not try to compete in price with inexpensive ready-made products. Your dresses do not come off an assembly line, and they don't have to be cheap. If your clothes are custom-made, however, you should make sure that they are up to professional standards. Your designs may be strange, but the work should not be slipshod. What looks good enough when *you* wear it (seam a bit crooked?) often isn't good enough to sell. This rule holds for any handmade product, and it is still another reason why you should limit the range of your production: if you make only long skirts, you will probably learn where you can cut corners without doing a sloppy job. Once again, buy materials (beads, yarn, yard goods) wholesale if it's possible.

Dresses and jewelry are only two of the handmade products that you can sell. Mobiles, pottery, sweaters, toys and stuffed animals, and silk-screen stationery and book plates, macramé items, stained-glass ornaments, painted wood boxes, children's clothes, wall hangings—almost anything that you make can be sold. The recent renaissance in crafts will bring you competition, but a wider market as well. Remember, though, that the more esthetic and less utilitarian your product, the smaller will be your market. More people buy clothes than buy abstract sculptures, and this is one reason that you hear more about struggling artists than about struggling commercial dress designers.

Travel

Weary from your entrepreneurial efforts? Want to get away from it all? The travel trade is booming and, if you still feel enterprising, you may be able to get your trip free, and perhaps even a share of the take.

On the most modest scale are the chartered bus services that were discussed earlier in this chapter, providing transportation to town, the Saturday football game, the nearest ski slopes, or the local women's college. If you're more ambitious, talk to a local travel agent or airline representative about organizing a group flight to Nassau or Barbados for spring vacation. Group rates are low, and your friends will be delighted; *you* will be delighted with your profit. Consider organizing flights from school to urban centers (New York, Los Angeles, San Francisco, Chicago) in June, September, and at vacation time. Or think really far afield and plan summer group flights to London, Rome, Tokyo, Israel, Africa, or the U.S.S.R.—the more expensive the flight, the higher will be your commission.

Despite the recent airline price war, group flights still represent a cash saving, and the airlines will be happy to provide you with information and assistance; they may even print some posters for you. Be sure, however, that you are cautious in your final commitment. You are often obligated to pay an airline in advance for group seats: be sure that you will sell at least enough seats to break even. Remember, too, that this field is competitive and very carefully regulated. It is *illegal,* for example, to make a profit on a "charter" flight (one where you "rent" the whole plane). *You* may profit only to the tune of a free ride—find out, and be careful.

Another travel possibility remains to be considered. This is the "special" excursion or tour—to the northern slopes, for skiers; to a nearby national park, for a weekend of hiking; or to a rural auditorium for a ballet performance or rock concert. You can prepare these packages with travel agents or hotel managers and include accommodations, guides with special skills, and box lunches for the journey if you wish. The possibilities of these trips depend upon your interests and the taste of your potential customers, as well as the points of interest in your area. Use your imagination. A dozen faculty families might be able to afford a trip to East Africa to photograph wildlife; fifteen of your class-mates might be equally eager to travel a hundred miles to watch the migration of the Olympic elk or to observe whales off California.

Room Cleaning Service

Most colleges discontinued maid service in dormitories during World War II. If you are energetic and don't mind other peoples' dirt, you should be able to earn money as a migrant housecleaner. Your equip-ment would be very simple: mops, pails, dust rags, and furniture polish—most dormitories provide vacuum cleaners for student use.

Alone, or with a crew of coworkers, you could go through rooms (either on or off-campus), thoroughly scrubbing the floors, polishing the furniture, washing the windows, and laundering the curtains and bed-spreads. Many students don't know how to clean efficiently, and your service could be very popular. You could charge by the hour or demand a flat rate per room. Package deals are risky—who knows what kind of inferno you may get stuck cleaning: some people really *do* grow plants on their floor with fertilizer—but such deals will appeal to your cus-tomers. (Of course, they may be especially appealing to really dirty customers; cleaner ones may rightly feel that they are paying for other peoples' dirt.)

Good publicity will remind people how much they need your ser-vice—"Cleanliness is next to godliness; we can give you the former for $5." Advertise seasonal specials: "Spring Cleaning," "Post-Christmas Cleaning," "Last-Exam Clean Sweep." If you were really enterprising you could sign people up for a "season clean ticket"—once every week or two weeks for a semester—at a reduced rate. And don't stop with the dormitories—if you can face kitchens and bathrooms, basements, attics, and garages, *your community needs you* and will pay you well to scrub up their private Augean stables.

Other Ideas

This section by no means describes the incredible range of busi-nesses that you might consider. Students have succeeded with many other types of business, although some are viable only in special cases. Open a store; open a restaurant; open a move theater. It's all been done before. Open an accounting service, a mimeographing service, a photo-copying service—open a service that takes over the office work of overworked student entrepreneurs. Open a rest home for exhausted student entrepreneurs. In theory, there is almost nothing that student enterprise cannot tackle. It permeates your entire college world.

Recovering from the children's party you gave the day before, you wake up one beautiful May morning and, savoring bacon-and-eggs in the dorm grill, you recall that Monday is laundry day. You scrunch together your filthy jeans and toss them outside the door to be picked up by the student who runs an on-campus laundry service (failing that, you take your things downstairs to the coin washers and dryers that another student has decided to operate). Monday is also linen day, and so you race downstairs to exchange your dirty sheets and towels for clean ones at the student linen service.

You have a paper due in a few days, so you give the student typing service a call; it has fifteen good typists on call to handle any load that might come up. Later you can have the paper xeroxed at the student-run copy center. What's more, now that you have heard from medical school, you can get rid of those hateful textbooks. "Should I burn them, or sell them?" Naturally, you decide to sell them to the student who deals in used textbooks (he's shrewd, and takes only basic texts that are always in demand—he won't get stuck with leftovers).

By now it's lunchtime, and you have some extra spending money from those discarded texts. You have enough records for today, so where should you spend the money? *Save* it—until tonight, that is, when they're showing a Chaplin flick in that comfortable lecture hall where you've so often dozed during class. Admission is only $1.00, but the student running the show probably earns a decent wage.

Lunch can't wait: you grab a sandwich and coffee from student-leased machines in the basement. There are still a few minutes left for a game on the pinball machine maintained by the student down the hall. On your way to the college ball field you pass student gardeners trimming a faculty lawn and student house painters putting a second coat on the fire station. In the swamp, students are milking the venom from water moccasins for $20 an ounce. You have a good day in the stadium, slamming out a two-run homer; the ball sails into the stands and barely misses smashing a tray full of cold drinks that an enterprising student is selling for an even more enterprising student sales coordinator.

The game goes into extra innings, which helps cold drink sales, and you lose. What's worse, someone from the rival school rips the wires out of your motorcycle. You have to push it back to the dorm. Fortunately, one of your dormmates has set up a repair service that's cheaper, faster, and friendlier than the professional one.

After supper and a movie, you have time to earn a little money yourself. You work for a consulting firm that does research for large companies—consumer interviews, library research, computer programming, and so on. Currently you're studying the development of a pollution-free automobile from a prototype developed by engineering students in your university's graduate school. Finally, a quick note home to the folks, to use up that four-year supply of school stationery that a sharp classmate sold you as a freshman.

And then—a chug of beer from your class mug, you remove your class ring, and settle into your fresh, clean linen—safe from student entrepreneurs until the morning.

Chapter Six

MAKING IT

This is our final chapter, but for you it is only the beginning. You have thought about a number of job possibilities and have considered them in relation to your own skills, interests, and wage requirements. You have set your sights high, but realistically, and now you have decided on the type of employment to look for. This chapter was placed last so that you would determine *what* you want before tackling *how* to go about locating and landing it. If you have already held a number of jobs, you know what job-hunting techniques work best for you. If you're searching and applying for a job for the first time, however, or if you're approaching a new employment area, the suggestions that are included in this chapter may prove helpful. The chapter discusses ways of organizing your search, applying for work, and accepting and terminating employment. The advice and procedures presented are, like the earlier chapters, the result of interviews with students who have been successful in finding and nailing jobs that rewarded them, financially and otherwise. That, after all, is "making it."

Timing

The right time to apply for a job depends upon the type of job that you have in mind, the individual employer, and when the job is to begin.

Colleges vary in regard to when they expect applications for the *on-*

campus term-time jobs that they administrate. In arranging jobs for incoming freshmen, some schools ask high school seniors to fill out employment papers at the time they send in their college acceptances. Other colleges distribute work assignments when the students show up in September; this system is likely to run on a first-come, first-served basis. Arrive early—or at the very least, not late—if you want a good choice of on-campus jobs. Still other colleges ask that students fill out on-campus job applications at the same time they request financial aid, which is usually in December or January preceding the fall term when the job is required. Note that all of these distribution schemes require some degree of advance planning on your part. Be sure to find out, as soon as you have been accepted by the college of your choice, the procedure that it uses in assigning work and follow instructions accurately and promptly.

Off-campus term-time jobs usually require that you be on the spot, first of all to learn of the job and then to apply for it in person. Check periodically at your student employment office for notices and leads, and don't overlook the classified ads in the student and local newspapers, particularly in the fall, the term break, and in late May. Employers know that these are the times when students come, go, and arrange new work schedules; for example, local merchants in a college town may count on an influx of a new labor supply in September. Remember, though, that you are one drop in a flood of undergraduates—by arriving a few days ahead of the rest you secure yourself a real employment advantage, especially for unskilled jobs. That "Help Wanted" sign in the bookstore window will hang there only until the first literate applicant bursts through the door.

Summer employment is associated with one powerful job-finding rule: start *early*. This cannot be stressed too much. Some employers, particularly those in factories and industries in which markets are unpredictable, do hire as jobs become available, but, in general, the best summer jobs are snatched up before the snow melts and lined up before the snow flies. Christmas vacation seems eons away from June, but you should keep in mind that many interesting or securely salaried positions, with the National Park Service or federal, state, and municipal governments may require Civil Service Examinations that must be taken in February and applied for even earlier. Camps and resort jobs may interview over the winter holidays or during the semester break. The farther away from your campus you wish to work, the earlier you must get started, to overcome the time lag of distance. If you expect to work in your home town, begin making inquiries around Thanksgiving weekend or at Christmas time. Remember that you are competing against hordes of classmates, students from other colleges, high school students, and unemployed older workers.

If you have enjoyed a job in the past and want to return to the same work or the same area, don't hesitate to begin arrangements in September for the following summer. Students who are continually anticipating the next employment season are generally better employed, with less last-minute frustration, than those who proceed on a catch-as-catch-can basis.

Should you plan to work in a city where you will have neither dormitory nor home living accommodations, you should remember that you must not only find a place to work but also a place to stay (unless, as at some resort hotels or summer camps, room and board are part of the employment setup). It is vital to arrange your living situation early, not only to avoid sleeping on strangers' floors for the first four weeks of the summer and spending your days off looking for a room but to make sure that you are not forced to drop most of your summer wages into the pocket of a landlord who is serenely lapping the cream off high summer rentals. As the job market declines, come June, so does the list of apartments to let and it becomes a seller's market. Plan ahead, to allow yourself as much of your salary as possible in addition to your summer vacation.

Along with the obvious advantage of getting ahead of your competition, you achieve at least three other gains by beginning your summer work search early. First of all, you have a chance to find out something about the companies or concerns for which you are interested in working. If you dash into the personnel office, out of breath and clutching the classified columns, to sputter, "I, uh, saw your ad and I see that you're looking for, uh [quick glance down], an administrative assistant, and I, uh, was wondering if . . ."—how impressed will the employer be with your poise and organizational ability? But what if you plan ahead: learn the personnel manager's name, the exact nature of the available position, and the function of the company? Your extra information helps you to prepare a strong approach.

Good morning, Mr. Smith. I phoned for this appointment with you because I understand, through your Sunday advertisement in the *News* that the public relations office of City Business, Inc., is looking for a summer administrative assistant. As a journalism major, I am particularly interested in the technical brochure preparation that accounts for a majority of City Business' activities. Last year I was the business manager for our college newspaper and I am interested in extending my knowledge of public relations procedures in publishing. We had one campaign that might be relevant to your company's market. . . .

Which is the most effective applicant? The first person might have had the same background and advantages; the difference is in their preparation.

If you begin early in your search for employment, you will probably receive several job offers. This makes it legitimate to tell one employer, whose position interests you, that you would prefer to work for him if he could match the salary offer of another potential employer, where the work seems less challenging.

Finally, you place yourself in a better position with an employer, even if he insists that he will not make his decision until May. This is rare in itself; most employers are as happy to resolve their summer staff opening as you are to seize it. But you will have time to contact an employer more than once, if he is not hiring immediately. He will feel that he "knows" and can count on you. By starting earlier than the others, and by following up on your initial interest, you have demonstrated a greater eagerness for the job.

It is true that, the earlier you commit yourself to a summer job, the greater is the possibility that you may regret not being able to take something better that has come along. See how good a strategist you can be. The less attractive jobs are usually the most plentiful and the last to be claimed, so concentrate your early efforts on first choices, and try to leave escape clauses if you feel you must pursue less acceptable leads at the same time.

Looking for a job is hard work, and the unemployment and economic slowdown that still plague the economy make the chore even less welcome. The longer you put it off, however, the worse it gets—literally *and* psychologically. Trudging with an armful of résumés from one mobbed employment agency to the next is truly a nightmare, especially when summer has already begun, emptying the job files and suffocating you with a work-search environment that is 92 degrees in the shade. Even if you begin your summer employment campaign in advance, you may be faced with little initial success. But think how you can minimize your discouragement and frustration—and maximize the chances of a contented spring term, anticipating your secure, satisfactory, summer job—if your first-time disappointments come in January, and not in June.

Leads and Sources

Once you have decided what type of work you are looking for and have committed yourself to the task of finding it, your next step is to scout out leads. You may have more job-finding resources at your command than you realize, so give some thought to identifying and best utilizing each one of them.

Contacts—

There is an easy way to do everything, and it usually involves knowing the right people. In looking for a job, don't minimize the advantage of sharing the project with other pairs of eyes: your father's, your mother's, your roommate's, his uncle's, the departmental secretary's, your friendly local politician's, and so forth. Anyone who is likely to know of employment—or to extend your possibilities, simply because he knows a lot of people—is worth pressing into service. Most people enjoy exercising their knowledge and power for the benefit of a struggling undergraduate, and a point made earlier is worth reiterating here: it is not so much how well you know a contact, but simply that you know him at all. Blood and acquaintance are thicker than plain air, and the most tenuous and obscure ties may bind you to a job: an architect may have ten qualified student applicants for an opening as an assistant draftsman—nine total strangers and the nephew of a next-door neighbor of his sister-in-law's best friend's boss's niece. Which will he hire? No connection is too slim to mention, especially if it's not your sole qualification for the job.

This example points up the fact that contacts are not only useful in locating leads and obtaining introductions to potential employers but are also among the most common reasons why any given individual lands a job. Like it or not, many of the best positions go, through patronage or nepotism, to people with connections, as our subsection on the category of "Pop" jobs, in the summer employment section, so poignantly demonstrates. Although working with or for Pop or Uncle Jack may not give you a sense of real independence, many other decisive and desirable contacts may be at your disposal. "A" work with a favorite professor may lead you to a job as his editorial assistant: an enviable position both personally and professionally. A breakneck summer of hard work as a busboy may result in your employer's giving you the nod for a waiter's jacket the next June—with $150 a week in tips as a fringe benefit.

Even if your contact does not control the job in question, his recommendation can serve you as a valuable reference. The fact that your seminar leader passes your name on to his thesis adviser, who is looking for a library research aide, vouches for your competence in advance. The director of Camp Piney Tiny-Tots may not know you from Eve, but he'll remember your older sister, who did such a good job as a waterfront counselor, and be more prone to hire you.

You may even land a job, through connections, that might ordinarily not be available to undergraduates. Uncle Harry's brokerage firm probably calls a temporary help agency to replace vacationing secretaries, but he will probably hire you instead if you ask him to. A surgeon's son, home for the summer, asked his father to help him find work. The father discovered by asking around, that one of the city hospitals needed a technician for its nuclear medicine department, and he sent his son in for an interview. Although the son was a fine arts major with little science background, and although the physician in charge of the department preferred to hire permanent employees only, the young man's intelligence was so apparent that he was hired as a summer technician. He learned quickly, returned to the position for two summers, and enjoyed the change of pace—although he did not shift his career expectations from museum director to doctor.

When you're looking for work, let people know about it. Whether or not they seem likely to be able to help you, you can at least give your friends and acquaintances the opportunity to contribute what they know. You may have valuable contacts of which you are unaware. An English major ran into her former Sunday School teacher and mentioned that she was looking for a summer job. Her ambition, she remarked wistfully, was to work for a newspaper. He was a reporter for the local daily, as it turned out, and got her an interview; she got *herself* the job as assistant to the theater critic. A freshman who vaguely hoped to find outdoor work, but who wanted to travel during his vacation, confided these wishes to a classmate—whose archaeology professor had just announced in class that there were openings on a summer excavation in Peru that included room, board, and expenses. This idea had never even occurred to the freshman, but he spent an exhilarating three months in Peru. A junior who did picture framing during the term never had to spend a penny on advertising; his friends simply circulated his name and skills, and he was always well-supplied with part-time work.

Some jobs are not even offered through any channels other than word of mouth. If a sociology professor needs data collected, or a biology researcher wants technical sketches to illustrate his latest article, he is likely to simply ask his secretary to "get someone." If she knows someone with the appropriate skills (you?), why should she advertise? One of the salesgirls at a particularly nice dress shop is about to quit: if her roommate has a friend who would love to work there, the "Help Wanted" sign will never hit the window. Like sunny seven-room apartments for $150 a month, desirable jobs are often handed down from friend to friend or are snapped up as soon as the vacancy is mentioned, without ever reaching the student employment offices or classified ads. Along with involving others in your search for work, you should keep your own eyes and ears open: "contacts" may appear where you thought none existed.

Once you have made your friends and relatives aware of what you are looking for, they will probably go out of their way to help you. If you have made a friend or relative into your employer, however, you may have to go out of your way for *him*. It is true that a job with Uncle Harry won't help you break those home ties that bind, but you may also find it harder to deal with excessive demands on the job if they are made by a relative or friend. Overtime hours, extra work, or unpleasant assignments may be much more difficult to decline if they are pressed on you by someone you know—or "owe."

Student Employment Office

Once you have marshaled your "connections" and put out your work-search bulletin along the grapevine of your acquaintances, the next step in looking for a job should be a visit to your student employment office. Most colleges run such an office, either independently or as a function of their financial aid program, and in this way provide listings of term-time and summer job offerings from local employers. These employers have contacted the college and have expressed their interest in hiring students, either as a spontaneous policy or as a result of solicitations by the student employment office; some offices contact potential employers several times a year to urge them to consider employing the students they serve. You can be sure that those offering the jobs you see posted, listed, or on file in the student employment office are predisposed to hire undergraduates. Moreover, many of these jobs are not publicized elsewhere, which cuts down on your competition. Many colleges, to protect their student bodies, do not allow students from other schools to consult the listings at their student employment offices.

On the other hand, if you are not enrolled at a particular college, you are not likely to risk more than a reprimand if you stroll in to pore over the cards on the office bulletin boards.

Student employment offices merely collate and list positions; they don't offer jobs. You will find sources of employment information and even definite job openings, but you will have to contact the employers directly and land the job yourself. By using the office as a reference, and thereby relying on your identity as a student-in-good-standing at Down-state Dependable College, you will, however, have a head start with potential employers.

Begin looking early at the listings in the office on your campus. Term-time jobs on campus may be distributed before school starts in September, particularly if the college itself supplies these jobs through its dining halls and libraries. Summer job offers may not begin to spring up until March, but special summer programs and internships with early deadlines will be listed earlier, for you to investigate. Volunteer, travel, and vacation study programs may be included, along with salaried possibilities.

Although student employment offices deal with college payroll positions and offers from outside employers, they are also clearinghouses for other on-campus jobs. Students in search of tutors may put in requests there, as may professors looking for research, laboratory, teaching, and secretarial assistants. Although many professors hire through the student employment office, others depend upon the initiative of prospective employees. Ask a professor whom you know, or whose work interests you, if he has a job that you can do for him; if not, he may recommend you to a colleague who does. Watch the campus newspaper for announcements of foundation or government grants to professors, projects, or departments. Grants for research proposals often generate the need for student help, both skilled and unskilled, but the recipients may show little interest until you do.

Coaches and athletic instructors may also have jobs for students; try direct contact if the student employment office presents no possibilities.

The bulletin board and current files at your student employment office are worth frequent scanning, but don't overlook the other resources of the office. Ask what other kinds of information are available there; you may discover literature on various types of employment, sources of past student job placements, and applications for internship and trainee programs. One New York City junior went through notebooks full of follow-up files in her college's student employment office that listed past jobs held by students at her school. She wrote to several law firms that had previously hired undergraduates with her background and landed a summer position with one as an administrative assistant. Her job, doing detailed research on cases, has helped propel her toward law school.

Private Agencies—

Private employment agencies can be helpful in finding openings in business offices, libraries, museums, publishing houses, hospitals, restaurants, resorts, and other enterprises. Like the student employment office, the private agency serves as a clearinghouse for employment offers, and it will make an attempt to match your qualifications with the requirements of potential employers. *Un*like your college office, private agencies expect to be paid for their services. Agency fees vary from state to state and, where local licensing prevails, even from city to city. Placement contracts also vary, and may be long and involved. *Study them carefully* for rates, contractual arrangements, and payment schedules.

Undergraduates should carefully weigh the advantages of utilizing private employment agencies against their disadvantages to the full-time student. Most placements by private agencies are immediate, so that whereas such an agency may help in your search for a term-time job, it should be the last resort in your summer job hunt. With the exception of a few positions in vacation towns, it makes no sense to apply for a full-time position through an agency until school actually ends and you are free to begin work. Most students will prefer to secure their place in the competitive summer employment market long before June, and for this routes other than agencies must be explored.

Consider the fee schedule before you commit yourself to an agency, particularly if you are looking for summer work. Many employers absorb the agency costs; the job is then listed as "fee paid." But many companies feel that—given the amount of time it takes them to train an undergraduate, and the limited period for which he will be employed—it is not worthwhile for them to pay, so that the number of fee-paid jobs for college students is decreasing. Some firms, although reluctant to pay the fees initially, will arrange to reimburse you after you have worked for them for a specified number of months. The most common practice concerning college students, however, is to have the student pay the agency fee. This may amount to most of your first month's salary, or to 10 per cent of your wages for the first ten weeks of your employment. Although the amount may not seem outrageous if you are taking on permanent full-time employment, for summer jobs it is prohibitive. Few students can afford to lose such a large portion of their vacation earn-

ings. Beware, as well, of unclear contracts. One Rutgers student was
sent to a New York City business concern by an agency, to be interviewed for a "no-fee" job. The company offered him a different position,
which he accepted—only to find himself bound by his contract to pay
the agency's fee.

Private employment agencies that specialize in *temporary* work may,
on the other hand, prove extremely helpful to students by providing
variety and flexibility in work schedules. Agencies such as Manpower,
Inc., and Kelly Girl, Inc., operate nationwide and offer you the option of
working odd hours and for short periods of time. Many such agencies
are set up to provide short-term clerical help for offices. These will
require you to take typing, shorthand, or clerical aptitude tests before
you are allowed to register, and your salary will depend upon the level
of your skills. Other agencies handle every conceivable type of job. In
the span of one month, a sophomore worked at three different assignments, scraping paint off steel beams, working on a packaging assembly
line, and sorting baskets of plumbing parts. All of these jobs were
obtained through a single agency. Another student worked for three
months in the purchasing department of an electronics company; jobs
that the employer classes as "temporary" may provide you with stable
summer employment. A senior received $2 an hour for two weeks of
taking inventory at a sporting-goods store during Christmas vacation,
and a young woman from the University of Buffalo, who demonstrated
ease with a stick-shift and in the company of longshoremen, spent two
weeks in August driving newly imported Volkswagens off a ship at the
Boston Wharf. If you have a short period of time to fill or want to
maintain the flexibility of short commitments, the services of a temporary employment agency may provide you with cash and surprises.

State Employment Agencies—

If you want more than the sporadic employment offered by temporary agencies, register with your local office of the state employment
agency. Every year, these offices assist thousands of students in their
search for summer work or for part-time employment during the
academic year—and their services are free. You may consult them for
job referrals and placement or just for helpful hints, but they also
administer occupational aptitude tests and offer professional job and
career counseling. Consider, also, the local Youth Opportunity Center,
which will teach eligible students job skills while they work. The
addresses and telephone numbers for both types of agencies can be
found in your local telephone book, among the state listings.

The Want Ads—

For sheer bulk, there's nothing like the Sunday newspaper want ads. But using the want ads well requires as much attention as researching a term paper. Giving the paper the once-over on a weekday morning and then slinking back to bed may be tempting, but it is not likely to be fruitful. Your best bet is to plan to comb through the Sunday classified ads, since those listings are the most complete, and weekday ads are often only a repeat run of some of Sunday's offerings. You will, theoretically, have a whole week to follow up on the jobs listed, but in practice you had better be prepared to rise early Monday morning for some telephone calls and leg-work, if you don't want Sunday's efforts to go to waste. Good jobs disappear fast because they are claimed by early applicants.

In general, help wanted ads are arranged with employment agency listings in the beginning, followed by specific job listings by individual employers in alphabetical order by job category. Don't stop after you've scanned the listings under just one category; if you are looking for a clerical job, for instance, you will want to check under "college grad," "gal/guy fri," "typist," "receptionist," and "secretary," as well as under "clerk." Employers are capricious in their listings, and it's best to run your eyes down all the columns, A to Z, before deciding that there are no more openings for ventriloquists, or whatever your heart desires. "Cute ventriloquist," "accomplished ventriloquist," "zany ventriloquist" all violate alphabetical logic, but they are possible employer approaches to a job you want. Under the law, newspapers are not permitted to publish sex-discriminatory listings. Although "male" and "female" job divisions may persist in the Help Wanted columns of your Sunday paper, they may legally reflect only suggested distinctions for organizational purposes—*not* sex requirements for particular jobs. Steamfitters', janitors', and executive openings will be listed under "male," secretarial and nursing positions under "female." Women should read all of the ads, however, and apply for what interests them, and for whatever they qualify. On the other hand, if you are a man interested in a job traditionally associated with women, do not hesitate to answer an ad for a "gal Friday." One Harvard man earned his college expenses working as a part-time secretary.

When you follow up a want ad, you have the advantage of knowing that an employer wants to hire; you thereby avoid the demoralization of sitting for hours in an employment office waiting room, only to be herded out with other frazzled college students and told that there are no jobs. But want ads cost money, and the employer may try to be brief, omitting details that, if included, would have told you that the job wasn't what you wanted (or that it was).

There are several different kinds of want ads, and different ways of following them up. In some cases, employers list their telephone numbers, making it easy for you to narrow your application field by a few judicious phone calls. Other employers obstinately refuse to do this, possibly because a secretary would be kept busy all Monday, answering tentative inquiries. One alternative is the "blind ad," which lists a job and gives a box number at the newspaper to which you write. These ads give the employer a chance to screen the applications before he starts interviewing applicants, and save him some time. These ads are perfectly legitimate. Respond to them by sending a copy of your résumé (discussed later in this chapter), with a covering letter explaining why you are interested in the job and how you found out about it.

Some ads list the job and the employer's name, location, and address. You can write or look up the telephone number and phone for an appointment. If it is a really large company with its own personnel office, such as a bank, corporation, or hospital, you can also just drop in. You make more of an impression if you phone for an appointment and arrange a personal interview; letters and résumés may be easily discarded. You, in the flesh, are more difficult to ignore. Many employers feel that demanding an in-person response will help separate the gold from the sludge—you make a point in your favor simply by showing up.

You may find, when you turn up for your interview, that the job you are being interviewed for is a far cry from the one you had in mind. When an employer advertises a job, he is trying to make it sound as attractive as possible. A job advertised as being "in an executive office" is likely to involve doing someone else's typing and filing. As you read the ads carefully, you will begin to get an idea of the classified jargon and be able to judge for yourself which employment ads are worth following up.

Employers whose ads offer the world with a string around it—"High pay! Short hours! Expense account!"—are often advertising for sales personnel to sell products. Like good salesmen, they are "selling" you the job. Most of these offers involve commission sales, and their fabulous world is legitimate *if* you can produce.

Look beyond the want ads in your city paper. You may find that your college newspaper's ads, or those of trade journals, list jobs that are better tailored to your hours and skills. One advantage of following up an ad in your college paper is that the advertising employer probably has contacts within the college community and has placed his advertisement with a student employee in mind. He will know the hours it is reasonable to expect from an undergraduate and may even be willing to arrange a schedule so that you will not be committed to working during exam time. He may have hired students from your school before; if so, it is a good idea to get their names from him and to see if you can find out what sort of an employer he is.

Trade journals often have some listings that are worth following up, especially if you have a particular skill (such as photography), which might not be listed under a separate heading in the city paper want ads. Specialized magazines (for example, sports, hobbies, library) often have ads with lucrative and exotic possibilities, but they may be far-flung: "Experienced crew sought for Bahamas yacht race," or "Sound recorder needed by African baboon study expedition." Remember that even city newspapers often carry job listings for other towns, particularly if the paper serves a metropolitan area as large as New York City or Washington. If your school is rural, by all means, purchase an edition of the nearest city paper. Small-town newspapers will give leads to the urban student who is able and willing to work in the suburbs.

If you would rather be on the receiving side of ad responses, consider listing your own ad in a trade journal or college paper. You're paying for this, so it's best to be brief; most newspapers charge by the word or by the line. It will be enough to list your name, address, and/or telephone number, and the type of employment you are seeking. It makes little sense to run an ad if you are interested in a very general field: who is going to respond to your ad for an available clerk-typist when he can fill his office with eager clerk-typists through his own ad? If, on the other hand, you have a particular skill or if there is a clever twist in your offer, advertising yourself may make sense. Depending upon your resources and the type of job you desire, concentrate your ads in local, national, or international publications. One student took an ad in the Paris edition of the International *Herald Tribune,* asking for a summer job as a tutor in English for French children. Within a month, he received five offers from French families; he accepted one on the French Riviera with full room and board, plus a small allowance.

Of course, not all job leads are in the classified section. It is useful to check the rest of the paper for news of new government and/or local programs that will require additional workers. One such example was Project Head Start, the federal program for prekindergarten children: the starting of this program created a sudden surge of openings for tutors, clerical help, and so on. Such programs often work with local agencies; by watching your newspaper, you can usually find out to whom you must apply. In addition, when such agencies receive additional funds, they are frequently used for summer help; read the front page and you may be one step ahead of the competition.

Direct Application to Firms

If you are interested in a specific kind of job and can't find what you want in the newspaper, through your student employment office, or from an agency, it is a good idea to go directly to employers. If you have the initiative to do your own writing and calling, you may turn up a job when the employer had never thought of hiring a college student, but is impressed enough by you to be willing to try you out.

Publications

The want ads are not the only valuable published source of potential employers. The Yellow Pages of your telephone directory is probably the most concise and readable listing of local businesses and industries, but the local chapter of the Chamber of Commerce can probably provide you with its own efficient directory of businesses—for large cities, the Chamber of Commerce listing looks like a long book. Certain associations of employers also have directories that list them explicitly, offering specific addresses and special qualities of individual businesses. *The Hotel and Motel Red Book* and *Sargent's Guide to Private Camps* are examples of such publications. You can use these listings to pinpoint appropriate employers in your area or to decide which companies it would be most worthwhile to approach. *Sargent's Guide to Private Camps,* for instance, has a section on Unusual Emphases that would be worth consulting if you are prepared to use a specific skill as a counselor and want to know which specialty camps will see you as a likely candidate.

Various books on student employment carry actual job listings; some of these are mentioned in the bibliography.

The direct approach can be a dazzling success or a depressing failure, depending upon how you go about it. One Wellesley junior interested in editing sent out her résumé with identical covering letters, to forty publishing houses, asking about summer employment. She didn't get a single response. A sophomore at Barnard called up the president of a small trade journal, one morning; she had never met him, but got his name from the masthead and his number from the telephone book. She described her qualifications and her desire to obtain summer employment as a writer. Result: she was hired and spent a summer writing copy for the company journal.

Why was there such a difference between the results of these girls' searches? The Wellesley student wrote to the most obvious source of editing jobs—the large publishing houses—whereas the Barnard student was clever enough to contact a company that was not well known and would not be flooded with applications from other eager undergraduates. The Wellesley girl also wrote to the director of personnel at each company. This was entirely proper, but it did not help her chances for a job that many students wanted. Personnel offices tend to be poor job sources if you are trying to get a responsible or sought-after job, because their officers are primarily interested in filling existing jobs, which executives list with them. An executive who appreciates the quality of your ideas or your résumé has the ability to create a job for you, or to fit you into a corporate structure that a personnel officer would probably treat more rigidly, feeling that his responsibility was to look for a permanent employee, or someone with more traditional experience.

Remember that your trump card, in approaching employers directly, is the chance it gives you to sell yourself. Make the most of this advantage, by concentrating your efforts on the businesses and officers who are most likely to pay attention to you. Present your qualifications forcefully and don't disguise whatever enthusiasm you may feel for the job, in the name of "cool." Companies get hundreds of mature, experienced, self-possessed applicants; if a potential employer is intrigued by *you*, it is more likely to be on the basis of your energy, adaptability, and imagination. Youth does have its advantages in the job market. If you convince an employer that his company needs you, it may well be because he foresees your putting the same eagerness and conviction to work for his business. When the employer is soliciting your services, you can afford to let him make his offer attractive; you have thousands of other job possibilities—mentally, at least. If you are soliciting employment, however, you must make yourself stand out. You have little to lose and, in approaching employers directly, self-assertion is an asset. You are initiating the encounter and pursuing what you want: don't stop halfway.

How to Apply

You have your leads. Your job search is organized; you have determined how much you want to earn, where you would like to work, and what jobs would fit in most easily with your interests, skills, and schedule. You know the possibilities in your chosen job market and have narrowed the list of employers to a key list of most likely candidates. It is now time to apply for the job.

No single method of application works for everyone, but once you have begun to plan your employment campaign, you will have to think about how you are going to present yourself to that potential employer, once you identify him.

Except in very informal situations, where you know your prospective employer well, or he is the owner of a small business, you will have to do more than drop in and ask for employment. If you mention at the corner diner that you need a part-time job, the owner may hire you on the spot for that cashier's opening. Your search for a lab research position *may* end the moment you confide it to your favorite biology professor. You may even land that $7.75 construction job, just by the right word to the right employer at the right time—especially if the employer is Pop, and he's just lighting up a cigar after a serene Sunday dinner. On the chance that a more complex approach is called for in your luckless case, discussion of the three main employment application techniques follow: namely, the preparation of a résumé, the covering letter, and the interview.

The Résumé—

In most cases, you will find that your most effective approach to a potential employer is to write and ask for an interview. You may feel more at ease over the telephone than behind a typewriter, but a formal letter is the traditional path to employment. If you are dealing with a government agency or a large corporation with dozens of secretaries, you can be sure that it is no imposition to ask for a letter and an appointment in return. With a small company, a department, or an individual professor, it might be better to state in your letter that you will telephone in a few days for an appointment. Give your potential employer enough time to read your letter and résumé, and then call him to follow up your contact.

Whatever your initial approach, you should prepare a résumé to send with all your letters and to take to all your interviews. A résumé (pronounce it rĕh′ zū may) is a capsule presentation of your vital statistics, education, and past experience that may be of interest to an employer. Although you may have to duplicate much of this information on a company's own personnel form, your résumé may save you some repetitive writing and can represent you in advance of your personal appearance. It gives your interviewer something to hold onto and provides him with a starting point for his questions. It also allows you to stress your good points while eliminating the discomfort of having to brag about yourself out loud. It ensures that no important point will be forgotten in the stress of an interview, and that none of your outstanding achievements will be left unmentioned, because of your shyness or overwhelming modesty.

A résumé should be no longer than a typed page. *Always* type your résumé and your covering letters as well. It is a rare employer who will be willing to decipher several sheets of illegible scrawl in his search for an employee, and even if your handwriting is graceful and clear, type makes a more professional impression. If you must, write your letters, but pay if necessary to have the résumé typed. Résumés may be photocopied, if you are sending out several identical ones; do not send carbons. Never send mere copies of a covering letter to more than one employer, even if you type in "individual" headings; this looks like exactly what it is, a nonspecific mass mailing, and the employer will not believe that you are interested in his particular firm. Clerical efficiency is important, but don't let your appearance to the potential employer be sacrificed to it.

This is the basic résumé format:

PERSONAL INFORMATION

Name	Year in College
School Address	Telephone (School)
Home Address	Telephone (Home)
College Major	Birthdate

JOB OBJECTIVE

EMPLOYMENT BACKGROUND

(Names and addresses of former employers)

EDUCATIONAL BACKGROUND

OTHER PERTINENT DATA

(Hobbies, skills that might relate to job)

REFERENCES

When you present your employment background, be sure to indicate the dates between which you held each job: "June 1, 1967–August 31, 1967, waitress, Wayside Resort, Saratoga, New York," or "September, 1971—present, library assistant, Casey College, Casey, Montana." Employers prefer that you list your most recent work first, and then your former jobs, in reverse chronological order. Although you will not have to elaborate on job descriptions such as in the examples given, a position such as "research assistant" or "case worker" invites a short sentence stating the nature of your duties and responsibilities, and any skills that you may have acquired.

Your educational background should also present first things first. List your college year and the name of your high school, and include in proper chronological order any summer programs, evening schools, skill courses, training, or internship projects in which you have participated. You may include details of your relevant school courses and extracurricular activities.

Volunteer work that has a bearing on the job you seek, or on the general question of your responsibility, may be included under employment background, educational background (if it took place during the term or in connection with a school organization) or "other pertinent data."

You need not include actual references with the résumé. You may either list the names and addresses of your references (ask them for permission, first!) at the end of your résumé, or indicate that references will be sent on request. Most employers prefer you to list past employers, supervisors, or teachers as references; personal friends, family acquaintances, and ministers tend to write nothing but praise, and the employer will obtain less concrete and balanced information concerning you. (If you are applying for a job at a Lutheran day camp, of course, by all means get your Lutheran minister to recommend you.)

Under pertinent data, include special prizes you've won or important positions you've held. Dean's list is impressive, as is cocaptain of the junior varsity soccer team. Competitive scholarships should be mentioned, if you've won them. Are you business manager of the school newspaper, art director for the yearbook, or one of the students on the curriculum committee? Put it into your résumé. Many of your achievements may seem unrelated to the job that you're applying for, but any employer will opt for the generally "strong" candidate in preference to the less active one. But don't burden your one typewritten sheet with every minor undertaking such as "Clean-up Committee for Junior Prom, 1969." The less cluttered your presentation is, the more effective it will be, and the more likely it will receive a careful reading.

As you compose your résumé, begin by presenting a total picture of yourself. This may give you a sense of some skills or interests that may suggest job possibilities that you previously overlooked. Prune the final document, however, for conciseness, clarity, and impact. Although you are expected to tell the truth and to present your record free from distortions, you may certainly adapt your résumé to the interests of specific employers. There is no point in going into an involved account of your studies in psycholinguistics if you are seeking a resort job as a waitress. Likewise, the student who is applying to both law firms and publishing houses may stress his history and political science major on the former résumé, and his English minor on the latter. Nor must you detail every one of your jobs, if your working experience is long: that job you held at the candy store as a sophomore in high school may be worth mentioning if you haven't worked since, but not if you have many more recent and responsible positions to list.

The Covering Letter—

Your covering letter can be a brief expression of interest in the job or it can be a creative five-hundred word sales pitch, depending upon your personal style and how much you know about why this business should hire you. In a large company, the director of personnel is the man to write to about the kind of work for which you are looking. Even if there is no director of personnel as such, your letter will seem businesslike and will find its way to the right man. Don't be afraid to start at the top. Letters to the president may find a flattered reception; at worst, they will be passed down to personnel, and no one will accuse you of pretentiousness. Set your sights high. If you have the name of a particular company official, known to you, or suggested by a friend, address your letter to him. Any piece of mail gets closer attention if it is directed to a specific person, and should it be rerouted through the personnel department, it will not hurt your application to have a company member on record as being interested in its fate.

If you have never held a job before, and feel queasy about the blanks in your formal résumé, your best bet may be to adopt an informal letter form. You can include in it pertinent interests, school activities, education, and odd jobs, which will make your lack of work experience seem less glaring.

It is also true that, particularly for unskilled summer jobs in resort areas, many employers are not eager to read a letter or résumé that presents the story of your life. If you want to work as a typist, waiter, or groundskeeper, your potential employer is likely to see your future career plans as irrelevant, and your need for funds as taken for granted (why else would a future Classics professor apply for a job as a groundskeeper?). So spare him the extra prose—and spare yourself. Stress your training, experience, willingness to work, and specific skills. Mention your age (some jobs have minimum age requirements) and the dates when you will be available. Indicate your intention to fulfill a season contract and suggest your punctuality, responsibility, and maturity, providing appropriate references (and their addresses). *Then,* if it seems helpful, add your reasons for applying, and whatever specific skills, ambition, or interests you think might help your cause. Many summer employers appreciate a recent, passport-type photograph, especially if they are too distant to expect an interview with you.

If you are at a loss as to how to begin your letter, tell the employer how you came to learn of his opening (a friend, a newspaper ad, and so forth). If you are forced to write a second letter, having received no acknowledgment of the first, start off with the explanation that your first letter must have been lost in the mails. This approach works best, of course, if you can include a carbon or photocopy of the "missing" missive. Keep copies of all the letters you send out, so that you will know whom you have contacted and when. You can then recontact prospects, if you get no reply, and can withdraw your applications to various firms, should you take another position. This is common courtesy, and ensures the good will of those potential employers—you may want to try them again next year.

If you expect to receive an application form from your prospect, your best insurance that you will get it is to enclose a self-addressed, stamped long envelope. Employers with many applicants may not send you their forms without one. If your letter is to a foreign employer, send it by air mail and enclose two International Postage Coupons to encourage his prompt reply. And by all means, write to him in his own language. Again, this is courtesy, but it also may be the only way to provoke a response.

Examples of a typical résumé and appropriate covering letter follow.

The Interview—

For certain specially skilled positions and summer internship programs, long detailed written applications may be the crucial factor. Recommendations may land you specific jobs. But, for most student employment purposes, it is the interview that carries the most weight. The majority of the students we talked to reported that for their term-time and summer jobs, the interview was the decisive point in the hiring process.

An interview makes sense both for you and for the employer. Put yourself in your prospective employer's place, and you will appreciate the difficulties of hiring by mail. One college junior sent off an application to a resort manager; his résumé was neat, complete, and impressive. The manager hired him, sight unseen, to man the reception desk, counting on a fresh-faced Joe College manner. But when the student appeared for his first day on the job, the manager was appalled. He realized that the application picture that the student had submitted must have been his high-school yearbook photograph; in three years the potential desk manager had grown at least a yard of hair—enough to induce apoplexy in the hotel's rich and elderly clientele.

25 Wyatt Hall
University of Kentucky
Louisville, Kentucky 69742
January 14, 1973

Mr. Alan Shapiro
155 Atlantic Avenue
New York, New York 10027

Dear Mr. Shapiro:

I am writing to you at the suggestion of my professor, Dr. Thomas Mudd. He has told me about the day-care center you are opening and suggested that you might be interested in hiring either an administrative aide or a counselor with my background for this coming summer.

I am interested in working with children in a new type of educational environment. Although my college major is English, you can see from my résumé that I have been involved in the field of education, both formally (through Dr. Mudd's course on Child Psychology) and informally (through summer jobs and extracurricular activities). Although I like to work directly with children, I would also be interested in doing organizational work as an administrative aide. I have had experience in keeping an office running smoothly, as well as many jobs or extracurricular activities involving public contact. Since I plan to go into the field of education after I graduate, I am interested in learning how a day-care center works, as well as in caring for children.

I will be home in Mount Vernon during semester break and would like to come in and talk to you about the possibility of employment this summer. (My address at that time will be: c/o Mr. and Mrs. Robert Macy, 12 Green Street, Mount Vernon, New York, 01607.) I will be available any time between February 14th and 20th. Please let me know when it is convenient to schedule an interview. I am looking forward to meeting you.

Sincerely,
Jean Macy

RÉSUMÉ

Jean Macy
25 Wyatt Hall
University of Kentucky
Louisville, Kentucky 69742
BU 8–4429

Home Address: 12 Green Street
Mount Vernon, New York 01607
495–7767

College Major: English

Birthdate: July 16, 1953

Employment Background:

June 7, 1972–August 21, 1972. Counselor, Wayside Camp for
Children, Mount Vernon, New York. Was in charge of a group
of eight ten-year-old girls; had general counseling duties, and
assisted drama teacher in coaching voice for camp play.

June 18, 1971–August 8, 1971. Receptionist-typist, Smith Apoth-
ecary, Mount Vernon, New York. Girl Friday type of position:
handling customers; miscellaneous typing; delivery within the
office building.

July 1, 1970–August 20, 1970. Mother's helper, Mrs. Louis
Stratton, Mount Vernon, New York; cared for two children, age
5 and 8; did general household chores.

Educational Background: University of Kentucky, Class of 1975.
Major in English, with a minor in education. Extracurricular
activities include being a Campus Guide, doing volunteer tutoring in reading for disadvantaged children, membership in College
Drama Society.

Bryant & Stratton School: Six-week typing course, summer 1969.

Skills: Typing: 50 words a minute on an electric typewriter. Have
had experience using other office machines: dictaphone, xerox,
mimeograph machine.

Hobbies: Drama and voice: have participated in dramatic societies
since high school; am able to coach voice and lead children
in improvisational drama.

References: Available on request.

It is difficult for you, as well, to size up your employer by mail. If
you are interested in resort work, you may want to know what the
provisions are for sleeping arrangements and board, how many students
will be working there, and what kind of tips you can expect—all questions that are difficult to ask and get useful answers to in a letter. An
interview helps you distinguish the considerate employer from the Simon
Legree of the sweatshop; clerical work is clerical work, but there is a
clear difference between a boss and an ogre. In addition, a personal
appearance is usually more impressive than just a letter. It lets the
employer know that you are genuinely interested in the job, and it will
make it hard for him to forget you.

A personal interview will give you an edge over other students who did not bother to show up and will also help to pressure your employer into a decision. In person you are a tangible, distracting reality, and you occupy someone's attention; a letter can wait until tomorrow, can easily be thrown out, turned down, and out-argued. One economics major, interested in getting an inside view of the stock market, took his résumé, with several copies of references, and simply walked into a large financial firm on Wall Street. Although most of the jobs required some skill in market analysis and usually went to graduate students, he was offered a job as a "runner," carrying securities, transfer receipts, and federal funds between various financial houses. Another student, who wanted to work for a large company "simply to see how one operated," started at the top by asking for an appointment with the vice president of General Motors. He was out, but the student managed to talk to his secretary, who sent him with a referral to the personnel department. He spent the summer in GM's data processing department.

It is in your own best interest, then, that you urge all potential employers to grant you an interview. There will be a few cases in which they will not respond favorably; one example is that of an incoming freshman seeking library or dining hall employment with the college. Most schools accept written applications in these cases. Off-campus term-time employment generally requires an application in person, and for summer jobs this is almost invariably true. This is yet another reason to apply early: vacations may be your only free "interview" weeks.

Once you have convinced yourself of the necessity and beneficial aspects of employment interviews, the next question is—how to handle them? A job interview is not styled after a college interview. The employer is not so much interested in the "whole you" as he is in how you will fit in with his particular enterprise. Less of you is under evaluation than you fear, and there is really not so much at stake—even in the worst years, there are other jobs. So relax, and be yourself. The topic of conversation will undoubtedly be you and the company. You are certainly well-versed on the former topic and should learn as much about the latter as possible before the interview so that you can tie the two together in a satisfying way.

Your potential employer is there to find out what assets his company can hire in you—what new insights you might bring to the job, whether you have the skills it requires, and so forth. Tailor your presentation of yourself to his particular needs, insofar as you can discover them. If it is a large business, you may know someone who works there, or there may be a company magazine you can read in the reception room. *Standard and Poor's,* which is available in many libraries, is also a source for information about large businesses. Ask around; you needn't have a detailed new idea for an advertising campaign if you are applying for a typing job, but it helps to know the kind of activities in which the company is involved. If you are applying for a job with more executive responsibility, you may want to sketch out some ideas about what you would do if you had the position. But don't "come on too strong." The company may want fresh ideas, but not a revolution.

Try to schedule your interview appointment for around 10:00 in the morning or 3:00 in the afternoon. By noon, a busy executive or office manager will be hungry—maybe irritable. By 4:00 on Friday he will probably be gone, or be hating you for keeping him from going home.

When you go to your interview, be sure to carry along a copy of your résumé; even if you sent one with your application letter, bring one—the first may be buried in your file. In this way, your interviewer will have a better idea about who you are and what the two of you should discuss, before the interview begins. It is as unnerving for many interviewers, especially people who are not often involved in hiring, to start out an interview cold as it is for you to go to one.

If you don't care about the job, dress as you please and arrive when you please. It may go without saying but it is important that you look presentable when you are interviewed for a job. One employment counselor we spoke to muttered, "I don't care what the job is. I'm allergic to men showing their hairy legs in shorts. I know some employers who would fall off their seats if I sent applicants in like that." This is Middle America speaking, but remember that you may be asking Middle America for work. Clean clothes and neatly trimmed hair are important to most employers. So is punctuality.

An interview is a two-way proposition. Do not be afraid to ask about the company or about specific aspects of the job for which you are being interviewed. A person with initiative is bound to be more interesting than someone who passively answers questions. Before leaving the interview, be sure you understand when you will hear whether you got the job. If you are not sure about some aspect of the job, such as salary, *ask* about it. Being clear about the terms of the job at the outset will spare you trouble later.

Show enthusiasm for the particular job you are being interviewed for, even if it is routine work. One Smith student once ruined an interview because her interviewer, the head of a theater library, assured her that the work was very dull and routine. The student replied that, with jobs so hard to find, she was willing to take the job anyway. What the interviewer *really* wanted to hear was that being near a theater collection would more than make up for the tedious side of things. The job went to a more "eager" applicant.

If it is apparent that the job you were seeking is unsuitable for you, or you for it, you can try to change horses in midstream. You are already in the office; you should try to explore other employment possibilities with the interviewer. This is a straightforward approach, and that is the criterion that should guide most of your reactions in an interview. If you are asked about your accomplishments, be honest and support your résumé, but don't lay claim to what you haven't mastered. If you mention an interest in biology, the interviewer may try to see just how much you know, but that may be his honest intent: to find out, not to test you or penalize you for your ignorance. If you exaggerate your command of biochemistry and then cannot define the term *amino acid,* he has every right to be skeptical of your other stated achievements. An honest claim of interest, not expertise, would have stood you in good stead. If you are asked to state your own salary requirements, be prepared to be honest about your financial needs and objectives, so that you can at least suggest a fair minimum rate of pay.

There are two exceptions to the rule of straightforwardness at an interview. The first is the situation involving tact. It is wiser, as seen in the previous example, to slightly overstress your enthusiasm for a job, if it comes into question. If later reflection shows your hesitation to be serious, you can always plead a previous offer, if the job becomes yours. During the interview, however, your prime object is to land the position. In case someone else you know is applying for the same job, a cunning interviewer may ask you what you think of him. Don't knock the man, even if he is your worst enemy. This is not only tactful, but dignified and cautious on your part.

The second exception is the interview situation involving time commitments to summer jobs. Many businesses are reluctant to hire students whom they know will quit at the end of the summer, even if the job is primarily clerical or otherwise routine and involves little training investment on the company's part. Students often resolve this problem by masquerading as permanent applicants, posing as dropouts if necessary, and then leaving in September. When you accept a position under false pretenses, you jeopardize your future employment if you intend to use your present employer as a reference for the next one. If you are not planning on a reference, then the ill will of the company will affect you only personally, not officially. Most of the students whom we surveyed insisted that they had disguised their college student status in the past and would continue to do so if they thought it would adversely affect their chances of being hired.

As stated earlier in this chapter, be sure to ask your interviewer exactly when you can expect to hear from him about whether you have been hired or not. This will give you some idea of where you stand, so that you won't pass up another job while waiting for this one if there's no hope. If you don't get a reply at the time agreed upon, wait for another day or two before you begin to press the Personnel Office about your application.

Landing a Job at a Distance

Exploring a new city or savoring rural life may be an exhilarating way to vary your summer employment, if you spend nine months a year on a suburban campus. In a tight job market, however, this plan entails risk. Success in finding a job is in part a function of your knowledge of the job-hunting territory. When you look for employment around your home town or campus, you have ready-made contacts and a good idea of what work is available. By deciding to work away from home and school, you're sacrificing valuable assets: "connections," and familiarity with the job market. Make up for this loss *before* you leave. A cautionary tale: a University of Michigan sophomore spent two months in Alaska job-hunting. He crossed and recrossed the tundra, résumé in hand—to no avail. Finally he landed a job in a fish cannery, which burned down three weeks later. He spent the rest of the summer far from the wild, camping on a friend's floor in an Ann Arbor apartment. This story should not discourage you from striking out on your own, but be aware: problems may arise if you don't plan carefully.

Try to make contacts in the area in which you want to work before the school year is over. Start writing for information early; the local Chamber of Commerce or State Employment Security Commission is usually happy to send you information about the kinds of employment that are available in the area for students, and will sometimes provide the names of local employers. One Alabama student got a job mining ore in Arizona through the Arizona State Employment Security Commission. Send for a local paper and read the want ads to get an idea of the kinds of jobs open in a certain area. If you have relatives or friends who come from the area you want to work in, talk to them; they may know cheap places where you can stay or people who might be hiring students. Once you have the names of prospective employers, send each a copy of your résumé, with a covering letter explaining what type of work you want. You might combine a vacation trip with an opportunity for an interview.

Remember that, from your own standpoint, the written application has one serious drawback: it doesn't give you a chance to look over your prospective employer. One young woman at N.Y.U., who applied by mail for a resort job, was hired as a waitress at a Nevada resort and, naturally, expected to find a number of other college students working there. As it turned out, most of the help were permanently employed older women. She was expected to work seven days a week, with no time off, for $60. In addition to waiting on tables, she had to prepare food and wash dishes.

This student's experience wasn't typical of jobs obtained by mail, but it serves to remind you that the chances for disappointment are great; after all, how many blind dates are successful? A well-phrased letter, filled with pertinent questions, will reduce the chance of ambiguity with respect to your pay, hours, and duties.

If you reach the end of the school year and still have no definite job, perhaps you should postpone your summer of far-away employment. If you are still determined to strike out on your own, however, be certain to take along enough money in that knapsack to support yourself during several weeks of job-hunting. Especially when unemployment is high, businessmen are likely to hire local students. If you have trouble finding a job, you should consider using temporary employment agencies in between spurts of searching for work so that you will not be too depressed by your dwindling hoard.

If you have taken time off from school and are looking for a job in another state, your search may be easier. Many employers are willing to hire undergraduates on leaves of absence for permanent positions. Carry with you a letter from your school stating that you have taken a leave of absence, and its duration. Many employers require such a statement when you apply for permanent positions; you will probably also have to account for your current draft status.

As pointed out in Chapter Four, Summer Employment, it is possible to find satisfying work even as far away as Europe, if you go about it correctly. As with most student employment, only two main guidelines should be followed: *start early* and stay with your search.

Accepting a Job

You've searched out your sources and run down your leads. Résumé submitted, application completed, references received, interview negotiated—and you're offered a job! Congratulations—but. Although it climaxes a long and elaborate pursuit, a job offer is not the end, but rather the beginning, of your employment experience. The employer has made his decision, and now you are faced with yours. Do I take it? Is it right for me? How do I choose between job offers?

Sometimes the search for employment is so involving that the double aspect of a job offer is lost. Students are often so preoccupied with nailing a job, *any* job, that they forget to ask themselves if they really *want* the work opportunity they've finally corralled. When one of your bids for employment does come through, you have every right to feel encouraged, but be sure to do some careful thinking before you accept or reject it.

In reflecting on your new possibility, you may want third-party information about the firm and the position. One good source of information is anyone who may have held the job before, or who has worked in other capacities for this employer. If possible, you should contact current employees, as well. If the company habitually hires undergraduates, your student employment office may have a file on it and be able to give you the names of other students who work there. Talk to everyone who might give you an inside view. If you are at all skeptical about the legality or appropriateness of any of a firm's procedures (as, for example, with a commission sales company), the Better Business Bureau or Chamber of Commerce will be glad to advise you.

The other rich source of insight is personal observation. When you went for your interview, did it seem like a friendly office? Were the secretaries discussing their boyfriends or the possibility of a strike? Did the waitresses in a restaurant seem harried and overworked? Did the children, at a summer camp, appear relaxed and active? Were you completely clear about what your work responsibilities would be and about the conditions under which you would do your job? Answering customer complaints by telephone at a giant department store after Christmas is exhausting, if you have your own office. In a cubicle, it becomes nerve-wracking; in an enormous room, desk to desk with a hundred other women at a hundred other nagging telephones—shattering.

Be sure you consider all of these elements—including your intuition and feeling for the job and the employer. Don't sell yourself short. If you know that you are qualified for a job involving responsibility and have a good chance of landing that job, don't settle for work in the mail room. On the other hand, work is hard to find. The current situation may change, but you should consider how many jobs are available and evaluate your offers accordingly. It may not take you long to pinpoint your true feeling about a semester of slinging hash in the steamy dining hall—but if the job market is poor, you may have to concentrate on the $2.95 an hour and the pleasures it will bring you, postponing your dream of glamour as a photographer's assistant to the bright days when photographers can again afford to hire assistants.

What if you have a tolerable offer but are still in the dark concerning the job you really hope for? If you're an undergraduate or a high school senior, you've already been through a similar dalliance: a second-string college mails you an acceptance, but you don't want to commit yourself until you've heard from your first choice. If the employer who replies first does not issue you a deadline, you may be able to stall him. It is also legitimate to explain your situation to the undecided employer, telling him that he is your first choice and that pressure from another offer has prompted you to ask him if he can yet evaluate your chances for the job. If he remains unable to give you his decision, you must choose anyway. How badly do you need a job? How bad is the definite job, and how desirable is the chancy one? You can settle on the sure thing or wait it out—double or nothing.

Bear in mind that once you have accepted a job, you are committed to it. You do not expect an employer to suddenly renege on his offer of employment, and you should let your other potential employers know, accordingly, that your applications are no longer to be considered. Likewise your employer, having hired you, will have rejected everyone else. You count on each other's good faith, and it is, therefore, unethical to change your mind *after* accepting an employer's offer. Not only does a reversal of your position inconvenience your employer, but it may mark you, if word is likely to circulate, as an undependable person and a poor employment risk. If you and your boss have signed a contract, as sometimes happens with resort employment, you may be held legally responsible if you default. Make sure of all the contract terms, when you accept employment. If you want to make a special provision for time off during exam period, for example, at that point is the time to discuss it.

There is more to accepting a job than merely saying "yes" to an initial offer of employment. To "accept" your job in the broadest sense is equivalent to making the most of it.

That first job is often the key to all the rest. Once you've finished your first year, or your first summer, you're an experienced member of the labor force, and that experience usually affects the kind of work you will get for about five years. Long after you finish that first job, employers will be asking your first employer what kind of a worker you were, or the chain of references, contacts, skills, and connections will still be operating, however subtly.

This hardly means that if you start out at age sixteen pumping gas, you can expect the same $1.65 an hour at age twenty-one. But if you do a good job then, you are investing in future successes. Even within a single position, your responsibilities may change according to how you fit into the job. Once you have been hired by a company, there is often an opportunity for advancement. A Kansas junior who began his summer as a busboy in a Cape Cod restaurant found himself in charge of food preparation when the head man suddenly left. His qualifications were minimal, but the owner had been impressed with how responsible a worker he was. His salary jumped from $1.97 to $5.50 an hour—in ten minutes.

If you are not able to change jobs within the company, you may be permitted to move on to more interesting projects, if you finish all your work early. A Milwaukee undergraduate who worked part-time in a local bank was allowed to write a manual for tellers after she had become involved in research during her spare time at work. This kind of assignment may not make more money for you, but it can be stimulating and may prove to be valuable experience for a future job. Taking the initiative will invariably prove to your credit, if you make sure that you do not appear to be seizing power—that is, someone else's job.

Companies want employees with ideas; rubber stamps may be useful, but any company would rather employ the man who designs them. Employers tend to prefer those people who are capable of making decisions and taking the responsibility for them. But just having a good idea isn't enough; you also must have the tact and finesse to get your idea across without offending too many people. Almost any really original suggestion comes at the expense of some "vested interest"; by taking responsibility, you may literally be wresting it away from someone else, who isn't likely to be overjoyed at the change. As a general rule, you should remember to channel your ideas through your immediate superior, rather than barging ahead on your own or going to *his* boss. Initiative must be tempered with respect for others and respect for the vulnerability of your position as a *student* employee. Learn to be innovative without bruising any senior egos, and you may emerge from your routine apprentice stage with independent projects and special assignments.

Terminating Employment

As a student, you have a certain advantage in that you can try out various jobs for periods of a few months and then terminate them, if you wish, with a plea of "summer vacation" or "return to school" or "new spring semester schedule." If you decide to quit a job, and don't want to wait until one of these convenient excuses becomes appropriate, you face a challenge. Clearly you want to maintain the respect, good will, and good reference of your present employer while extricating yourself from his payroll.

Why do you want to leave? Before you actually quit, you should think through what you expected from the job in the beginning. If the work is too boring, talk over the problem with your employer; he may be able to work out some new responsibilities that would make your job more satisfying. If this proves to be impossible, at least you have demonstrated your concern to him, and hard feelings between you will be minimized.

If you want to leave to take up a more attractive or better-paying position, this is understandable, but you should try not to alienate either employer by behaving utterly opportunistically. Give your present employer notice, in writing, that you have decided to leave. Two weeks is the courteous minimum, but longer notice will be appreciated and is particularly important if you hold a highly responsible position. You should offer to stay until your current assignment is completed, or until a replacement for you can be hired and/or trained. Make sure that your present employer knows that you appreciate his firm and the job that you have worked at for him; recognize that your new employer will judge your reliability, in part, on your reference and on your treatment of your former employer.

No matter what your reasons for quitting, you should, obviously, keep the discussion of your motivation in leaving low-keyed and impersonal. If you are quitting for personal reasons, minimize the conflict and muzzle your hostility. This job will be part of your employment record. It may be too unpleasant to stay with, but don't make any parting remarks that may haunt you in your dealings with potential employers in the future.

This guide is about to finish its job. It has attempted to provide you with the basic tools for financial survival as an undergraduate. You have

surveyed your possibilities for scholarships and loans, and have reviewed your skills and their marketability. You have checked over the
employment opportunities open to you during the school term, and the
summer, and have considered the advantages of going into business for
yourself. You have digested the information on job-finding and job-
landing. Whatever this guide could offer has passed into your mind, and
there ends the task of this book, as a far more important task begins.

All of this data, all of these statistics and examples and distillations
of student work experience were brought together for a single reason: to
help you in your financial and employment plans. The achievement of
that goal is out of our hands, and in yours alone. This is your job—the
best of luck with it, and with the rest of the jobs in which you invest
yourself as an undergraduate. We wish you high pay, benign bosses, and
a sense of achievement in your work. With any luck on our part, we
have communicated to you, *not* expertise in the field of student employment but a mastery of tools, the most important of which will turn out
to be your own imagination and initiative.

If courage should ever fail you, call back to mind the following
story, and console yourself with its poignant lesson. A penniless English
major, down and out in Cambridge and Boston, once wandered the
brown brick pavements, which were crowded with engineers, nuclear
physicists, and other wraiths in the shiftless mass of the unemployed.
The lines of Ph.D.'s at the state employment office had begun to quiver
visibly: Christmas was close, and the air was sharp. Our heroine was
shivering on a Harvard Square street corner one bitter evening, proffer-
ing matches for sale between her little blue fingers when—lo! and
behold, a former classmate swept her off to the toasty offices of the
Harvard Student Agencies, where she enjoyed permanent fame and
fortune as the editor of *Making It: A Guide to Student Finances.*

No one is unemployable.

APPENDIX I

Job	Description	Skills Needed	Where to Apply
Auto Mechanic Helper	Makes minor repairs and adjustments, replaces worn or broken parts.	Thorough knowledge of automobiles, plus mechanical aptitude. Usually requires driver's license.	Gas stations, independent repair garages.
Automobile Service-Station Attendant	Pumps gas, and checks oil, tires, water and batteries, and replaces them when necessary. Often installs automobile accessories.	Some mechanical aptitude.	Gas stations.
Bank Clerk	Performs specialized functions at bank, such as bookkeeping, clerical work, office machine operations, and messenger work.	Varies according to specific function. General knowledge of business helpful.	Banks, trust companies, and savings and loan companies.
Bank Teller	Performs basic business functions at bank, such as cashing checks, making changes in depositors' accounts, etc.	Ability to deal with public, some aptitude with numbers.	Banks, trust companies, and savings and loan companies.
Bellhop	Escorts guests to rooms, carries baggage. Performs other services, such as delivering messages, packages, etc.	Ability to lift heavy suitcases and packages.	Hotels, motels, and vacation resorts.
Bookkeeping Clerk	Prepares and maintains records of business transactions, payroll, etc.	Knowledge of bookkeeping procedures and methods.	Bookkeeping departments of large businesses and accounting firms.

Job	Description	Skills Needed	Where to Apply
Bookkeeping Machine Operator	Copies and posts figures from one record to another using a bookkeeping machine.	Ability to operate bookkeeping machine.	Bookkeeping departments of large businesses and accounting firms.
Busboy or Busgirl	Removes dirty dishes, table cloths, etc. Carries trays, fills glasses with water.	None.	Restaurants.
Calculator Machine Operator	Operates adding and calculating machines, keeps records.	Ability to operate calculating machine.	Bookkeeping departments of large businesses, banks, and accounting firms.
Cashier	Takes payment for various services and merchandise and enters payment on a cash register.	Ability to deal with public and ability to operate cash register.	Retail establishments, theaters, and restaurants.
Child-Care Worker	Performs tasks such as babysitting, feeding, etc.	Ability to deal with children.	Largely self-employment. Register at student employment office.
Commercial Art Worker	Does lettering, decorating, coloring, and drawing.	High degree of artistic skill.	Sign companies and art studios. Also chance of self-employment.
Computer Programmer and Data Processor	Prepares computer, runs and checks programs.	Knowledge of and ability to use computers.	Computing labs and businesses with computers.
Construction Laborer	Assists other workers by holding material and tools, loading and unloading materials, etc.	None.	Contractors, local and state government public works and highway departments.

Job	Description	Skills Needed	Where to Apply
Cook	Prepares meals.	Ability to cook.	Restaurants, hotels, hospitals, and drive-ins.
Display Man Helper	Assists display man and prepares window displays, trimmings, etc.	None.	Department stores, retail outlets, and independent display companies.
Dry Cleaner Helper	Loads and unloads dry-cleaning machines, extractors, and tumblers.	None.	Large dry-cleaning establishments and plants.
Elevator Operator	Operates elevator.	On-the-job training usually provided.	Management of large buildings, hotels, and apartment houses.
Factory Operative	Operates machines used in manufacturing.	Varies with function.	Factories.
Faculty Aide	Assumes a number of tasks and duties that may include abstracting articles, translating, etc.	Varies greatly.	Various academic departments, institutes, and student employment offices.
Farmhand	Does general farm work including planting, harvesting, etc.	Ability to perform strenuous tasks.	Farms.
Floor Boy or Floor Girl	Carries supplies to operators or assemblers and removes finished product.	None.	Manufacturing companies.
Fountain Clerk	Takes orders for and serves food at lunch counters.	None.	Diners, cafeterias, drug stores, etc.
Gardener's Helper	Assists gardener in planting, weeding, spraying, etc.	None.	Private gardeners, nurseries, and cemeteries.

Job	Description	Skills Needed	Where to Apply
Hospital Worker	Tasks may include laboratory work, being a night receptionist, etc.	Varies greatly.	Hospitals and clinics.
Hotel Clerk	Greets and registers guests, issue keys, and provides addition services as required.	Ability to deal with public.	Hotels, motels, and vacation resorts.
Keypunch Operator	Transfers information from written word to tabulator cards by operating keypunch machine.	Ability to operate keypunch machine.	Large industrial and business firms.
Library Worker	Attends desk and shelves books.	None.	College, public, and private libraries.
Medical Laboratory Assistant	Performs various tasks in lab including labeling, sterilizing, etc.	General knowledge of a physical science.	Independent medical laboratories, pharmaceutical laboratories, clinics, and hospitals.
Nurse's Aide or Orderly	Assists physicians and nurses to provide care, feed and bathe patients, make beds, etc.	None—willingness to help people.	Hospitals and college infirmary.
Office Boy or Office Girl	Performs general office tasks such as sorting letters, delivering messages, answering the telephone, etc.	None.	Businesses, professional firms, banks, etc.
Parking-Lot Attendant	Parks cars and collects fees.	Driver's license.	Parking lots, restaurants, hotels, etc.
Photographer ·	Takes and sells photographs.	Skill in photography.	Largely self-employment. Possible jobs at weddings, graduations, etc.

Job	Description	Skills Needed	Where to Apply
Post Office Worker: Substitute Carrier or Clerk	Clerk: sorts letters, sells stamps, etc. Carrier: delivers mail and makes collections from mail boxes.	For carrier, ability to lift heavy sacks.	Applicants must qualify on Civil Service Summer Employment Exam or regular Post Office Exam.
Receptionist	Receives visitors, clients, or customers at a business or professional office.	Pleasant personality, ability to deal with public, attractiveness.	Business or professional offices. Most vacancies filled through employment agencies.
Repairman's Helper	Assists repairman (television, appliance, household, etc.).	Mechanical aptitude.	Repair shops and appliance stores.
Route Man's Helper	Helps load trucks and make deliveries.	Ability to lift heavy objects. May also require driver's license.	Wholesale and retail stores, moving companies, dry cleaning stores, etc.
Salesclerk	Performs sales and sales-related functions in retail stores.	Ability to deal with public, ability in salesmanship.	Retail stores.
Sports Instructor	Teaches various sports.	Skill in a particular sport.	Schools, recreation programs, camps, etc. Also chance for self-employment.
Stenographer	Takes dictation in shorthand or by machine and transcribes notations by typewriter.	Knowledge of stenography and typing.	Business and professional offices. Most hiring done through employment agencies.

Job	Description	Skills Needed	Where to Apply
Stock Handler	Receives, unloads, and distributes merchandise.	None.	Department stores and man- ufacturers.
Stock Man or Stock Woman	Fills shelves with mer- chandise, opens ship- ments, etc.	None.	Grocery stores and large dis- count stores.
Surveyor's Helper	Transit man: measures land boundaries, etc. Rodman: holds rods to assist transit man. Chainman: measures dis- tances using measuring tape.	Knowledge of geometry and trigonometry, plus some physical strength.	Architectural and engineering companies.
Taxi Driver	Drives customers to de- sired location.	Driver's license, knowl- edge of streets in city where one plans to work.	Taxicab com- panies.
Tour Leader	Conducts tours of muse- ums, universities, histor- ical sights, etc.	Knowledge of area in which tour is to be con- ducted.	Museums, uni- versity informa- tion offices, etc.
Truck Driver, Light	Transports goods by truck.	Appropriate driver's li- cense.	Factories, wholesale and retail stores, and construc- tion companies.
Tutor	Teaches subjects and sup- plemental material.	Knowledge of field in which one wishes to tutor.	Largely self- employment. Register at stu- dent employ- ment and coun- seling offices.
Typist	Uses typewriter to pre- pare letters, memos, en- velopes, etc.	Ability to use typewriter. Usually must be able to type in excess of 50 wpm.	Business and professional of- fices. Also chance for self- employment by typing term papers, etc.

Jobs	Description	Skills Needed	Where to Apply
Waiter or Waitress	Works in restaurants taking customers' orders, delivering the prepared orders, and preparing bills.	Ability to deal with public.	Restaurants, lunch counters, etc.
Watchman	Guards buildings, industrial plants, and businesses.	None.	Guard and watchman companies.

APPENDIX II

School	Enroll-ment	Tuition	Room & Board	Scholar-ships Awarded 1970
THE AMERICAN UNIVERSITY Washington, D.C.	10,225 M 5,101 F	$2,220	$1,250	$ 344,89
AMHERST COLLEGE Amherst, Massachusetts	1,250 M	$2,825	$1,075	$ 580,00
BARNARD COLLEGE New York, New York	1,950 F	$2,550	$1,400	N.A.
BELOIT COLLEGE Beloit, Wisconsin	850 M 850 F	$3,100	$1,000	$ 650,00
CALIFORNIA INSTITUTE OF TECHNOLOGY Pasadena, California	681 M 31 F	$2,565	$1,225	$ 502,46

Loans 1970	Per Cent Scholarships or Loan Holders	Per Cent Students with Term-Time Jobs	Average Student Wage on Campus	Student Employment Office?	Student Business Organization?	Enough Term-Time Jobs?
529,050	20%	N.A.	$2.00/hr	Yes	Yes	No
110,000	45%	70%	$1.70/hr	No	No	No
N.A.	60%	50%	$2.50/hr	Yes	No	Yes
350,000	33%	15%	$1.60/hr	No	No	No
185,378	66%	50%	$2.20/hr	Yes	No	No

School	Enroll-ment	Tuition	Room & Board	Scholar-ships Awarded 1970
UNIVERSITY OF CALIFORNIA AT BERKELEY Berkeley, California	10,318 M 7,703 F	$ 638	$1,485	$ 1,700,00
CARLETON COLLEGE Northfield, Minnesota	808 M 582 F	$2,265	$1,185	$ 673,00
UNIVERSITY OF COLORADO Boulder, Colorado	18,631 M 12,150 F	$ 423* 1,691	$1,080	$ 2,683,00
UNIVERSITY OF CONNECTICUT Storrs, Connecticut	550 M 650 F	$ 305* 705	$1,110	$ 303,16
CORNELL UNIVERSITY Ithaca, New York	10,627 M 3,725 F	$2,800	$1,600	$15,181,45
FISK UNIVERSITY Nashville, Tennessee	400 M 700 F	$1,750	$1,125	$ 400,28
FLORIDA STATE UNIVERSITY Tallahassee, Florida	9,285 M 7,725 F	$ 450	$ 980	$ 320,41
GEORGIA INSTITUTE OF TECHNOLOGY Atlanta, Georgia	8,000 M 300 F	$ 504* 1,209	$1,000	$ 200,00

* *Where two tuitions are listed the lower amount is for state residents only.*

Loans 1970	Per Cent Scholar- ships or Loan Holders	Per Cent Stu- dents with Term- Time Jobs	Average Student Wage on Campus	Stu- dent Employ- ment Office?	Stu- dent Busi- ness Organi- zation?	Enough Term- Time Jobs?
3,000,000	25%	10%	$2.50/hr	Yes	Yes	No
240,000	42%	50%	$1.60/hr	Yes	No	No
937,000	14%	20%	$2.00/hr	Yes	Yes	No
684,720	65%	26%	$2.20/hr	No	Yes	No
3,095,328	70%	40%	$2.00/hr	Yes	Yes	No
242,750	42%	27.6%	$1.60/hr	Yes	Yes	Yes
1,676,776	32%	13%	$1.60/hr	Yes	No	No
400,000	20%	30%	$1.90/hr	Yes	No	No

School	Enroll-ment	Tuition	Room & Board	Scholar-ships Awarded 1970
UNIVERSITY OF HAWAII Honolulu, Hawaii	5,922 M 5,963 F	$ 233* 843	$1,375	$ 357,22
UNIVERSITY OF IOWA Iowa City, Iowa	12,544 M 8,060 F	$ 620* 1,250	$1,114	$ 2,484,59
UNIVERSITY OF KANSAS Lawrence, Kansas	10,239 M 6,806 F	$ 460* 1,050	$ 900	$ 1,119,73
UNIVERSITY OF MARYLAND College Park, Maryland	14,932 M 11,779 F	$ 589* 1,289	$1,030* 1,130	$ 2,088,00
MICHIGAN STATE UNIVERSITY East Lansing, Michigan	23,425 M 17,086 F	$ 504* 1,188	$1,200	$ 5,000,00
UNIVERSITY OF MICHIGAN Ann Arbor, Michigan	23,195 M 23,394 F	$ 660* 2,140	$1,250	$ 2,500,00
UNIVERSITY OF MINNESOTA Minneapolis, Minnesota	17,583 M 11,708 F	$ 600* 1,428	$1,150	$ 2,000,00
UNIVERSITY OF MISSOURI Columbia, Missouri	12,600 M 8,400 F	$ 500	$ 940	$ 1,500,00

* Where two tuitions are listed the lower amount is for state residents only.

Loans 1970	Per Cent Scholar- ships or Loan Holders	Per Cent Stu- dents with Term- Time Jobs	Average Student Wage on Campus	Stu- dent Employ- ment Office?	Stu- dent Busi- ness Organi- zation?	Enough Term- Time Jobs?
737,023	12%	25%	$1.75/hr	Yes	No	No
$ 5,083,050	67%	50%	$2.10/hr	Yes	No	No
$ 3,418,945	34%	N.A.	N.A.	Yes	Yes	No
$ 2,030,000	20%	50%	$2.00/hr	Yes	No	Yes
$10,000,000	40%	62%	$2.00/hr	Yes	No	Yes
$ 3,500,000	33%	50%	N.A.	Yes	No	Yes
$ 3,000,000	25%	65%	$2.30/hr	Yes	No	No
$ 3,000,000	30%	20%	$1.85/hr	Yes	No	No

School	Enroll-ment	Tuition	Room & Board	Scholar-ships Awarded 1970
UNIVERSITY OF MONTANA Missoula, Montana	5,576 M 2,935 F	$ 414* 1,081.50	$1,050	$ 477,921
UNIVERSITY OF NEBRASKA Lincoln, Nebraska	8,771 M 5,094 F	$ 267.50* 630.50	$ 940	$ 1,250,000
UNIVERSITY OF NEW HAMPSHIRE Durham, New Hampshire	4,866 M 3,540 F	$ 810* 2,000	$1,000	$ 1,100,000
UNIVERSITY OF NORTH CAROLINA Chapel Hill, North Carolina	11,802 M 5,765 F	$ 225* 950	$1,000	$ 1,161,347
UNIVERSITY OF NORTH DAKOTA Grand Forks, North Dakota	4,898 M 3,231 F	$ 446* 1,024	$ 780	$ 159,834
OHIO STATE UNIVERSITY Columbus, Ohio	34,000 M 17,000 F	$ 620* 1,240	$1,215	$ 2,100,000
UNIVERSITY OF OKLAHOMA Norman, Oklahoma	13,856 M 7,630 F	$ 448* 1,280	$ 900	$ 699,600
UNIVERSITY OF OREGON Eugene, Oregon	17,611 M 13,125 F	$ 408	$ 900	$ 1,002,000

* Where two tuitions are listed the lower amount is for state residents only.

Loans 1970	Per Cent Scholar- ships or Loan Holders	Per Cent Stu- dents with Term- Time Jobs	Average Student Wage on Campus	Stu- dent Employ- ment Office?	Stu- dent Busi- ness Organi- zation?	Enough Term- Time Jobs?
$ 232,960	25%	20%	$1.80/hr	No	No	No
$ 1,000,000	35%	50%	$1.75/hr	Yes	Yes	No
$ 508,000	25%	15%	$1.80/hr	No	No	No
$ 798,309	38%	34%	$1.65/hr	Yes	No	No
$ 3,753,044	62.5%	20%	$1.75/hr	Yes	Yes	No
$ 2,500,000	20%	40%	$1.90/hr	Yes	No	No
$ 1,170,000	20%	20%	$1.70/hr	Yes	Yes	Yes
$ 3,500,000	50%	50%	$2.00/hr	Yes	No	No

School	Enroll-ment	Tuition	Room & Board	Scholar-ships Awarded 1970
PENNSYLVANIA STATE UNIVERSITY University Park, Pennsylvania	29,899 M 12,928 F	$ 675* 1,350	$1,035	$ 1,417,742
UNIVERSITY OF PITTSBURGH Pittsburgh, Pennsylvania	7,800 M 6,000 F	$ 850* 1,250	$1,250	$ 4,377,722
POMONA COLLEGE Claremont, California	715 M 585 F	$2,520	$1,400	$ 1,048,312
PURDUE UNIVERSITY Lafayette, Indiana	17,158 M 8,416 F	$ 700* 1,600	$1,100	$ 2,356,625
RHODE ISLAND SCHOOL OF DESIGN Providence, Rhode Island	625 M 560 F	$2,350	$1,175	$ 316,798
RICE UNIVERSITY Houston, Texas	1,699 M 598 F	$2,100	$1,270	$ 1,423,000
UNIVERSITY OF ROCHESTER Rochester, New York	N.A.	$2,600	$1,450	$ 1,644,304
RUTGERS COLLEGE New Brunswick, New Jersey	6,644 M	$ 400* 800	$1,328	$ 1,241,912

* *Where two tuitions are listed the lower amount is for state residents only.*

Loans 1970	Per Cent Scholar- ships or Loan Holders	Per Cent Stu- dents with Term- Time Jobs	Average Student Wage on Campus	Stu- dent Employ- ment Office?	Stu- dent Busi- ness Organi- zation?	Enough Term- Time Jobs?
$ 9,049,526	35%	25%	$1.75/hr	Yes	No	No
$ 1,200,000	60%	N.A.	$2.25/hr	Yes	No	N.A.
$ 46,400	50%	25%	$2.00/hr	Yes	Yes	Yes
$ 1,380,000	20%	30%	$1.60/hr	No	No	No
$ 46,900	20%	25%	$2.00/hr	Yes	No	Yes
$ 182,000	50%	N.A.	N.A.	Yes	No	Yes
$ 362,251	35%	25%	$2.12/hr	Yes	No	No
$ 2,182,950	34%	42%	$2.00/hr	Yes	Yes	No

School	Enroll-ment	Tuition	Room & Board	Scholar-ships Awarded 1970
SARAH LAWRENCE COLLEGE Bronxville, New York	144 M 609 F	$3,200	$1,600	$ 248,648
SCRIPPS COLLEGE Claremont, California	560 F	$2,400	$1,400	$ 350,000
UNIVERSITY OF SOUTH DAKOTA Vermillion, South Dakota	3,399 M 1,949 F	$ 414* 990	$ 800	$ 93,150
UNIVERSITY OF SOUTHERN CALIFORNIA Los Angeles, California	4,680 M 2,522 F	$2,150	$1,300	N.A.
UNIVERSITY OF THE SOUTH Sewanee, Tennessee	750 M 220 F	$1,950	$ 900	$ 240,000
STANFORD UNIVERSITY Stanford, California	4,118 M 2,185 F	$2,400	$1,210	$ 4,531,342
SWARTHMORE COLLEGE Swarthmore, Pennsylvania	649 M 515 F	$2,510	$1,135	$ 682,000
TUSKEGEE INSTITUTE Tuskegee Institute, Alabama	1,550 M 1,512 F	$1,075	$ 725	$ 145,000

Where two tuitions are listed the lower amount is for state residents only.

Loans 1970	Per Cent Scholar- ships or Loan Holders	Per Cent Stu- dents with Term- Time Jobs	Average Student Wage on Campus	Stu- dent Employ- ment Office?	Stu- dent Busi- ness Organi- zation?	Enough Term- Time Jobs?
$ 37,852	28%	14%	$2.00/hr	Yes	No	Yes
$ 100,000	35%	65%	$1.85/hr	Yes	No	Yes
$ 1,889,833	30%	25%	$1.75/hr	Yes	No	No
$ 7,514,902	60%	N.A.	$2.00/hr	Yes	No	No
$ 140,000	40%	30%	$1.60/hr	Yes	No	No
$ 690,684	42%	40%	$2.00/hr	Yes	No	No
$ 62,925	36%	30–40%	$1.80/hr	Yes	No	No
$ 230,000	75%	40%	$1.75/hr	Yes	No	No

School	Enroll-ment	Tuition	Room & Board	Scholar-ships Awarded 1970
UNIVERSITY OF VERMONT Burlington, Vermont	4,075 M 3,220 F	$ 950* 2,400	$1,000	$ 427,000
WEST VIRGINIA UNIVERSITY Morgantown, West Virginia	9,643 M 5,249 F	$ 292* 1,122	$1,100	$ 400,000
COLLEGE OF WILLIAM & MARY Williamsburg, Virginia	1,700 M 1,600 F	$ 660* 1,594	$ 950	$ 300,000
UNIVERSITY OF WISCONSIN Madison, Wisconsin	21,094 M 13,294 F	$ 508	$1,200	$ 2,814,536
YALE COLLEGE New Haven, Connecticut	4,000 M 1,000 F	$2,900	$1,500	$ 3,371,000

Where two tuitions are listed the lower amount is for state residents only.

Loans 1970	Per Cent Scholarships or Loan Holders	Per Cent Students with Term-Time Jobs	Average Student Wage on Campus	Student Employment Office?	Student Business Organization?	Enough Term-Time Jobs?
$ 250,000	30%	7%	$1.75/hr	Yes	No	No
$ 1,000,000	30%	20%	$1.80/hr	Yes	No	No
$ 150,000	30%	40%	$1.60/hr	Yes	No	Yes
$ 3,930,025	25%	12%	$1.80/hr	Yes	Yes	No
$ 787,000	50%	35%	$2.20/hr	Yes	Yes	No

INDEX

American Home Economics Association, 49-50
American Indian Youth Scholarships, 45, 62
American Laymen and Churches Overseas, Committee of, 207
American Legion Educational and Scholarship Program, 33, 37-38, 43-44, 55-56, 63, 65, 77
American Medical Association, 51
American Newspaper Publishers Association (ANPA) Foundation, 54
American Nurses Association, 52
American Optometric Association, 65
American Pharmaceutical Association, 51
American Society of Medical Technologists, 51
American Student Tours, Inc., 202
American Study Tours, 206
American Youth Hostels, Inc, 202, 207
AMVETS Scholarship Program, 37
Annapolis, U. S. Naval Academy at, 41
Apprenticeships, serving of, 88-90
Aptitude tests, 44, 46-47, 53, 76, 82, 264
Aristo Craft Company, sales opportunities with, 132
Arizona, 21, 74; State Employment Security Commission, 280
Armed Forces, The, 31, 35, 37-38, 59-61, 65
Armed Forces Relief and Benefit Association, 66
Army, Department of, 36-38; commissions in, 40; recruiting command, 42; Relief Society in, 37; Reserve Nurses Corps, 42; Reserve program, 39-41; Student and Registered Nurse Program of, 41
Artistic and creative skills, 97-100
Association Internationale des Etudiants en Sciences Economiques et Commerciales, 201, 207
Athletic instructors, 135, 262; scholarships, 15, 75; skills, 95-96, 126, 157
Austin College, 16
Avon Company, sales opportunities with, 132

Banks and banking, 61, 63
Baptist Church, 48
Barbizon Model Agency, 117
Barnard College, 268-269
Bartending services, 136, 164, 236-237
Beehive Fashions, sales opportunities with, 132
Behavioral Sciences, 53
Belgian Educational Travel Service, 206
Benefits: fringe, 175; student, 33
Bennington College, 88
Better Business Bureau, 179, 282
Big Ten schools, tuition at, 14
Black students, 45-47
Blind students, 42
Board expenses, college, 20-22, 58
Books, cost of and allowance for, 20-21, 39-40, 77
Borrowing, 59-60. See also Loans
Boy Scouts of America, 161
Boys Club of America, 70
Brokerage houses, 69
Brown University, 16, 85
Budgets, balancing of, 20-21, 71-72, 140, 217
Buffalo, University of, 264
Business: administration, 40; agencies, 114, 117, 234; assets, 26; boom, 10; and the economy, 22, 182, 197, 201, 224, 243-246, 258; office, 263; schools, 59, 67, 69-70; skills, 82, 92; student run, 115, 212-213, 225

California, State of, 65, 183 186
California, University of, 17, 22
California Institute of Technology, 16
California Rural and Legal Assistance (CRLA), 178-179
Cameron, Robert G., cited, 29
Camp Counselor International Exchange Program, 199, 207
Camp Fire Girls Camps, 161
Camps, 162, 167; counselors for, 144, 157-160, 163, 183, 199, 207; day, 141; European, 199, 207; summer, 95, 141
Canada, 166, 173
Cape Cod National Seashore, 153
Capital, need for, 223-224
Career Planning Program, 30
Carine, Edwin, T., Jr., cited, 28